Star in the East

Star in the East

——— ✳ ———

Krishnamurti
The Invention of a Messiah

ROLAND VERNON

palgrave

FOR ST. MARTIN'S PRESS

STAR IN THE EAST
Copyright © Roland Vernon, 2000.

First published 2001 by PALGRAVE™
175 Fifth Avenue, New York, N.Y. 10010
Companies and representatives throughout the world.

PALGRAVE is the new global publishing imprint of
St. Martin's Press LLC
Scholarly and Reference Division and Palgrave Publishers Ltd.
(formerly Macmillan Press Ltd.).

ISBN 0-312-23825-8

Library of Congress Cataloging-in-Publication Data
available at the Library of Congress.

First published in Great Britain by Constable,
an imprint of Constable & Robinson Ltd.

First PALGRAVE edition: March 2001
10 9 8 7 6 5 4 3 2 1

Printed in the United States of America.

This book is dedicated to my friend

NARADA

who reveals to me

no thing

Contents

List of Illustrations

Author's Note and Acknowledgements

Compiling this book has involved me becoming very intimate with the teachings of Krishnamurti, and this in itself has been a remarkable adventure for me. There is no immunity from his demand that a reader probe and question the deepest reaches of his or her accepted world view, and one cannot but emerge at the other end of a journey such as this with a readjusted perspective of life and living. It has been a thoroughly illuminating experience for me, which has at times challenged my objective stance, as an author, yet water-tight impartiality has been my one and only creed from beginning to end. It is this very degree of historical neutrality that is bound to raise objections from certain quarters, because feelings about so charismatic and influential a person run high. I have encountered both supporters and detractors of Krishnamurti who will doubtless feel that my portrayal contradicts their own well-grounded experience, perhaps offensively so, and I apologise in advance, especially to those who have helped me, if this is the case. There were several occasions when I received directly contradictory reports about the same events, or about traits in the teacher's character, and at no time has it been my agenda either to reinforce his credibility or the opposite. I have attempted to take the balanced, detached position, listening to as many authoritative voices as have become available, and in no case, to my knowledge, distorting the picture with half-truths or untruths. This book will surely not detract from the phenomenon of Krishnamurti. An honest and open debate is the only way to uncover a true picture and gain insight, as he himself was the first to advocate.

On a similar note, I apologise for my free use of words such as 'guru', 'messiah', 'disciple' and 'following' in relation to Krishnamurti and his companions. The terms may be inappropriate, but it would involve some very artificial and unnecessary wordsmithery to avoid them altogether.

No one could write about Krishnamurti without relying to some degree on the extensive and invaluable work accomplished throughout a lifetime of experience by Mary Lutyens, who sadly died shortly before this book went into production. I acknowledge my debt to her, with humility and admiration.

Many people have helped me, steering me in the right direction, contributing reminiscences, enrichment, inspiration, contacts, goodwill and enthusiasm. The staff and students at Brockwood Park not only equipped me with material for the book, but fired my imagination and taught me much about education, for which I thank them, especially Bill, Len, and Jerome. Harsh Tankha and his assistants at the Krishnamurti Foundation also kindly supplied me with several leads, answered many queries and gave me access to archive material.

Interviewees who gave their time and recollections included Scott Forbes, Colin Foster, Sebastian Lange, Clare Harvey, Elsie Ridley, and Peter Boughton (National President of the Theosophical Society in England). Representatives from the Krishnamurti schools in other parts of the world who also agreed to be interviewed, included Gautama (from The School, Madras), Satish Inamdar (The Valley School, Bangalore), Swaminathan Gopalam and Meredy Maynard (the Oak Grove). My thanks extend to many others who contributed in one way or another: Barry Thompson and the library staff of the Theosophical Society in London (quite the best and most accessible library for religion and philosophy I have used), The Very Rev Fr. Lloyd Worley, Provost of the American Province of the Liberal Catholic Church, Canon Peter Spink, F David Peat, Radha Sloss, Nick Consoletti, and the many academics who responded to my requests for copies of their papers. A few contributors have elected to remain anonymous, and yet others deserve mention, but space will not permit.

Permission to quote from the correspondence of Krishnamurti,

Nityananda and their circle, together with all Krishnamurti's teachings published prior to 1968, was kindly granted by the Krishnamurti Foundation of America. The Krishnamurti Foundation Trust, of Brockwood Park, England, are gratefully acknowledged for granting permission to quote from Krishnamurti's works published after 1968 and for allowing the reproduction of photographs from their collection. Excerpts from *Loving and Leaving the Good Life* are copyright 1992 by Helen Nearing. Reprinted with permission from Chelsea Green Publishing Company, White River Junction, Vermont, and the Good Life Center, Harborside, Maine. John Saltmarsh and the Good Life Center also kindly gave permission to use photographs from Helen Nearing's archive. All other sources are acknowledged in the endnotes and bibliography. In some instances copyright holders, despite much searching, have been impossible to trace. If notification of any copyright transgression is received by the author or publisher, every effort will be made to accommodate acknowledgement in future editions.

On a personal note I would like to thank Connie and Wayne Burke, of Athens, who have probably forgotten that they introduced me to Krishnamurti fifteen years ago, by lending me a (now) tatty edition of his *The Flight of the Eagle*, which although baffling and to some extent unnerving me at the time, has led a direct path to the text I now write. Several of my friends here in Somerset have galvanised me with their own interest in Krishnamurti, fanning the fire of my enthusiasm, especially after the three arduous marquee seasons that interrupted my winter writing work. John Wilks, Dominic Quarrell and Narada spring to mind. I owe a huge debt to my agent Caroline Davidson for her constancy, and my editor at Constable, Carol O'Brien, who could not have been more accommodating and enthusiastic.

Finally, perhaps predictably but none the less genuinely, I pour out my soul in thanks to Helen, light of my life, heart of my home, warmth of my bed. She unhesitatingly gave and continues to give me space to pursue my interest in the sorts of things covered in this book, even though it at times means herself taking on more than her share of domestic drudgery. She and my boys have lived with the spectral presence of Krishnamurti in their home for three long winters, through photographs, books, films, tapes, kitchen table discussions and hearing endlessly repeated the basic facts about his life. At times it apparently seemed as though their husband and father had been quite overshadowed by a person whom they had not invited into the house, but generously accommodated, and indeed grew to know a little.

1

The Boy on the Beach

———— ✳ ————

Headquarters of the Theosophical Society, Adyar, near Madras, South India.

Newcomers to the Theosophical Society in 1909 could not fail to be struck by the sheer magnitude of Charles Webster Leadbeater. In every sense he was larger than life. Massively built, he oozed strength and vitality, even in his mid-fifties, with a chest broad as an English oak, a muscular, unbroken slope between his forehead and nose, a thick silver beard and powerful shoulders. The loose pyjama-bottoms and white muslin shirts he preferred to wear in the hot climate were somewhat incongruous on so stately an Englishman, whose frame seemed better suited to frock coats, embroidered waistcoats, spats and golden watch-chains. But it was his presence, more than his physique, that tended to dwarf all who came near him. Unpredictable, like a fairy-tale ogre, at times benign, at others fearsome, he possessed the sort of personality that refused to be ignored. When he entered a room all heads turned, when he opened his mouth to speak all other voices were hushed. He laid claim to vast knowledge, spanning both the sub-atomic and the infinite, the etheric and spirit world, the far reaches of history and the unveiled mysteries of the future. His ideas were monstrous, his ambitions uncontainable, and his assuredness incontestable. He was a fortress of conviction. Brave was the man who contradicted such a colossus.

The newcomer would also have been aware of Leadbeater's bizarre history, his long-standing prominence within the Theosophical Society, and the recent turn of events that had cast a sinister shadow on his reputation. After the rumoured adventures of his youth, Leadbeater had become an Anglican clergyman before abandoning Christianity for the more exotic spiritual quest of Theosophy, with its alluring motto, 'There is no religion higher than Truth.' He had worked alongside Madame Blavatsky herself, the legendary mystic, traveller and clairvoyant who founded the Theosophical Society, and it was with her that he had first travelled to India, back in 1884. This had led to what he claimed was a clairvoyant awakening of his own, since which time he had dedicated his life to shaping the Society's philosophy through his many books, articles and lecture tours. Thanks largely to his energy and conviction, Theosophy had by now established itself as one of the most exciting and influential religious alternatives of the western world.

A recent scandal had threatened to scupper the entire project. Leadbeater had been accused of indecent behaviour towards a series of adolescent boys. Some of the charges were substantiated, but not to such a degree as to fell this towering pioneer. Enemies he had many, but he gave them little consideration, and their weapons glanced off his hide like paper darts. In his own little world, at Adyar, in South India, he ruled like a moghul. Although not Theosophy's nominal leader, he had the Society president's complete confidence, and his every utterance was treated as infallible. To the newcomer he was every inch the wise patriarch. Despite his faults, it was impossible not to be impressed by so commanding and vigorous a personality.

Embedded within the luxuriant gardens of the Theosophical Society estate, right at the river's edge, lay Leadbeater's private residence known as the Octagon Bungalow, an elegant little structure with a white stucco exterior and a covered verandah on all eight sides of its circumference. Here he would retire with hand-picked helpers to work on his various esoteric and literary projects, sometimes deep into the night, until his colleagues (though rarely he himself) could barely hold up their heads or push their pens. He did allow a break in the day's labours, for a swim, at about five o'clock in the afternoon, when the trees and shrubs had begun to cast long shadows over the garden's terracotta paths, and the air at Adyar was thick with the sound of crickets. Bounding barefoot out of his quarters, towel in hand, he would lead a small masculine team at the double along the river path that went down towards the coconut plantation and out to the beach. As his secretaries and assistants scampered to keep up with him, he would stride past the groups of admirers who often hung around the Octagon Bungalow at this time of day, hoping to ingratiate themselves. Famously misogynous, he was particularly dismissive of elderly European ladies, of whom there were a number at Adyar, frequently to be seen cross-legged under a banyan tree, frail and uncomfortable, earnestly attempting to meditate or raise themselves to higher spiritual planes.

On one particular hot evening, in the spring of 1909, Leadbeater was sitting in his bungalow with a bright and ascetic-looking young Englishman called Ernest Wood. They had been working continuously since early morning, with Wood acting as the older man's amanuensis, spurring on Leadbeater's occult imagination with incisive questions, and recording the results on paper. Wood was expected at some stage to compile and formulate their jumbled reams of notes into a book, a daunting editorial task that he somewhat dreaded. They paused from their toils at five, as usual, for the late afternoon swim, and proceeded, with a few others, down to the Adyar sea-shore, a broad, pale length of beach that stretched for miles in both directions, south towards the flat expanse of the Coromandel Coast, north to the city of Madras, and faced out eastwards into the Bay of Bengal. They stripped quickly and raced down to the surf, plunging straight in and splashing each other with shouts of laughter.

Near to the water's edge a group of Indian youths gathered to watch the curiosity of naked Europeans cavorting. Separate from the others, two young boys squatted in the sand, one of them, the smaller of the two, smiling as he tried to catch the attention of the Theosophists. His hair was shaved at the front, up to the crown of the head, but grown long at the back, and worn in a pigtail, in the traditional style of Brahmin boys. Behind him sat the other boy, taller and thinner, who seemed hardly aware of his companion's excitement, but turned away in a daydream, his mouth hanging open in a moronic expression. They were both very thin, with their shoulders and ribs clearly visible through the skin, from

3

months, perhaps years, of inadequate nourishment and unresolved ill-health. They hardly noticed the flies that gathered at the moist corners of their eyes, or the mosquitos that feasted on their swollen ankles.

Ernest Wood and one of his companions recognised the boys, and waved back at the younger, beckoning him to join them. This was all the encouragement he needed, and he took off like an unleashed puppy down to the sea. The other child, his elder brother, did not even notice that he had been left alone, his large dark eyes staring into the distance, absorbed and yet apparently sightless.

While Wood and his companions pulled the younger boy into the water, encouraging him in English and broken Hindi, neither of which he appeared to understand, Charles Leadbeater turned his attention to the other boy. He had always been drawn to children of this age, fascinated by their standing on the threshold of maturity. It was a crucial stage of life, Leadbeater believed, the point of transition between childhood magic and adult judgment. This gateway was vital in defining the child's future outlook; given the right guidance, and placed in the care of wise hands, the adolescent might avoid a life of misery by stepping onto the path of divine discipleship, which led to salvation itself. To Leadbeater it was the difference between a life spent in heaven or hell. But it was not pure altruism that fed his attraction for teenaged children. He felt his own power boosted in their company, in what amounted to something of an occult trade-off. The magisterial knowledge he passed on to them was to be repaid unwittingly by pupils with doses of their youthful virility, on which he became increasingly dependent as he aged. Young people, particularly boys, acted on him like a tonic, and kept alive the spirit of wonder and vitality for which he was so admired. The practical methods he employed to extract this tonic had been, and were to become still further, the subject of much debate and scandal.

The other Theosophists noticed Leadbeater's distraction. They were familiar with his ways and knew the signs. It was the older boy, Wood suddenly realised, who had sparked fire in his leader's eyes – young Krishna, the half-wit, the little brother's awkward shadow. Leadbeater had quite obviously been gripped by something he had seen, to which none of the other bathing Europeans, as mere Theosophical footsoldiers, had access. His ability to see beyond the physical veil, to delve into the world of subtle bodies, spirits and astral planes was well-credited in the community; indeed, it was the very keystone of his authority at Adyar. As he silently exercised his arms in a symmetrical breast-stroke, neck-deep in the Indian Ocean, his occult imagination took wing.

Oblivious of his companions in the sea, Leadbeater had eyes only for the boy, because what he beheld was breathtaking, quite unprecedented in his experience. The child appeared to be surrounded by an etheric substance of gorgeous luminescence. It was what Leadbeater would describe as his 'causal body', his higher mental capacity, or aura, the accumulation of lifetimes of occult development. There was 'a radiant globe of flashing colours, its high vibrations sending ripples of changing hues over its surface – hues of which earth knows nothing – brilliant, soft and luminous, beyond the power of language to describe . . . filled with living fire drawn from a higher plane'.[1] Here before him, housed within the form of a scrawny native, he recognised an ancient and wise soul, who had reached, through multiple reincarnations, a degree of rare development, completely lacking in selfishness, one for whom desires and feelings were petty abstractions in comparison to the spiritual work he was destined to undertake. The child's body was nothing – a mere shell adopted for the practical business of living this life. But through that shell, Leadbeater foresaw that the boy might 'be able to work for the good of humanity, and to pour out at these levels influence which otherwise could not descend thereto'.[2]

Leadbeater did not take any immediate action. For once in his life he did not act on impulse. He brushed aside the comments of Wood who, having once or twice in the past given Krishna some help with his homework, maintained the lad was retarded. There were pressing constraints. It was a bad time for Leadbeater to be seen in the company of adolescent boys, as the furnace of scandal surrounding him was far from exhausted. And yet the possibilities opened up by what he had seen were too thrilling to be ignored. The more he mulled over the encounter, the more he was convinced that both brothers, indeed their whole family, had been brought to Adyar for a specific purpose, and that purpose was the product of a divine will. He, Charles Webster Leadbeater, was to be a central player in that plan, though exactly what was expected of him was as yet unclear. He would have to get to know the boys a little and, crucially, win the support of his President, Annie Besant, who was currently lecturing abroad. Tact and patience were essential – neither of which he possessed to any great degree.

During the course of the next few weeks he invited the brothers for regular interviews at his bungalow – awkward, one-sided affairs, as they stood tongue-tied in front of the formidable Englishman, understanding little of what he said. Gradually, through kind words and reassuring pats on the head, Leadbeater succeeded in winning their confidence, and the further he delved into the occult abyss the more convinced he became that his original hunch was correct. It was almost unimaginable and too exciting even for him, bluff and confident as he was, to spell out. And yet it fitted perfectly – it made absolute sense of what he and the Theosophical Society had been working towards for the past quarter of a century. Such were the mechanics of the divine Logos, he told himself – mysterious, unpredictable, but yet inevitable. It was the destiny of the world and mankind. In his boundless vanity he now glimpsed the ultimate prize and determined that nothing would prevent him reaching it. Like the sun that rises for the life and glory of the world at every dawn, so the beauty and clarity of his own role in the divine plan now manifested itself before him. It was to be his task to pluck young Krishna from obscurity, to mould and prepare him for the great mission that was his to accomplish. For into that child's body, at the appropriate time, for all the world to see, would descend the spirit of Christ himself, and mankind would behold a new messiah.

2

The Melting Pot

———————— ✳ ————————

The Theosophical Society's lifeblood, its very source and inspiration, derived from the work of one individual, a woman whose magnetic personality, exoticism and learning have earned her a place as one of the most controversial spiritual adventurers to have challenged the authority of mainstream religion: Helena Petrovsky Blavatsky. Foul-mouthed, volatile, grotesquely fat, and reeking of the cigarettes she continuously rolled and smoked, Madame Blavatsky's influence was seminal in the development of what is today known as the New Age movement. Her claim was that she had rediscovered a primordial wisdom, the key to life and divinity, which pre-dated and superseded all religions, cultures and theologies; her revelation of this 'secret doctrine', she maintained, would transform religious consciousness in the western world, and signal a new era in the history of humanity.

Blavatsky spent her life amassing information on a whole spectrum of religious philosophies, specialising in obscure sects, secret societies, ancient disciplines and exotic manuscripts from the orient. While her storehouse of knowledge lent a certain plausibility to her claims, it was her breathtaking demonstrations of spiritualist phenomena that were to add irresistable spice to her public appearances, with the result that few who encountered her failed to depart unconvinced of her uniqueness. She was the archetypal nineteenth-century occultist, swathed in black shawls, bulbous-eyed, gravel-voiced, sporting a thick eastern-European accent – part witch, part priestess, with a dash of the eccentric academic, a woman who could combine blatant showmanship with genuine scholarship, and although swamped by scandal and accusations of fraudulence during her own lifetime, repeatedly proved herself resistant to assault. The force of her personality was enough to silence would-be critics at face-to-face meetings, but those who did summon the courage to grill Blavatsky usually retreated with their fingers burnt. No stranger to coarse manners, she appeared to enjoy obliterating her opponents, lashing them with her intellect, which, unlike the virtually immobile hulk of her body, was athletic and lucid.

Born in the Ukraine in 1831, Helena Blavatsky left home and then husband at the age of seventeen to pursue a life of mystic quests and adventures, which are said to have included working as a Russian spy and fighting for Garibaldi's Red-shirts. Towards the end of the 1850s she visited India, travelled north to Kashmir and made the mountainous journey north-east to Ladakh, a Himalayan outpost with a Tibetan culture. She later claimed to have visited Tibet itself, and to have studied there for several years with her Master, a spiritual Adept, at his home in a remote cave. Here, she would later have it believed, she received the instruction that was to form the backbone of her doctrinal outlook and the founding platform of the Theosophical Society's mission, although it would appear that the story of her Tibetan sojourn was in fact a hoax, fabricated to enhance the mystery of her Master.

Blavatsky's travels took her to New York in 1873, where she blazed a trail through occult circles with her litany of romantic tales and theories. Dabblers in the supernatural were entranced by her spiritualist tricks, such as precipitating letters from her Master out of thin air or causing objects to materialise, all performed with casual panache as a kind of after-dinner entertainment, to the accompaniment of husky incantations and appropriate ceremonies. Bewitched by her hypnotic pale blue eyes, her outspoken claims and gargantuan physical presence, occultists in New York society began to turn to Blavatsky as a seer.

She had declared that her purpose in America was to coax people away from the trivialities of mere spiritualism and generate an interest in the higher occult powers. Through study and effort, she maintained, an individual might enter onto the path of wisdom, and thereby, with the help of a spiritual Master, engage with the metaphysical source of creation. The path would lead, through multiple incarnations, to spiritual adepthood for the aspirant, and a final resting place for the soul in nirvana. This lofty ambition appealed to Blavatsky above the contemporary fad for spiritualism, which she condemned as sentimental and indulgent, nothing more than a childish thrill for serious seekers of wisdom. Yet it was spiritualism that brought her together with her co-founder of the Theosophical Society, Henry Steel Olcott. She had been impressed by a popular series of articles written by Olcott, describing interesting spiritual phenomena that had been occurring at a farm in Chittenden, Vermont. Determined to meet and forge an alliance with the articles' author, she hastened to the Vermont farm when she knew Olcott would next be there, and instantly achieved her purpose without difficulty, as was her way. The impressionable Olcott was captivated, and the two formed a friendship that was to continue after their subsequent return to New York. Drawing together a circle of like-minded esotericists, they would host meetings to debate occult issues and present lectures. It was at one of these, on 7 September 1875, that the Theosophical Society spontaneously took shape.

Theosophy[1] literally means 'divine wisdom', and although the term is today usually associated with Blavatsky's organisation, it has links with philosophical schools that date back to antiquity. Pythagoras' sixth century BC religious community at Croton, in southern Italy, is said to have embodied theosophical ideals, which later influenced the work of Plato, who in turn paved the way for the neoplatonist philosophy of Ammonius Saccas and Plotinus, in the third century AD. All three can justifiably be described as forefathers of modern Theosophy. At the root of theosophy lies the conviction that everything, manifested and unmanifested, created and uncreated, divine or material, emanates from a state of unity, immeasurable, incomprehensible to the intellect, yet all-pervasive. This transcendent reality, or godhead, is accessible to physical man through a process of mystical realisation, or union, and it is only within the experience of this unity that true wisdom is to be found – primordial wisdom, the ground upon which all the religions of the world have been modelled. According to theosophical thought, independent religious dogmas, rituals and priestcraft misrepresent the essential underlying wis-

9

dom which brooks no division. During the course of western history, adherents of such radical spiritual ideas have tended to compile their speculations and conduct their experiments in secret, to avoid persecution from the established religions. Clandestine orders, brotherhoods and heretical sects were formed, which made it their duty to safeguard 'the wisdom' for future, perhaps more enlightened, generations; in liberal political climates these found expression in better-known organisations like freemasonry.

Blavatsky and Olcott epitomised, with their new Society, the spirit of nineteenth-century adventurism, tapping the contemporary mood while at the same time bringing together several strands of religious enquiry from the past into a cohesive movement. Sectarianism and agnosticism had been on the rise in the Victorian era, fuelled both by the proliferation of charismatic non-conformist clerics, and exciting new breakthroughs in science. The dimmer recesses of cultural mythology were being explored and questioned in the name of progress, and the biblical texts themselves became the subject of academic scrutiny. In the privacy of their homes, the social elite and even royalty were known to dabble in occult practices, hoping to gain insight into the mysteries of life and death. The ancient seats of ecclesiastical authority were challenged to defend their traditional claims against the evidence of scientific pioneers like Darwin and Lyell, while at the same time splinter-group congregations began to swell under the influence of tub-thumping tirades from chapel pulpits. Religious opportunists prospered. Meanwhile, intellectuals and political radicals were spear-heading a secularist revival, based on the ideals of eighteenth-century enlightenment thinkers, and they formed agnostic chapel movements, complete with Sunday assemblies, secular hymns and heretical sermons questioning the very existence of God. The moral conscience of the times was clear-cut, but in terms of the religious status quo there was an uncertain public mood.

Blavatsky's Theosophical Society was a melting pot for these prevalent movements and fashionable preoccupations. Her catchment was wide, encompassing spiritualists, dissenting Christians, atheists, agnostics, and political subversives, together with freemasons, occultists, and members of Hermetic, Rosicrucian and alchemical societies. Their common ground was millenarian, a shared belief that the old order was passing and that human knowledge, power and consciousness were on the cusp of a golden age, a new epoch that would be facilitated by the rediscovery of ancient 'theosophy' – the very wisdom which Blavatsky claimed as her qualification.

Three central objects for the Society were settled upon:

1. To form a nucleus of a universal brotherhood of humanity, without distinction of race, creed, sex, caste or colour.
2. To study comparative religions, philosophies and sciences.
3. To investigate the unexplained laws of nature and the psychical powers latent in man.

However, the breadth and indeterminacy of these pursuits concealed Blavatsky's other important agenda for her Society, which was both idiosyncratic and dogmatic: to proliferate belief and dependence upon a hierarchy of 'Masters', an occult brotherhood of semi-divine entities, who, it was claimed, could travel on the astral plane to visit pupils, either through dreams, or occasionally through spectral appearances. Blavatsky taught that the Masters were Great Souls (or *Mahatmas*), spiritual adepts, who had survived beyond the normal life-span of human beings in order to pass on divine wisdom to the initiated. Their existence was thus potentially real, or corporeal, but their bodies were believed to be too vulnerable to travel from their rarified homes so that, in practice (to their pupils), they were metaphysical and communication with them was dependent on flights of the imagination and a giant leap of faith. None the less, the plans and machinations of the Masters were to form the core of Theosophy's doctrinal system, and members of the Society would aspire to become enrolled as pupils of a particular Master as a prerequisite for their ascent on the mystic path.

A defining point in the the Theosophical movement, and one which was to cause an early division within the Society, emerged from Blavatsky's insistence that her Masters' philosophy was rooted in the religions of the east, and that members who sought true wisdom should turn their attention to the teachings of Hinduism and Buddhism. Indeed, the founders made plans, shortly after the Society's inauguration, to emigrate to India, where it was intended that a Theosophical headquarters would be established. It was not an entirely unexpected deviation. Blavatsky had visited India twice already, in the 1850s and 1860s, and felt a strong sympathy with the philosophy she encountered there. The acknowledgement in Hinduism's sacred texts that all creation springs from, returns to, and exists united within an unimaginable godhead, beyond measure and name, was closely parallelled by theosophy's own theory of primordial divinity. And Blavatsky's gravitation eastwards also reflected a prevailing fashion for orientalism that had been growing since the early part of the century. The exotic, mysterious and richly perfumed allure of the east had captivated painters such as Delacroix and Ingres, and thence spread to the other decorative arts, while at the same time, empire-builders, bound for or returning from India, began to generate public interest in the culture of the distant colony. Indian philosophy had also at last reached western shores, received, albeit, by an intellectual minority, particularly through the works of Rammohan Roy and Keshub Chunder Sen.

According to the orthodox Theosophy that Krishnamurti would one day inherit, the Great White Brotherhood of Masters, Blavatsky's brainchild, had a very distinct Indian slant. High up in the hierarchy, above the Masters who retained their bodies in order to teach, was an elite quintet of entities, angelic in substance, who, it was claimed, acted as a bridge between ignorant humanity and all-knowing, unnameable divinity. At the head of the hierarchy was the Lord of the World, who was said to have the physical appearance of a teenaged boy, perceptible to a privileged few, and then only on the most auspicious occasions and in a state of trance. Beneath him came the Buddha, followed by a trinity of Lords: the Mahachohan, the Manu, and the Maitreya, whose appearances were similarly rare. The Maitreya was the World Teacher, who was said to 'descend' into human incarnations, for the advancement of mankind, at various times in history. His 'vehicles' had included both Jesus and Krishna. After the Lord Maitreya, in the hierarchy, came a series of other Masters, two of whom were to play a particularly important role in the direction of Blavatsky, the Theosophical Society and, later, Krishnamurti: Kuthumi (the Master KH) and Morya (the Master M). These entities, according to Blavatsky, had kept their ancient bodies, and lived near to each other in a remote Tibetan valley, where she herself had allegedly studied. Kuthumi had the looks and colouring of a fair-skinned Kashmiri Brahmin, whereas Morya was a dark Rajput prince. Their physical appearance was important to Theosophists. Devotees, including the young Krishnamurti, would carry idealised portraits of the Masters on their travels, as an aid to forming corporeal images of them. The portraits (particularly of the Aryan Kuthumi) were not unlike images of Jesus printed in Victorian children's Bibles.

Unknown to any of her disciples, the mythical Masters Blavatsky created were modelled not on deific Himalayan hermits steeped in wisdom, who could travel magically to and from the minds of their pupils, but on very real figures in public life, the most prominent of whom were involved with political reform in India.[2] The Master Morya was modelled on Maharajah Ranbir Singh of Kashmir, a cultivated philanthropist, and the Master Kuthumi on Thakar Singh Sandhwalia, leader of a Sikh revivalist organisation. Blavatsky transformed these real men into supermen, colossi of her imagination, and transcribed in books and letters not just the essence of their particular ideologies, but the sum of her own scholarship and experience as well, with frequent recourse to both Hindu and Buddhist scriptures. She would later feel entrapped by the unwieldy edifice of fact and fiction she had created; but it is doubtful that she ever contemplated the influence her Masters were to have after her own lifetime, within both the Theosophical Society and the various religious organisations that derived from it. It is an influence that can be felt in New Age movements to this day.

Blavatsky and Olcott set sail from New York on 18 December 1878, arriving in Bombay the following February, and by 1882 had moved the international headquarters of the Theosophical Society to a twenty-seven-acre estate known as Huddlestone's Gardens, at Adyar, a suburb of Madras, in south-east India. The Society had enjoyed a boom, and membership reached 100,000. During the course of the next fifty years, there would be other high points, and the Adyar compound would grow vastly; but disaster was at hand for Blavatsky, and in 1884 it arrived in the form of a deluge of scandal. A string of accusations led to the revelation that many of her so-called 'manifestations' of the Masters, or their letters, were faked. Puppets, secret drawers, doors and cabinets had apparently been employed to dupe the gullible, all with the assistance of a housekeeper, now turned Judas. Ailing and disgraced, Blavatsky left India in 1885 and settled in London. But this indomitable woman was by no means finished. The remaining fifteen years of her life saw her directing the activities of numerous influential disciples, and, liberated from the hot-seat of official leadership, she produced her greatest written work, *The Secret Doctrine*.

If the mention of Blavatsky in certain circles nowadays arouses mixed feelings, a touch of scepticism and no little amusement, the name Charles Webster Leadbeater can give rise to open vehemence. Leadbeater, the single most important influence on Krishnamurti's education, is still revered by some as a saint of modern times. Many others respect his work as that of a prophetic scholar; but equal numbers revile him as a demonic exploiter, a hilarious fraudster or a sexual pervert.

Leadbeater was born in Stockport, Cheshire, in 1854, the son of a railway bookkeeper. Not a great deal is known about his relatively humble background, because in later life he fabricated an elaborate and thrilling alternative to the truth. This false account remained the accepted version of his life-story until a biographer published an exposé in 1982.[3] A devoted fan of the novels of H. Rider Haggard, Jules Verne and H.G. Wells, Leadbeater concocted a personal history that read like a nineteenth century romance.

He claimed to have been born in 1847 (probably to twin himself, in terms of seniority and occult synchronicity, with his future Theosophical colleague, Annie Besant, who was born in that year). As a youth, the story goes, he emigrated to deepest South America with his father, supposedly the chairman of a railway company, and a younger brother, Gerald, who, in fact, never existed. There they lived lives of perilous adventure and heroism. One tale has them ambushed by Indians in the Brazilian jungle and held captive by rebel bandits; young Charles is roasted alive over a fire and wounded by gunshot, while his mythical brother Gerald is put to the sword for refusing to trample over a crucifix. On another occasion he is led underwater in Peru to a secret stockpile of Inca treasure. Returning to England, his claims extended to matriculating at Queen's College, Oxford (sometimes St John's College, Cambridge), witnessing supernatural tricks performed by his father's 'good friend' Edward Bulwer-Lytton, the most influential occultist of his day, and stabbing a werewolf in the Scottish isles. The truth is that Leadbeater would only have been an infant at the time he was claiming to have been doing battle in the jungle, that he never went to South America at all, that he never attended any university, and that his father was a back-office pen-pusher who died at the age of thirty-six, leaving his wife and only son almost destitute.

Leadbeater's later bombastic confidence belies the sensitivity and shyness of his younger days. He first comes to attention in 1878 as curate of Bramshott, a small parish in Hampshire. Bored by the routine of parish chores, the young curate preferred to engage himself in lay activities with his flock. He felt particularly comfortable in the company of children and they for their part were drawn to him as if to the Pied Piper. He tirelessly organised outings, clubs, sports events and holiday trips for them, thus early discovering the role to which much of his life's work was dedicated. His talents as a captain figure for young people, especially boys, were to be marred later in his career by recurrent rumours of sexual impropriety, but he none the less inspired their confidence and devotion, even as an old man.

Like so many other young clergymen of his generation, Leadbeater felt uneasy about orthodox Christian theology. So much so that he took himself to London to attend lectures given at the Hall of Science by that virulent secularist, socialist and sworn atheist, Annie Besant. Little did the curate suspect that the speaker, whose words were heresy to the ears of his superiors in the Church, would one day become his closest ally and colleague on the other side of the world. He simultaneously developed a fascination for the supernatural and soon stumbled across some fashionable new books that appeared to combine all his interests. They sprang from a young organisation, the Theosophical Society, which Leadbeater determined to investigate. On 16 December 1883 he was formally inducted into the Society, along with the distinguished physicist Professor (later Sir William) Crookes, and in the presence of several luminaries, including Oscar Wilde. He immediately volunteered his services as a work-horse, and was assigned to answer the Society's burgeoning correspondence, explaining as much he could about Theosophy.

His curacy soon took second place to this new vocation, in which he felt very much at home.[4]

The following year he encountered Blavatsky herself, who had arrived on an unexpected visit to the London Lodge of the Society. Turning to be introduced to her new disciple, she dryly commented, 'I don't think much of the clergy, for I find most of them hypocritical, bigoted and stupid.'[5] Nevertheless, it was a significant meeting for both of them. Leadbeater, ripe for the picking, was swept off his feet. A subsequent letter, supposedly from the Master Kuthumi, recommending him to visit India was all that it required to dissolve his tenuous attachment to the Church. Enflamed with a desire to encounter the Masters personally, he made his excuses at Bramshott, packed his belongings, gave up eating meat, and set sail with Blavatsky for India. For her part, Blavatsky felt it would be something of a prestige coup (in the face of enemy fire) to arrive in India with a converted clergyman at her heels.

Leadbeater arrived at Adyar on 21 December 1884, brimming with enthusiasm, and soon began to have visions of the Masters. His buoyant optimism was tempered by a gruelling period of introspection when he was left for several months alone at Adyar. It was a period of learning, hard toil and considerable discomfort, but at the end he felt himself to have established 'astral consciousness'.[6] From that time on, Leadbeater never wavered in his confidence of the Masters, nor of his own authority as their clairvoyant channel.

After Adyar, Leadbeater served Olcott for three years with the Theosophical Society in Ceylon, but by 1889 was keen to return to England. He had become inseparably attached to a thirteen-year-old Singhalese boy called Jinarajadasa, and claimed that the lad was a reincarnation of his murdered (mythical) younger brother, Gerald. Leadbeater persuaded himself that he must become the boy's guardian, and was determined to see him properly educated. To this end he staged an elaborate plot to spirit the boy away from his family on a departing schooner. After a near-murderous confrontation with their son's abductor, Jinarajadasa's heart-broken parents gave their consent for his departure. He was to be the first of three Indian boys to become Leadbeater's protégés,[7] Krishnamurti being the second.

Back in London, Leadbeater took it upon himself to rear and educate

Jinarajadasa, a task he accomplished so successfully that within a few years the boy had graduated with honours from Cambridge University. Amongst other achievements, Jinarajadasa became the author of several eloquently argued books, and ultimately served as President of the Theosophical Society. Both he and another of Leadbeater's pupils at this time, twelve-year-old George Arundale, were to become central figures in the story of Krishnamurti.

Meanwhile, Theosophy's mentor, the ailing Madame Blavatsky, showed little interest in seeing Leadbeater in London, and he likewise kept his distance. Perhaps there was an element of personal antipathy; but it is just as possible that Blavatsky was genuinely alarmed by Leadbeater's very literal interpretation of her Masters doctrine. Leadbeater claimed intimate personal knowledge of the Masters she had created, frequently citing messages he had personally received, without the aid of her own mediumship. This was Blavatsky's monster taking on a life of its own. As she settled down to a retirement of outstanding literary activity, she may well have felt Leadbeater to be, at best, something of a loose cannon, or at worst, a crackpot zealot.

But his star was on the rise. Theosophists began to take note of his articles, and his enthusiasm for the Masters acted like a healing balm for those distressed by the scandals that surrounded Blavatsky. One person, in particular, found herself fascinated with the former clergyman's work. She was one of the Society's latest and most notorious converts. Her record to date was as a leading socialist, secularist, social reformer, hero of the trades union movement, campaigner for women's rights, and a scourge of the British establishment. In collaboration with Leadbeater she was about to embark on a new life – one which would result in her becoming the other major impetus in propelling Krishnamurti's career and defining his early outlook.

Annie Besant's role in the making of the World Teacher began in the early weeks of 1889. She had been commissioned by the *Pall Mall Gazette* to write a review of Madame Blavatsky's seminal work, *The Secret Doctrine*, and the more she read, the more she realised that her life was on the brink of a shattering transformation. It was as if her own hidden convictions about human existence were being brought out into the light through someone else's words. It was a spine-chilling revelation, and there began for Besant a rediscovery of her own inner self, the dawning of a fabulous new adventure.

Besant was just forty-one when she read *The Secret Doctrine*, but she had already proved herself one of the more outstanding personalities of the nineteenth century. Brought up as a devout Christian, she early discovered an instinct for missionary altruism that was to permeate her life's work. At first, not unlike George Eliot's Dorothea Brooke, she thought the best opportunity for her to serve lay in marrying a clergyman and working for the needy of the parish. But the twenty-year-old bride of the Rev. Frank Besant was shortly to find life unbearable at their Lincolnshire rectory. Her husband's brutal authoritarianism, coupled with her own sexual reluctance and sheer boredom, led to a breakdown of the marriage after a mere six years. Annie's greatest regret about the separation was not the Victorian social stigma, but the ultimate loss of both her children to her husband's care.[8]

Free of the rectory, Annie took up writing and began to question the fundamentals of Christian faith. It was not that she had lost her desire to serve mankind, but that her vocation had dissociated itself from what she saw as an unjust religion. Along with a growing crowd of nineteenth-century dissenters, she could not equate social deprivation, pain and cruelty with the kindly personal God upheld by traditional Christian doctrine. She emerged as a leading light in the world of Free Thought and political radicalism. Espousing the claims of Darwin and modern science, she publicly defied Christianity and eloquently questioned the very existence of God.

Although admired today for her pioneering work, Annie was viewed by many in her time as a threatening zealot. Her work in the area of birth control (the first woman to make public statements on the issue of contraception) led to her being tried in 1877 for attempting to corrupt the nation's morals. In November 1887 she led a vast crowd of the hungry unemployed in a demonstration at Trafalgar Square that subsequently turned into the street-battle with the police, known as Bloody Sunday. A year later, she led 1400 women out on strike at the Bryant & May match factory in a protest against poor working conditions and wages that was to become a landmark in the history of the trades union movement.

Despite the apparent effectiveness of her work as a reformer, Annie felt increasingly during the 1880s that there was something fundamentally missing in her life. Socialism had to some extent quenched her thirst for missionary service, but it had not replaced the spiritual vacuum left by her abandonment of Christianity. She began to feel that her campaigns were geared only towards economic ends, towards material solutions. Socialism would not change peoples' inclinations to love and care for one another, she decided; it would not ease psychological suffering or bring about the Brotherhood of Man.

Blavatsky's Theosophy appealed to her intellectually. Central to its attraction was the doctrine of karma: the theory that a person's actions (and thoughts) in this life affect his or her opportunity for upliftment in the next – a cyclical path of spiritual improvement leading ultimately to Adeptship and nirvana. This corroborated Annie's conviction that evolution was not just a physical progression (along the lines of Darwin), but also a spiritual, and thus social one as well. As mankind passed through multiple lives to achieve perfection, pain and suffering would evaporate, to be replaced by philadelphian unity. This was human equality, this was freedom from a vengeful God-figure, this was the modern science of evolution, this was the dignity of man endorsed by natural law. In short, Theosophy provided a meeting point for her spiritual and political impulses.

The opportunity for Blavatsky to ensnare the militant socialist came in March 1889, when a reverential Annie, having recently submitted her book review, called to visit. After a cordial conversation, the magnificent Russian turned her powder-blue eyes full on the visitor, and pleaded, 'Oh, my dear Mrs Besant, if you would only come among us!'[9] Annie nearly crumpled on the spot in a swoon of devotion, such was the engaging power of the wily old occultist. She then astonished the public and her friends by formally joining the Theosophical Society on 10 May 1889. She resigned her membership of the National Secular Society and the Fabian Society, and went on to give a series of public speeches in defence of her decision, one of which was heard by the young (and as yet unknown) Mohandas K. Gandhi, later to become her sparring partner in the cause of Indian Home Rule.

There developed a relationship of intense mutual fondness between Blavatsky and Besant; within a few months of their first meeting, she became the old Russian's closest aide and spokesperson, and the two lived together at Annie's house on Avenue Road, north London. The tired and bronchial founder preferred to let Annie answer questions on her behalf at public gatherings, while she sat back in an armchair, rolling her cigarettes. By 1890 Annie was president of the Blavatsky Lodge, a separate section of the Society, and co-editor of Blavatsky's journal, *Lucifer*. She had also become a member of the Esoteric Section of the Society, or ES, a hardcore occult committee, consisting of Blavatsky's pet circle of disciples. Annie took over control of the ES in the 1890s, and by the time of Krishnamurti's appearance had turned it into something of an elite inner club, the aristocracy of the Theosophical Society. It was while Annie was in America on a lecturing tour that she heard the news of Blavatsky's death on 8 May 1891. She had finally succumbed to influenza, having struggled to combat Bright's disease for some time.

Annie Besant resolved soon after to follow in the footsteps of her deceased guru and visit India. She had for many years taken an anti-imperialist stance with regard to British rule in India and had been a vigorous campaigner for Indian Home Rule. As such, her reputation preceded her. When on 16 November 1893, she finally set foot in the country that was to be her home for the remaining forty years of her life, she was given a tremendous reception and her first tour around the country was nothing short of regal. Stepping into the shoes of Blavatsky and bringing with her a prodigious reputation for fighting tyranny in the name of political freedom, she was seen by nationalists as a potential saviour. She felt she had come to the greatest challenge of her life, and was ready to martyr herself for the cause. The suffering of the poor in India touched her social conscience; and the iniquity of Britain's colonial rule offended her sense of political fair play. Yet interwoven with these missionary impulses came her fascination with Hindu philosophy, and her conviction that India was to be the cradle of a new world religion.

The happy union of these interests in the person of Annie Besant made her an unstoppable force in Indian cultural life, much to the annoyance of her compatriots in government. The British Raj, which had viewed Blavatsky with deep suspicion and placed her under police surveillance, was not sympathetic to the Theosophists. Their fraternisation with locals, their encouragement of social reform, and their infatuation with native religions did not endear them to the colonial administration in Calcutta. The incorporation of Annie Besant into their ranks merely added fuel to the fire. Quite aside from her formidable record as a political agitator, she was on cordial terms (socialist or not) with high-ranking members of the government and judiciary in London. British officials in India were indignant that a member of so exalted a social set should be seen to champion the interests of the subject race.

But tact and colonial etiquette were not at the forefront of Annie's mind at this time. She was beginning to experience frequent visitations from the Masters, and was more convinced than ever of her occult calling. Enthralled with Theosophy she allowed many of her past interests and friends to fall by the wayside. George Bernard Shaw had been one of her closest friends, perhaps even a lover. He regretted her conversion, but summarised his own explanation of her departure in a shrewd, if rather cynical paragraph: 'She was a born actress. She was successively a Puseyite Evangelical, an Atheist Bible-smasher, a Darwinian secularist, a Fabian socialist, a Strike Leader, and finally a Theosophist, exactly as Mrs Siddons was a Lady Macbeth, Lady Randolph, Beatrice, Rosalind, and Volumnia. She saw herself as a priestess above all. That was how Theosophy held her to the end.'[10]

Besant first met Leadbeater at a gathering of the London Theosophical Lodge in 1890, but their collaboration did not begin until April 1894, after Annie had been to India. She was drawn by his dynamism and his infectious confidence, as well as to his looks, bearded and sharp-eyed, not unlike her friend Shaw. Her life to date, including the India experience, had equipped her to explore the first two objectives of Theosophy (to form a universal brotherood and to study comparative religions), but as regards the third object (to investigate the unexplained laws of nature and the psychical powers latent in man) her education was as yet deficient. In this arena Leadbeater was now to become her guru.

In August 1895, Leadbeater and Jinarajadasa were invited to live at

Avenue Road, and so began a period of close collaboration and experimentation with Annie Besant. That first summer together was marked by a series of expeditions, some of them to the countryside, during which they would concentrate their investigative powers on a particular area. Striding through the lush Sussex meadows, Leadbeater would talk continuously, pouring forth a stream of occult observations, occasionally aided by comments from Besant at his side, while Jinarajad-asa ran along at their heels, earnestly taking notes. At Box Hil in Surrey they laid out a rug on the bracken and spent the day delving into mythological history. While staying at Lewis Park Farm in Sussex they explored distant reaches of the solar system, identifying four as yet undiscovered planets. Later, seated on a grassy bank beside the Finchley Road in north London, they initiated a study known as 'Occult Chemistry'. This involved a diminution of the occult eye so as to allow clear vision at a sub-atomic level. They sought, thereby, to identify the fundamental building block of matter and, from that, to correct, expand and reinterpret the periodic table itself.

In the summer of 1895, Besant and Leadbeater formed the partnership that would dominate Theosophy until the mid-1930s. The pooling of their respective interests into a single movement represents a culmination of theosophical history. No longer a society for learned debate, Theosophy now appeared to offer a viable religious alternative that might, in time, change the world. Their claims were extravagant, but their delivery was plausible, and in the person of Annie Besant, they had an eloquent, much-respected spokesperson.

Coming as it did, at a time of religious uncertainty in the west, Theosophy had a promising future. All that was needed was a focus for the movement; a heart, a mascot upon which to pin the high passions of devotees; an authority, immaculate and uncorrupted, before whom unquestioning faith could be laid.

3

Make Straight the Way

———— ✳ ————

On 11 May 1895, while Annie Besant and Charles Leadbeater were consolidating their friendship in London, Jiddu Narayaniah was travelling home by cart in the blistering South Indian heat. The landscape around him was baked hard from months of relentless sunshine and hot winds. On either side of the dust track thorny green scrub and brush were punctuated with rocky outcrops. They rose up in masses, heavy with gargantuan boulders and surrounded by a spread of infertile red soil. It provided distant views that were both desolate and beautiful; arid but still yielding to the hardiest kinds of vegetation. This was typical of the terrain in this inland district of the Madras Presidency, where the vast coastal plain gives way to the higher ground of the central Indian peninsula.[1] The monsoon was due in about a fortnight, and daily temperatures, though cooler here than in the nearby river basin, had risen to around 35° Celsius. As Narayaniah trundled through small farming settlements on the uncomfortable trail back to his home town, all but those compelled to toil in the sweltering sunlight were hiding in the shade.

The huge majority of workers in this part of India laboured in the grain fields and rice paddies, but Jiddu Narayaniah was rather better off. As a literate high-caste Brahmin, and having graduated from the University of Madras, he had been accepted for employment by the British administration. He was a junior civil servant, though he was later to be promoted to full tahsildar (tax collector) in the provincial capital. The people of the district were proud with a rich literary and artistic heritage, and there was a strong nationalist current latent in the culture. The good name that Narayaniah may have lost in selling his services to the foreign regime was compensated for by the material comfort he derived from its paymasters. Besides, the male members of his family had for many years worked as officials on behalf of the British. His father had held a responsible post within the Madras Presidency civil service and his grandfather had been in the judicial department of the East India Company.[2]

Narayaniah was relieved to arrive at his house in Madanapalle that same evening. The demands of his job meant that he was frequently away – he was used to that – but this was a particularly critical time for another reason. His wife, Sanjeevamma, was due at any moment to produce their eighth child. The pre-monsoon heat had added to her discomfort, and although they had organised a female relative to be at hand night and day, Narayaniah wanted to be present to ensure that all the post-natal ceremonies were carried out correctly, as befitted a strict Brahmin household.

Stepping over the sewage drain that ran outside his house, he entered its dark, low-ceilinged hall, where the air was stale and suffocatingly hot. It was a comfortable house by local standards, with a number of chambers, an open yard within, and two storeys, topped with a thatched roof. Its rooms were small and claustrophobic, and at this time of year his wife and children spent most of their time on the verandahs.

His wife greeted him affectionately in their native language, Telugu. Sanjeevamma was a pretty woman with a full-lipped mouth, high cheekbones and gentle eyes. Despite her discomfort she radiated the warmth and contentment that all reports of her emphasise. She and her husband were cousins, and their marriage, though arranged at a young age, according to caste tradition, was a happy one. Narayaniah asked if arrangements for the birth were exactly as she wanted them. Satisfied that this was the case, the couple retired to the upstairs terrace, where Sanjeevamma lay back on a comfortable chair and sang songs to her husband in her 'very beautiful melodious voice'.[3] They then had supper, prepared for them by Brahmin servants downstairs, and afterwards slept out on the open terrace.

It is doubtful Sanjeevamma slept for long, bearing in mind the heat and her condition. Just before midnight her contractions began in earnest, and she woke Narayaniah, asking him to help her downstairs. She had a strange request. She wanted to go into the puja room, a sanctified area of the house set aside for ritual devotion. It was against custom to enter the puja room after having eaten in the evening or before the ritual morning wash; but Sanjeevamma was a devoutly religious woman, and proceeded to meditate at the shrine, calmly mouthing prayers between her spasms.

Their relative then helped her to the room that had been set aside for the birth, and Narayaniah waited outside, sweating and gazing at his pocket watch by the light of oil lamps. All he could hear were the encouraging words of the midwife and his wife's repeated prayers, muttered like a mantra between gasps, 'Rama, Rama Anjanaya.' At 12.30 a.m. on the morning of Sunday 12 May,[4] the relative opened the door and told Narayaniah, 'Sirasodayam,' the traditional Sanskrit word used to announce a birth. It means 'the head has appeared,' and Narayaniah checked his watch once more to record the precise moment, so that the astrologer would be able to piece together the birth-chart – another important tradition.

Sanjeevamma's eighth birth was surprisingly swift and painless, when compared to her previous ones. The new baby was a boy and, although the name-giving ceremony would not be conducted for several days, he would clearly have to be named, in accordance with tradition, after the Lord Krishna, who was himself an eighth child. The baby would therefore be called Krishnamurti – incarnation of Lord Krishna. The following morning the astrologer was invited to the house, where he performed his scholarly task, after having completed the appropriate rituals at the household shrine. He was both surprised and pleased at his findings. The child would grow to be a very great man, he informed the boy's father, collecting his fee. It might involve crossing some difficult hurdles, but he would definitely rise to great heights. Sanjeevamma needed little convincing. For some time she had expressed strange feelings about her unborn child, a sense that he would possess unique, outstanding talents. And all the reports of Sanjeevamma that have come down to us testify that she was known for her psychic gifts.

*   *   *

There is little definitely known about Krishnamurti's early life, or about the lives of his older siblings, several of whom had left home by the time he rose to prominence. Almost everything compiled about his childhood was written from the perspective of his later status, and is therefore awash with imaginative mythology. The occasional solid fact stands out like a marker in the flood, but much of it has been ornamented with half-truths, and imbued with the perfume of scripture. Until recently, for example, it was commonly maintained that Krishnamurti had in fact been born in the puja room of his home. It was thought that this contravention of Brahminic rules pointed to the child's future religious prominence. However, this was no more than a fable. Iconology is a powerful instrument for wooing the faithful but it can be hazardous for the historian, as demonstrated by popular depictions of an even more celebrated nativity – at Bethlehem.

Part of the problem derives from Krishnamurti's own memory loss in later life. He frequently let it be known that he could recall nothing about his past except what others had told him. His philosophy stressed the importance of living in the present, free from the conditioning engendered by past experience, and for this reason reminiscing was an irrelevance. Some facts and incidents he certainly did retain, if only on a subconscious level, and these occasionally surfaced as disjointed ramblings during his later mystical 'processes'. They were like cinematic stills, or flashbacks, but aside from these incoherent glimpses, we rely heavily on Narayaniah's testimony for details of his son's life up until 1909, and this is far from reliable.

Six months before Krishnamurti's birth, Narayaniah had been appointed stationery sub-magistrate for Rayachoti, a town fifty miles north east of Madanapalle.[5] As a sub-Magistrate he ranked alongside deputy Tahsildars on the bottom rung of the government's civil administration machinery, earning a mere 100 rupees per month. He served in several of the district's towns over the next decade, rising in status and more than doubling his income. He was required to travel a good deal, and sometimes took his family with him, depending on where schooling was available,[6] but they returned at least three times to Madanapalle, which one can assume was the family base. Situated 2,250 feet above sea level, Madanapalle enjoyed a cooler, healthier climate than many towns of the area; its wild hills and nearby forests provided Naryanaiah with a welcome refuge from his work in the malaria-infested valleys of the region.

Madanapalle (which in Telugu means 'the god of love's hamlet') lay within the district of Cuddapah, which had been ceded to the British in 1800 and had enjoyed relative peace thereafter. Despite the opening of two railway lines through the area in the late nineteenth century, almost all Cuddapah's trade was internal and confined largely to the weekly grain markets. Surplus of rice and millet was minimal, due to the scarcity of level agricultural ground in the area, and a bad harvest often led to drastic food shortages. Cuddapah had already suffered seven devastating famines during the nineteenth century, and three years before Krishnamurti's birth, in 1892, emerged from yet another, which was by no means to be the last.

As Brahmins, the Jiddu family belonged to a high caste minority of one in fifty-five Hindus, but this was no guarantee of financial security. Brahmins represented a spiritual rather than material elite. They were the caste from which temple priests were selected, guardians of the sacred scriptures, and they represented the mainstay of Hindu religious scholarship. According to the tenets of Hindu orthodoxy, Brahmins were those who had arrived, through the law of karma, at the last and highest stratum of spiritual evolution. The significance of Krishnamurti belonging to this caste, both for the Theosophists and for his subsequent devotees, cannot be overstated. Brahmins were considered purer in mind and body than other people, and were therefore subject to strict taboos in order that their spotlessness be safeguarded. Marriage outside the caste was unthinkable, as was the eating of meat, or physical contact with the lowest caste, the Untouchables. Foreigners (as non-Hindus) were deemed equivalent to Untouchables. Food could not be shared with, accepted from, or even prepared in the presence of Europeans, for fear of contamination; nor was physical contact with them thought healthy – a sacrifice Narayaniah had to make regularly in the course of his employment. When British visitors called in to visit the Jiddu household, their departure was followed by a full-scale scrub of both premises and inhabitants. Like most young Brahmin boys, Krishnamurti was well-schooled in the principles of religious practice. The rituals, theology and ethics of Hinduism would have been second nature to him, a matter of domestic routine. From the moment of his birth through to 1909 his life was circumscribed by the conventions of caste, and he was an active functioning member of his cultural group.[7]

As he grew beyond infancy, Krishnamurti showed a natural inclination towards religion, perhaps because of a strong bond with his mother, whose devoutness bordered on the mystical. She is said to have communicated with her dead daughter as well as being able to detect people's auras;[8] Krishnamurti apparently shared this facility, and was encouraged to develop it by his mother, until he, too, reported having visions of his dead sister. After Sanjeevamma's own death, Narayaniah was astonished to see his ten-year-old son blindly following empty space around the house, claiming that his mother was just there, in front of them, eating, washing and changing her sari. 'I frequently saw her after she died,' Krishnamurti wrote in 1913. 'I remember once following my mother's form as she went upstairs. I stretched out my hand and seemed to catch hold of her dress, but she vanished as soon as she reached the top of the stairs.'[9]

These visions are believable in the light of what else we know of the boy Krishnamurti. He was a quiet contemplative lad, content to sit for hours, often at lonely temples and shrines, watching and dreaming. He loved to settle himself in the shade of a large tree and observe the movements of insects and reptiles creeping in the grass around him. In these quiet states he would slip into a world of dreamy imaginings, picturing friendly fairies hopping and playing. His mother was the one person who cherished his singularity, who saw his empty-headedness not as stubborn resistance to schooling, or unintelligence, but as a gift of sorts. Few others detected in his wide-eyed gaze the contemplative insight of a future religious philosopher, although one doting aunt did suspect a store of hidden wisdom behind the vacancy, and dubbed him Dronachari, after a spiritual master in the *Mahabharatâ*.[10]

Aside from appearing somewhat half-witted, the boy Krishnamurti suffered from recurrent bouts of ill-health, and there were times when his survival seemed doubtful. The first of these followed a severe attack of malaria when the family was living temporarily at the district capital, also called Cuddapah, situated beneath the hills in a river basin, an environmental hell-hole of heat and pestilence, well-known as a breeding ground for malarial mosquitos. His fragile life was threatened again when another bad harvest brought a return of famine to the area in 1896–7, again claiming thousands of lives.

Krishnamurti's poor health persisted throughout his childhood. He was so ill at one stage he had to be kept out of school for an entire year, a situation that antagonised his teachers, who already considered him something of a moron. Schooling was a luxury in the Cuddapah district, where literacy extended to just 4.3 per cent of the population (almost exclusively males). As the Jiddu family were so much on the move, Narayaniah's boys could not enjoy a settled, uninterrupted education; but Krishna (as he was known) was the source of particular worry to his ambitious bureaucrat father, because he seemed determined to remain uneducated. He would capitalise on his mother's softness and invent illnesses just in order to stay away from the classroom. There are stories of his giving away pencils and slates to beggars on the walk home from school, of his staring aimlessly into space during class, or being thrashed and sent out of the classroom for inattention, whereupon he would remain dreaming until dark, unless his sparky younger brother came to collect him.

He early came to depend on Nityananda, three years his junior, who seemed to possess everything that Krishna lacked. Intelligent, alert, full of humour, Nitya impressed and charmed his teachers, thus throwing his older brother's deficiencies into even stronger relief. The only area in which Krishna appeared to display any degree of aptitude was mechanics. He was fascinated by machinery, its intricacies, movements and logistics. On one occasion he broke his father's clock down to its constituent parts, probably causing Narayaniah to assume the thing was lost for good, but proceeded to reassemble it diligently and perfectly without a pause for food or rest. In all other practical matters the boy Krishna had Nitya at his side, the perfect streetwise guide. Their team chemistry survived the extraordinary changes of environment they were to experience together over the ensuing years, and their differences in character proved to be mutually complementary. Nitya was destined to become Krishnamurti's closest friend and companion until death separated them at a crucial stage of the latter's spiritual development. They had a younger brother, Sadanand, the tenth and last of Sanjeevamma's children, who was born mentally handicapped in 1902.[11]

In 1901 Narayaniah was transferred to another settlement in the area, Kadiri, and the following year to Vayalpad, just a few miles away from Madanapalle. The family probably returned to their nearby home base at this time, as Krishna is registered as having attended Madanapalle school in September 1902. But in 1903 they were off to Cuddapah once again, where they settled for four years. Narayaniah, though hardly an eminent government officer, was now a senior tahsildar on an income of 225 rupees per month. At the peak of his career he was responsible for an area of 800 square miles, consisting of 160 settlements which he would regularly have had to tour.

It was in disease-ridden Cuddapah that the family suffered two tragedies; first, the death of Krishna's eldest sister in 1903 and then, shatteringly, that of Sanjeevamma herself in 1905. Krishnamurti wrote in 1913 about the event. 'My mother's death in 1905 deprived my brothers and myself of the one who loved and cared for us most, and my father was too much occupied with his business to pay much attention to us.'[12] Of Narayaniah's ten children, five now survived, and the only girl amongst them had married and left home. It was a time of painful readjustment for the three younger boys, Krishna included, who now had to rely on their own pitifully weak resources. There began a period of domestic decline which, had it not been interrupted by the events of 1909, might well have claimed the lives of the boys.

Within a few years of his wife's death Narayaniah had begun to dedicate his working life to a cause that had been close to his heart for many years – Theosophy. The pious Sanjeevamma had also supported the Society's activities, and Krishnamurti recalled seeing a cross-legged portrait of Annie Besant hanging in the family puja room, alongside images of traditional Hindu deities. By the early years of the nineteenth century, Blavatsky's plan for the revitalisation of Hindu religious awareness was beginning to bear substantial fruit, thanks principally to the efforts of Annie Besant. Educated Brahmins applauded the Theosophists' efforts to revive Vedantic philosophy, and appreciated the Society's resolve to stem the tide of India's westernisation. Theosophy aspired to religious neutrality (although it clearly supported Hinduism and Buddhism against Christianity) which meant that devout Brahmins could enlist themselves as members with impunity. Narayaniah joined in 1882, and thereafter regularly attended the Society's annual Conventions at Adyar, as well as hosting provincial Theosophical gatherings at his own house.

His career in the revenue department of the Madras Presidency came to an end in 1908, when his thoughts and longings turned increasingly south-east towards the Theosophical Society's leafy idyllic compound at Adyar. It was then that he wrote to Annie Besant pleading for employment and some form of family accommodation at the headquarters. He waited eagerly for a reply.

Consolidation achieved through unswerving labour was the Theosophical Society's unofficial motto during the early years of the twentieth century; and no one embodied it more than Annie Besant, the Society's inspiration and power-house, if not, as yet, formally its leader. Her mission was to re-educate India, to revive a sense of national pride and culture at the same time as reforming certain indigenous traditions, such as child marriage, which she felt to be barbaric. In 1898 she founded the Central Hindu College, constructed, symbolically, on the Ganges at Benares, Hinduism's sacred city. This was to be the first of several schools, colleges and universities she planned, both within and outside the government system, which would give birth to a new generation of Indian youth. To this end Besant toured wide and far, from the Maharajahs' palaces of northern India to the lecture halls of European cities, raising money and public awareness for her immense educational programme.

Under the leadership of the aging Olcott and his mighty lieutenant, Annie Besant, the Theosophical Society, with its ever increasing Indian slant, appeared to be thriving as never before. However, it was the oriental bias, and the abandonment of ideological neutrality that caused some of its more conservative membership concern. A major rift had already taken place with the American division, which was now led by the powerful Katherine Tingley from her community at Point Loma, California. Tingley claimed direct succession from Blavatsky, and went so far as to disrupt the progress of Besant's colleagues whenever they ventured onto American soil for lecture tours.

There were also disapproving murmurings from within Besant's own ranks about the burgeoning personality cult that was beginning to focus on her. She was revered, virtually deified, with an ardour that only India knows how to bestow upon its popular heroes. It was thought by some that the adulation had found its way to her head and caused her to think herself above criticism. Her personal penchant for ceremonial orders and vestments did little to allay their suspicions. She had taken to wearing white saris, often swathed in shawls and paraphernalia appropriate to the various organisations, clubs and sub-sections to which she belonged (most often as president). Thus attired, she posed for the photographers – once, famously, guru-style, cross-legged on an animal skin – and framed images of her were hung in puja shrines across South India, including that at the Jiddu house in Madanapalle. Amongst the many organisations she sponsored was Co-Masonry, originally a French Masonic order, unique in that it was open to both men and women. Many devoted Theosophists feared that enrolment in the new order and subscription to its rituals was a requisite for anybody hopeful to be admitted to Besant's inner circle of activists.[13] After 1906 the timid voices of dissent against Besant's regime were given greater impetus when two momentous events threatened to split the Society to its roots. First came the Leadbeater scandal; and then there was the discovery of the World Teacher.

Charles Leadbeater's Theosophical career since the close of the previous century had been almost as dazzling as Annie Besant's. Whilst Olcott was tied up with administrative tasks and Besant was busy forging her education strategy, Leadbeater concerned himself, through his writings and lectures, with extending the frontiers of Theosophy's occult pursuits. He was a self-professed clairvoyant of the most accomplished rank, and claimed thereby to have intimate knowledge of the Masters, their hierarchy, plans and wishes. He maintained that his psychic investigations and astral-body travels had revealed to him the structure of the universe, and he wrote convincingly of his experiences and facilities; of how he could identify auras as clearly as another man might see a material object; of how he possessed perspicacity as to the several planes of existence – those rungs on the ladder that stretches between base matter and formless divinity.

The greater Leadbeater's confidence and eloquence on these matters, the more Besant came to depend on him for her own clairvoyant experience. She was cast more in the mould of a pragmatist, a woman of action, rather than a contemplative. It was hardly her style to act the exotic medium, in the manner of Blavatsky, much to the disappointment of some Theosophists who longed for material proof of the occult. Instead, she gave the impression, to observers like Ernest Wood, that her clairvoyance was received second-hand. Wood suggests the existence of a kind of contract between Leadbeater and Besant, whereby she would accept his clairvoyance without question, if he would support her decisions in all practical and policy matters.[14] Thus Leadbeater emerged as the authority behind Theosophy's doctrinal system in the early years of the twentieth century. His philosophy, though founded on Blavatsky's Masters, was more rigorously dependent on their immanence than anything proposed by the Society's original founders. He presented his scheme in a mathematically logical format, through diagrams, symbols, tables and didactic prose which, though fashionably scientific, belied the mystical speculation on which it was based.

Leadbeater's public presentation and style proved enormously popular, and he established himself as an indispensable ambassador for Theosophy, especially in the United States, where he lectured tirelessly during the first five years of the century. He was frequently seen on these tours accompanied by one or more adolescent boys, some of whom became his constant travelling companions. Ever since his curacy at Bramshott Leadbeater had made it clear that he preferred the friendship of boys to any other, a partiality that had apparently passed without much suspicion. He was regarded as one who could inspire and excite the young, and cultural taboos of the time precluded the idea that he might harbour more sinister motives. His organisation of the Lotus Circle, a society for children of Theosophists, and his several articles on education were seen as proof of his laudable interest in young people. Hence the willingness of several leading Theosophists to assign their sons to his care. Their discreet and polite trust was shattered to devastating effect in 1906, when charges of gross perversion were fired against Leadbeater by appalled parents in America.

It came to light that Leadbeater had been teaching his boys masturbation, and had encouraged them to practise it regularly as a means of advancing their occult training. A certain amount of what was euphem-istically referred to as 'indicative action' had taken place. In other words, Leadbeater had manually demonstrated to his pupils how the practice was to be performed. The scandal caused a tremendous uproar within the Society, whose principal ideologist was now being exposed as an exploitative demon. Leadbeater had in the past repeatedly stated the importance of sexual purity for those on 'the Path', yet here he was, allegedly using the teachings of the Masters to ensnare and pervert the minds of innocent boys.

He defended himself by claiming that his motive had been to protect young boys from psychological torment and distraction. Inducing regular sexual discharge, he said, would relieve a boy's sexual tension and lead to greater purity of thought rather than the opposite. He answered the accusations calmly, never once stooping to admit personal shame, but claiming to the end that his methods had always been chaste and well-intentioned. The evidence that Leadbeater frequently shared beds with his pupils, and the recurrence of further accusations over the years, together with his well-documented misogyny, lead one to suspect that he may well have been motivated by a homosexual impulse. However, those who knew him well and worked with him on a daily basis for years, professed his innocence and claimed never to have witnessed any signs of sexual impropriety. The 'martyr or pervert' debate raged on throughout Leadbeater's life, and rages still, above his scattered ashes.

More important was the effect the scandal was to have on Annie Besant and the Theosophical Society as a whole. Her first reflex was to spring to his defence, her sense of loyalty characteristically taking pre-cedence over any short-term sensation, no matter how abhorrent it might have seemed. The Theosophical Society without Leadbeater would have been unthinkable to her, as would an admission that her own guide in matters occult had deliberately abused the sacrosanct doctrine of the Masters for his own gratification. He had erred and given his boys the wrong advice, she conceded, but his motives and character were unstained. It is no wonder that Leadbeater's opponents have branded him Besant's Svengali.

The question of the Society's presidential succession now arose, as Henry Olcott appeared to be on the decline. Annie Besant, so closely associated with Leadbeater, was no longer everybody's first choice as successor. Nevertheless, Olcott himself publicly appointed Besant in January 1907, having apparently received a visit on his sick-bed from the Masters M and KH instructing him to do so. The reaction of some senior Theosophists in England to news of this visitation, was disbelief and outrage. There was doubt about Olcott's mental state, especially as the formidable Mrs Besant along with two of her closest female acolytes had been the only witnesses of the Masters' supposed visit. Nevertheless, after Olcott's death in February, and despite some opposing factions within the British and American sections, Annie Besant was voted in as Theosophy's new President. She then retired for an occult holiday in Germany, where she was joined by no less a colleague than Leadbeater himself.

By 10 February 1909, Leadbeater was back at Adyar, fully reinstated, as a result of Besant's determined persuasiveness. She had published her opinion that freedom of thought and speech was of paramount importance to a Society that valued Truth above all else. Leadbeater's behaviour throughout the crisis, she said, had proved his integrity of purpose. She went further, presenting his tribulations in the language of Christian martyrdom: the ordeal had been a 'symbolic crucifixion through which every candidate for the Arhat Initiation must pass'.[15] As ever, unflinching in the face of enemy fire, she did not allow various eminent members' resignations to influence her resolve. Leadbeater must be returned to the fold if Theosophy, under her direction was to advance.

She and the whole community at Adyar were emotionally dependent on Leadbeater's clairvoyance, ebulliently confident as it was. Then there was the matter of her emerging ideology, monumentally grandiose in its ambitions. She proposed nothing less than the birth of a new cosmic order, based on universal brotherhood, spawned in the world's religious heartland, India, and led by a World Teacher, a messiah, as yet to be discovered. Leadbeater was to have an indispensable role in this project.

Under Annie Besant's direction, the Theosophical Society was increasingly to adopt something of the missionary evangelism that had characterised her entire life's work. She and other political radicals had earlier been enthralled by Darwin's contention that evolution, governed by natural selection, was leading humanity inexorably on a path towards perfection. Fired by her typically Victorian belief in progress and social service, she now adjusted these evolutionary theories to corroborate her own millenarian project. Theosophy provided her with a platform, and from this she propounded her design for the future of mankind: the creation of a heaven on earth, the bringing about of a better age in which harmony, justice, equality and peace would reign. Crucial to her plan was the beneficent presence of superhuman agents, her Masters; and at the core of their divine intervention was the concept of a messianic figure, an incarnation of the World Teacher, sent by the Masters to mediate between humanity and the godhead. Besant saw her own role as that of John the Baptist, preparing the world for this great event, sowing in the minds of all people Theosophy's ideology which the World Teacher would one day translate into the new world law. Salvation was attainable, she maintained, according to the precepts of evolution and the perfectability of man.

Theosophy's prime task, and crucial to the preparation for a new age, was the regeneration of India. The Indian subcontinent was destined, according to Besant's scheme, to provide a religious philosophy for the new civilisation. Within Hinduism, she maintained, were to be found the closest and purest elements of Divine Wisdom – that primordial truth, so long the focus of theosophical speculation, which lay at the centre of all world religions. Fundamental to this was Vedantic Hinduism's emphasis on the oneness of creation, the multiplicity of the manifest world having emanated from divine unity. In pursuing universal brotherhood through the tool of global pantheism, she was fulfilling the Theosophical Society's first stated objective. It would have thrilled Besant to imagine that she was at last putting into practice a philosophy that had been longingly envisaged since the days of Pythagoras and Plato. Through all the centuries of persecution and religious perversion, the flame of truth had struggled to stay alight in the hands of mystics and heroes, and only now, under the guardianship of Annie Besant, did its implementation appear to be within sight. Her courage and vanity were more than equal to the task.

Drawing on Blavatsky's work, Besant and Leadbeater perfected an elaborate matrix to explain the logistics of Theosophy's evolutionary theory. It proposed that humanity was evolving, over a period of millennia, from its original, crudest form towards a divinely enlightened species. This gradual evolution would be marked by the arrival, in sequence, of seven Root Races, each developed on its own continent, or land mass, and each bearing its own distinctive character. The present Root Race was the fifth: the Aryan, or Indo-European.

These broad Root Race epochs were each further divided into seven sub-races, which were said to succeed one another after a period of some hundreds of years. So far, within the span of the current (fifth) Root Race, four sub-races had come and gone, and the fifth, known as the Teutonic was still prevailing at the time of Besant. This Teutonic era encouraged the potentiality of Nordic peoples, and was characterised by sophisticated mental activity, self-interest and competition. However, its time was nearly up, Besant declared, and it was about to be outshone by a sixth sub-race, the era of which was just dawning. It was the responsibility of the current generation of Theosophists to usher in this sixth sub-race, and great excitement accompanied the prospect.

The sixth sub-race was expected to appear in California and would embody the subtler aspects of human nature, principal amongst which was intuition. This would dispose the race as a whole towards brother-hood and communal harmony. Great significance was attached to this attribute, because the specific character of the sixth sub-race was said to define the orientation of the sixth and next Root Race, a cataclysmic evolutionary milestone, still far away. Thus, the orientation of human-kind, according to Theosophy, was on the cusp of a historic change, and this concept was integral to Besant's preparations for the new age.

As her theory evolved, during the first quarter of the century, Annie Besant developed a set of arguments as to why the Coming was immi-nently expected. First was the evidence of certain American ethnologists who claimed to have 'proof' of a new racial type developing along the Pacific coast of California. The Bureau of Ethnology's report included descriptions of 'a new conformation of skull and face . . . a new pre-cociousness of mind'.[16] Then there was the matter of the land mass which some scientists proclaimed was rising gradually out of the Pacific Ocean. This was one day to be no less than the home of the Sixth Root Race, Besant declared. Further to these physical indications, there were cultural signs that the old epoch had come to its natural end. Everywhere,

Besant maintained, there was evidence of cultural decay. Western religion had been outmoded and rejected; science had reached a deadlock through its inability to penetrate the secrets of metaphysics; industry and automisation had destroyed humanity's concept of beauty, the result of which was decadence in art and music; and the gross injustice of society, the chasm between rich and poor, had shown mankind to have lost sight of its values. The sudden convergence of evidence from so many quarters was more than coincidence. The time had come for a change, she claimed, and quoted numerous other cultures and religious organisations that shared her sense of expectancy.

The concept of a returning messiah proved intriguing to Besant's generation. Theosophy's western membership was made up to a large extent of educated religious dissenters, people who had stepped outside the mainstream of their culture's traditional faith, yet still cherished the iconology of their upbringing. The notion of the divine man, an embodiment of humanity's highest ideals, sent to usher in the Kingdom of God, was deeply ingrained within the religious conscience of the entire Judaeo-Christian world. By the same token, Besant's role, as John the Baptist, was regarded as the appropriate precursor to the 'Coming'.

Theosophy had transplanted this western religious conviction into an eastern context. The messiah, or World Teacher, was made to correspond with the traditional Hindu figure of the Avatar, a deific person sent to the world at certain crucial times to watch over the dawn of a new religious era. Theosophical doctrine (derived again from Hinduism and Mahayana Buddhism) contends that the current overlord of humanity's spiritual welfare was the Lord Maitreya. At precise historical points, and in accordance with the cyclical emergence of new race types, he takes over the body of a man, his 'vehicle'. Thus comes into the world one who will direct the religious destiny of the new race. Previous vehicles of Maitreya had included Jesus and Krishna.[17] It was the Theosophical Society's responsibility now to discover and nurture the new one. This was to be the Society's most ingenious invention: the unification of differing religious traditions into a single aspiration, centred on the universally applicable Christ principle – man made perfect.

As early as 1899, the Coming of the World Teacher and the evolution of the new race-type had become prime amongst Annie Besant's obsessions. They were the subject that year of her four Theosophical Convention lectures at Adyar. By 1908, she was in a position to announce the imminent return of 'the Christ'. The human figure of Jesus was seen as a close parallel to the figure who would soon emerge. She rightly thought that western audiences would comprehend her message more clearly if put into the language of their own religious heritage, whereas in India she tended to replace 'Christ' with 'Maitreya'.

1909 was dedicated to lectures on the same subject. Besant toured Europe and America holding forth on her theories of the new age, the new civilisation and the messiah who would come to steer its course. It was a bold move. The credibility of the Theosophical Society and the loyalty of all its members was staked on this one issue – and this at a time when the Society was recovering from two severe blows, the Leadbeater scandal and the controversial election of Besant as Olcott's successor. Unshaken by the implications, she preached her message like a veteran stage actor, with tremulous conviction adding drama to her prophetic words. She was every inch the holy mother.

The same year a new note of excitement entered her usual millenarian diatribe at a lecture in Chicago. 'I can say,' she pronounced, 'that we look for him to come in the western world this time – not in the east, as did Christ two thousand years ago.' The authority behind this thrilling announcement came from researches conducted by Leadbeater in 1906. They centred on an eleven-year-old boy, Hubert van Hook, the son of a prominent Chicago Theosophist. Young Hubert, bright, advanced and handsome, was said by Leadbeater to possess the aura and intellect suitable to groom him as Avatar for the new age. Annie Besant was also much taken with the lad, though, as we have seen, she would have deferred to Leadbeater's judgement in such matters.

In retrospect, the choice of Hubert appears to have been made in the hysteria of the moment. Such was the atmosphere of frenzied expectancy generated by their millenarian theory, the pressure must have been great to find a suitable candidate for the role of saviour. It also cannot be ruled out that Leadbeater was very attracted to young Hubert, and subsequent evidence would tend to suggest that his plans for the boy were not entirely spiritual. None of this appeared to affect the decision of his parents (firm Leadbeater supporters throughout the scandal years) to sanction Hubert's departure for India, where, it was expected, he would be prepared for his great role. Mrs van Hook and her son arrived at Adyar in November 1909. It is unclear whether or not she had been warned in advance about the dramatic turn events had taken during the course of their long voyage from Chicago. But it was clear to both Leadbeater and Besant, by the time Hubert set foot in India to take his place within the Theosophical Society, that their identification of an American boy as the vehicle for the new messiah had been an embarrassing mistake.

By 1909, the Theosophical headquarters at Adyar was home to a growing community of Europeans and Indians, accommodated either in simple monastic rooms or private villas which affluent members were allowed to have built on the compound, so long as they agreed to let the Society use them when they were not resident. Since Blavatsky and Olcott's original acquisition of the twenty-seven-acre estate, a further 124 acres had been purchased, and several extravagant building projects were being planned to provide devotional shrines, together with accommodation for ever greater numbers of visitors. Finance for these, and all the Society's activities, derived from the sales of Theosophical books (scores of which were published every year), and donations from the coffers of munificent patrons.

   Jiddu Narayaniah had set his heart on retiring to the Adyar estate and would not be put off by Annie Besant's polite but curt refusal of his request. He persisted, reiterating his qualifications and civil service record. But to every application the same reply would come: there were no employment vacancies, and the Theosophical compound was not a place to rear a family of boys. Narayaniah's insistence, however, at last bore fruit. A member of staff at the Theosophical headquarters interceded on his behalf, and after meeting Annie Besant at the December 1908 Convention, Narayaniah was offered some secretarial work. Nevertheless, the boys would not be allowed to live on the compound, she ruled, and the family would have to make do with a small, run-down house just beyond the estate boundary. Undeterred by the prospect of domestic squalor, Narayaniah moved to Adyar with his four sons on 23 January 1909.

Conditions in the overcrowded little cottage were appalling. Worst of all was the absence of adequate sanitation and sewage facilities. Narayaniah bore the discomforts stoically but repeatedly asked for a toilet to be installed, to which request the Society remained deaf. The degradation took its toll on Narayaniah's sons. They were soon covered in insect bites, infested with lice, and severely under-nourished. While their father proved his efficiency at work and earned himself a good reputation amongst Theosophists, the boys' lives sank into squalor.

The nearest government licensed school was at Mylapore, a hot and dusty three-mile walk away. Both Nitya and Krishna were registered there as soon as they moved to Adyar; their elder brother, Sivaram, attended college in Madras, while young Sadanand stayed at home. Annie Besant had made it clear in advance that the Society would not provide transport for the boys' schooling, and Narayaniah could not afford to pay for it, so there was little option for them but to face the daily trek on foot. It was hardly made better by what lay in store for them when they arrived. Lessons were conducted in English or Tamil, neither of which the boys spoke, making them appear like backward country bumpkins. Krishna, still dreamy-eyed and remote, suffered more than his wily younger brother. Never one to endear himself to schoolmasters, Krishna was punished brutally for his inadequacies and branded an imbecile.

The Theosophical Society estate, with its lawns, flowerbeds and tree-lined avenues must have seemed a paradise to the boys after the misery of school. Although they lived outside the perimeter, they were allowed to come in as they pleased, so that they could enjoy the gardens. A favourite destination in the early evening was the nearby beach, where European and Indian men in the Society would go for their daily swim. It was here that the boys would sit on the sand, watching the white men splash around in the shallows. Well-behaved, overawed and a little afraid, the boys never made a nuisance of themselves and exchanged friendly greetings with one or two of the Europeans they met regularly. Amongst these were two well-educated young men who had abandoned promising careers at home for the excitement of the Theosophical spiritual adventure: an Englishman called Ernest Wood, and a Dutchman, Johann van Manen. These two took an interest in Narayaniah's sons, at first offering them swimming lessons, and then helping them with their homework.

Krishna and Nitya thus tentatively edged themselves into the fringe of the Theosophical family, a move of which their ambitious father doubtless approved. It was inevitable that they would sooner or later come into the orbit of Charles Leadbeater, who would pause from his work at five o'clock and proceed down to the broad Adyar sands in the company of Wood and van Manen.

The ever-buoyant Leadbeater had burst back upon the Theosophical scene at Adyar just eighteen days after the arrival of Narayaniah and his boys, and his commanding presence on the estate released Annie Besant to undertake a prolonged summer tour of Europe and America. A few days after her departure, in late April 1909, Leadbeater had his first fateful encounter with young Krishna on the beach.

Krishnamurti was hardly typical of the sort of child usually drawn into Leadbeater's circle. Scrawny, vacant and humourless, he was invariably outshone by Nitya – far closer to the Leadbeater type, though perhaps too young. Yet it was Krishna rather than his brother who possessed the qualities that set Leadbeater's occult imagination on fire, imperceptible as they were (at this stage) to others in the Society. Central to these qualities was the luminescence of what Leadbeater referred to as his 'causal body'. This is an etheric radiance, or aura, that is present within, but not dependent upon the physical body of a mortal person. According to Leadbeater, individuals who have developed spiritual Adepthood over the course of many lives, possess a causal body that is 'filled with the most lovely colours, typifying for us the higher forms of love, devotion, and sympathy, aided by an intellect refined and spiritualised, and by aspirations reaching ever towards the divine'.[18] Leadbeater claimed to possess the gift to identify this iridescent matter in much the same way as ordinary people can make a visual distinction between solid and liquid, land and sea.

Ernest Wood was astonished at the impression Krishna made upon Leadbeater on the beach. Returning to the compound after their swim, Wood mentioned that he had watched the boy struggle with his homework and that he was a simpleton. Never one to listen to the opinions of others, Leadbeater affirmed that the boy would one day be a great spiritual master. 'As great as Mrs Besant?' asked Wood, the story goes. 'Much greater,' came the pregnant reply.[19]

At this time Wood, van Manen and Leadbeater were working intensively on subjects closely related to millenarianism and the perfectability of man. They would shut themselves away in Leadbeater's Octagon Bungalow, next to the river, and forge the central theories upon which new Theosophy was to be focussed. Leadbeater was the source of authority and provided all the material for the finished work. He would lie trance-like on a couch, while his assistants encouraged him with probing questions, taking written notes of his words before assembling them into order. Their completed work was printed as articles in *The Theosophist* magazine, and then prepared for publication in book form. Favourite topics for occult investigation included the formation of the sixth Root Race and the evolution of individual souls over the course of multiple lives. Leadbeater's comments were for the most part spontaneous and inclined towards prophecy.

Wood later recalled one occasion, shortly after the beach encounter, when he posed the question to Leadbeater as to whether individuals who currently occupy the bodies of Hindus might, in past lives, have belonged to different races and religions. The point at issue was the revulsion felt by devout Hindus at the idea that they might return in a future life as non-Hindus. Leadbeater was intrigued by the question and wanted to explore it further, but balked at the idea of investigating past lives of existing Hindu Theosophists. Wood therefore suggested they use the two Jiddu boys as their occult guinea pigs, a choice that Leadbeater thought most appropriate.

The boys were then summoned to present themselves at the Octagon Bungalow. Krishnamurti arrived in a state of paralytic shyness, 'easily startled, shrinking into himself at the smallest provocation'.[20] Before meeting Theosophists he had come to expect a degree of dismissive condescension or even cruelty at the hands of Europeans. Leadbeater sat him down on the couch, said a few reassuring words, none of which Krishna understood, and laid his hand gently on the boy's head. Thus began Leadbeater's well-documented investigations into the past lives of Krishnamurti, beginning with the first thirty, and stretching back over tens of thousands of years. As the months went by, his discoveries proved sensational and confirmed his hunch that Krishna was indeed a highly advanced spiritual being. So excited was Leadbeater, he went as far as to intimate confidentially to one or two close associates that the true vehicle for the Lord Maitreya had been delivered into their hands.[21]

It was decided that a symbolic name should be given to the boy, both to protect his identity until the appropriate time, and to add a mythological flavour to the project. All the other key players who featured in one way or another in the past lives were similarly renamed. The system of nomenclature employed was astronomical, Krishna being called Alcyone, the brightest star of the Pleiades, with Nitya as Mizar and Leadbeater as Sirius.

Almost all prominent Theosophists were found to have played a role in the vast and complex network of past lives that now began take shape. Gender, race, religion and personal relationship varied from life to life, but the principal protagonists had invariably encountered each other during previous incarnations, either as well-known historical figures or as close relatives. It was a monumental work, first aired publicly in serialised evening instalments given by Leadbeater on the rooftop of the headquarters building. It then took rather more formal shape in a series of articles in *The Theosophist*, and was eventually published in two large volumes entitled *The Lives of Alcyone*. Its subtitle ran: *A Clairvoyant Investigation of the Lives throughout the Ages of a Band of Servers*.

Such was the hunger for spiritual revelations at Adyar, *The Lives* soon became the focus of cult fascination. Members of the resident Theosophical community felt that events were moving fast and that the summit of all their hopes might be within reach. They began to compete with one another as to who featured more prominently than whom in the unfolding drama. They would listen to Leadbeater's utterances, spellbound, each in the hope that he or she might have experienced some close brush with the mysterious Alcyone centuries before, or played some vital part in civilisations that had long since vanished. This would endorse a member's spiritual stature and encourage a sense that they were in some way advanced along the path to perfection.

Leadbeater was in his element while working on *The Lives*. His energy and imagination were given free rein, and he would frequently work with Wood deep into the night, pacing round and round to stop himself from dozing off. Ernest Wood, although an enthusiatic collaborator at the time, later expressed doubts as to Leadbeater's complete integrity. There were occasions, he noted, when the stream of clairvoyance was aided by some surreptitious cheating at the bungalow's bookshelves. Human nature, he wryly added, was streaky, like bacon.[22] But as the sole authority for a document which was taking on biblical significance within the Society, Leadbeater established for himself a seat of unassailable power.

Despite the commotion at Adyar, Leadbeater refrained from sharing the full extent of his aspirations in his correspondence with the absent Annie Besant – at least for the time being. He first draws attention to Narayaniah and his family in a letter dated 2 September 1909, deploring the abysmal accommodation allocated to 'one of our best and most reliable workers'.[23] Mention is made of one of the sons, and the investigations into his past lives, but Krishnamurti is not identified by name until 6 October, around six months after the beach encounter, by which time Besant had been sent a number of *The Lives* to peruse for herself.

Annie must have felt that the ground was shifting under her feet. She had just completed extensive tours of Europe and America, prophesying the imminent arrival of a new Christ, and intimating very strongly that he would appear in the west. If Leadbeater was hedging his bets between May and October 1909, and was still holding the door at least partially open to Hubert van Hook, he was leaving his President, who had staked all on the messiah issue, on an uncertain footing. Nevertheless, Besant, trusting, as ever, Leadbeater's clairvoyant discrimination, rallied enthusiastically to the call of Alcyone, and prepared to meet the neophyte upon her return to India.

Meanwhile, Leadbeater suggested to Narayaniah that the two brothers be given private tuition at home by members of the Theosophical Society. Narayaniah hesitated, caught between the flattery of having so much attention heaped upon his offspring and practical considerations as to the boys' future. Unless they attended a government registered school they could never hope to qualify for the sort of careers that would set them apart from the rabble, careers such as his own and his father's, in government service. Leadbeater eventually persuaded him by suggesting the eventual likelihood of an education in England, considered the best possible opportunity for an Indian boy at that time. However, in a letter to Annie on 14 October Leadbeater claims that the boys were removed from school because of 'a providential difference of opinion' between

Narayaniah and the teacher.[24] Whatever the reason, Krishna and Nitya were now placed firmly under the guidance of Theosophist tutors.

They were soon to be joined in classes by a rather mystified Hubert van Hook, who arrived in Adyar during November 1909. Hubert discovered his great future role had been usurped and, although still considered an important player in the coming golden age and allocated the star name Orion, his precise position was unclear. A few years later he became the subject of yet more sexual allegations against Leadbeater, although this time they were kept secret by an appalled but loyal Annie Besant. In later life he was to become a Chicago lawyer and was so embittered about the Theosophical Society, he forbade his wife and family even to mention the subject.

Leadbeater for the time being kept a slight distance from the Jiddu brothers, so as not to allow for the start of fresh rumours and scandal. He did, however, mastermind the boys' occult progress, most significantly taking their astral bodies to visit the Master Kuthumi in the mountains of Tibet. The credibility of these sorts of events, of course, relied not on any material evidence of their happening, but on the extent to which Theosophists would accept the infallibility of Leadbeater's word. On the night of 1 August 1909, he claimed, while the brothers' physical bodies slept, the Master performed his customary ritual of welcome, admitting them onto the occult path as his probationary pupils. Though the boys recalled nothing of the event afterwards, Leadbeater wrote it up in graphic detail.

On 27 November 1909 Annie Besant arrived back in Madras, and was met at the station by a huge crowd of admirers. The venerable snow-haired lady stepped on to the platform to be greeted by her faithful members and a host of others, most of whom regarded her as their honorary mother. They had been waiting, unprotected, in the midday sun for hours because of a delay on the railway line. A group of senior Theosophists stood near the front ready to present their fascinating young discovery, now well-groomed, gaining weight and with at least a smattering of conversational English. His bare feet had been scorched by standing for too long on the baking platform, and he had had to balance himself on the feet of an adult Theosophist standing nearby. When the moment arrived, the boy was almost overwhelmed by a sudden

46

rush from the enthusiastic crowd behind, and he was just able to lunge forward and throw a garland of flowers around Annie's neck. Later, back at the Society's compound, the brothers were formally introduced to their President and prostrated themselves at her feet.

Thus Annie Besant began her relationship with the man who was to outshine all the many brilliant, powerful and talented luminaries she had encountered in the course of her long and eventful life. Her affection for Krishna sprang from a blend of maternal love, spiritual reverence and ideological conviction. It was a happy mixture, the one dovetailing indistinguishably into the other. Everything to which her religious, emotional and intellectual life had so far been directed was from this moment pinned upon this one individual. Her titanic loyalty towards him was unflinching in the years to come, even when tested to the full, and she died still resolute in her devotion. Krishnamurti, for his part, found in Besant a replacement of sorts for his mother. She was also an exalted public figure, to whom he felt he should always defer, and this in some ways prevented a real, spontaneous friendship developing between them. His future correspondence with her is tinged with respectful formality, and this reflects the quiet awe with which he regarded his eminent sponsor. Years later, when the ideological edifice of Theosophy crumbled under the weight of his own reasoning, and he began to clash with many of his former associates, Besant was the one person he could never say a word against.

Annie immediately insisted that the brothers be moved from their squalid accommodation outside the estate to a small apartment right next to her own quarters. Narayaniah was dazzled by the interest this magnificent woman was showing in his sons, and they were forthwith transferred to an environment that just six months before would have seemed beyond the reach of their dreams.

Within a matter of days after her return, however, Annie Besant had left Adyar bound for the sacred city of Benares, purportedly on Society business. It is possible that the main motive for her mission might have been something rather different. There is evidence that she was in contact with a group of tantric holy men in Benares, who practised an obscure form of *siddha-yoga*. Besant, like Blavatsky before her, was highly influenced by the scholarly pandits of Benares, whose knowledge, oozing with the flavour of ancient wisdom, offered her a model for the future world philosophy. Theosophy's well-defined Hindu bias at the time would appear to be consistent with this. The wisdom she gleaned from her clandestine Benares visits was her equivalent of the inspiration received by Blavatsky from her so-called Masters.

Two of Besant's Benares gurus, Swami Vishudhanand and Gopinath Kaviraj, apparently predicted to her the imminent appearance of a vehicle for the Lord Maitreya. They gave as their evidence certain lines from a Tibetan sacred text, the *Kala Chakra Tantra*, and went so far as to say that the messianic teacher would be called Krishnamurti.[25] It has been suggested that Besant proceeded to Benares so soon after her arrival back in India to consult her holy men as to the authenticity of Leadbeater's discovery. If their findings, quite independent of Leadbeater, had revealed the appearance of an Avatar called Krishnamurti, Besant would have been in no doubt as to the boy's significance. She would have felt thoroughly vindicated in having spread the message of his Coming, endorsed, as she now felt herself to be, by two quite distinct and reliable occult authorities. Such might well have been the case, as it was from Benares, a few days before the end of 1909, that Annie posted a letter to Leadbeater confirming her conviction that the Lord Maitreya had chosen Krishnamurti to be his vehicle.

Krishnamurti had by now changed in appearance, largely through his having abandoned the traditional haircut of Brahmin boys: shaved at the front up to the crown of the head and grown at the back down to knee-level. He now had it cut to an equal shoulder-length all round, and parted, Christ-like, in the middle. Others in the compound began to wear their hair in a similar manner, keen to imitate this spiritual icon to whom their leaders appeared to attach such great significance. At this stage, however, the matter of Krishnamurti's vehicleship was still supposed to be kept secret.

Meanwhile his occult training progressed rapidly, under the close direction of Leadbeater, a veteran psychic conjuror, who rarely failed to convince those close to him as to the authenticity of his visions. When Society members complained to Leadbeater that they could remember nothing of the astral extravaganzas they were supposed to have experienced, he would encourage them to let their imaginations fly, spicing their fancy with colourful imagery of his own. Thus Krishnamurti, sensitive and imaginative, would begin to focus his daydreams not so much on the fairies of his childhood musings, but on the panoply of Theosophical Masters.

His early training was brought to a climax on 11 January 1910, shortly after the arrival of Besant's letter from Benares, when it was decided that he should be initiated into the Brotherhood, his first step on the path to becoming an Adept. It was to be an occasion of the highest import, and great were the expectations of those privileged enough to be involved in its preparation. Annie Besant, writing from Benares, had instructed that her own room should be made available for the ritual, and the headquarters building was closed off so as to maintain complete quiet. So it was that Leadbeater and Krishnamurti locked themselves away there on the evening of 10 January, guarded outside by Nityananda and recent arrival from England, Dick Balfour-Clarke. The event was to continue until the morning of 12 January, during which time the two participants remained in the room, dropping in and out of a state of trance. Leadbeater lay on the floor and Krishna on Besant's bed, while their astral bodies were put through great ceremony and adventure. The whole procedure was later apparently remembered by Krishna and written down on his behalf by Leadbeater (who adamantly maintained he had added nothing of his own except for a few grammatical corrections).[26]

The experience began with a visit to the Master Kuthumi's house in Tibet, where Krishna was cordially received and briefed about the forthcoming Initiation. He then proceeded to the house of the Lord Maitreya himself, where, in the company of a host of other Masters, he was ceremonially admitted to the Brotherhood. Besant and Leadbeater were also astrally present, and they were charged with guiding the neophyte along his spiritual path. After a number of routine tests (one of which involved the act of forgiving his bestial schoolmaster), he was given the Key of Knowledge and congratulated by the whole assembly. The following night he was presented to the King of the World at Shamballa.[27] Krishnamurti described this sovereign of the occult hierarchy as 'a boy not much older than I am, but the handsomest I have ever seen, all shining and glorious, and when He smiles it is like sunlight.' The King 'told me that I had done well in the past, and in the future I

49

should do still better; and if my work should be difficult I must never forget His presence, for His strength would be always behind me, and His star would shine over me.'

After this portentous induction, Krishnamurti returned to his body and recovered consciousness. Leadbeater brushed his hair, dressed him from head to toe in white silk, and prepared him to be viewed by an expectant public. Then, with great sense of occasion, he opened the door to release Alcyone, the Masters' Initiate from Annie Besant's bed-chamber. As Krishna appeared at the doorway, his eyes still glazed from thirty-six hours of intense spiritual imaginings, the effect he had on those who received him was spell-binding. He seemed somehow transformed – majestic and unearthly. His brother Nityananda, his father, and several others who beheld him, threw themselves spontaneously to the ground at his feet, overwhelmed by the sanctity of the occasion.

It was a magnificent piece of theatre, orchestrated to perfection. Towering above all the complexities of Theosophy, with its sophisticated theories, its scientific and doctrinal niceties, there now stood a spotless child, a pure and innocent Brahmin figurehead. Standing beautiful and dreamy-eyed on his pedestal, he perfectly symbolised for Theosophists the ineffable godhead that ruled above the teeming multitude of material diversity. The eager seekers who had been drawn into Theosophy's broad embrace, thrown up by a century of religious, scientific and social revolution, had at last found their focus. They had found their Christ.

4

At the Feet of the Master

——————— ✳ ———————

The question must inevitably arise: why was Krishnamurti chosen for this extraordinary role? What were his qualifications over and above those of, say, Jinarajadasa, Hubert van Hook or his own brother, Nitya? Much has been reported about the electrifying effect he had upon audiences in later life, but was he already displaying the qualities of a rare mystic at the age of fourteen, mute and withdrawn as he was? Or was he merely a convenient pawn in somebody else's machinations, the possessor of just the right combination of attributes that would make him an unquestioning and suggestible collaborator in Theosophy's master plan?

Evidence of his displaying mystical gifts before coming to the attention of Leadbeater is scant and rests largely on Narayaniah's hazy reports of his son's psychic awareness. Leadbeater's vision of wonderful colours emanating from Krishna's aura on the beach must, at best, be seen as a personal experience, and one not substantiated by anyone else's testimony. Stories of the boy's quiet and uncomplaining acceptance of his schoolteacher's beatings doubtless brought to the minds of Theosophists images of Christ before Pilate, but they are hardly, in themselves, concrete indications that the child was divinely inspired.

His orientation from earliest childhood was religious, and he had the sort of cultural background that might allow him to develop into a spiritual master, should the right circumstances present themselves. Just as Mozart quickly picked up the skills of musical virtuosity, brought up by his father – an exceptional violinist – in an exclusively musical environment, so did young Krishnamurti absorb the fundamentals of a spiritual life. This does not prove that he was a mystic, but it shows evidence of a logical and unbroken continuity between his childhood influences (religious) and his adult preoccupations. The Theosophical environment into which he was ushered encouraged this continuity. Few can boast such consistency, and it goes some way towards explaining his development of exceptional skills as a religious thinker.

It is more difficult, however, to establish at what point his religious training was superseded by genius. The same could be said, again, in relation to Mozart and his compositions. In view of the events of subsequent years it would be hasty to attribute all young Krishna's charisma to his Brahminic and Theosophical education. Another ingredient appears to have been present, which did not even require verbal articulation to achieve its effect, but which was soon to sway the hearts and minds of thousands. He possessed an innate personal magnetism, not of a warm physical variety, but none the less emotive in its austerity, and inclined to inspire veneration. Observers throughout his life noted its effect, and labelled it in a number of ways, most frequently 'benediction'.

Quite apart from the boy Krishna's qualifications for the role of messiah, his aura or mystical gifts, the most important attribute he possessed, as far as Leadbeater was concerned, was emptiness. This offered Leadbeater the opportunity to conduct the crowning experiment of his career: a blank sheet, apparently without a will of his own, pliable and passive, perfect material to be shaped and programmed. Leadbeater began to fill Krishna's head with the basic tenets of Theosophy, starting with vivid descriptions of the Masters. He gave glittering accounts every day of how Krishna had fared at the previous night's encounter with the occult brethren in Tibet, to which the boy would listen, open-mouthed and wide-eyed. Many Theosophists remembered Leadbeater's talent for telling stories and how he breathed life into his descriptions of the Masters with his hushed, atmospheric tone of voice and sparkling eyes. It cannot be wondered that Krishna's impressionable imagination was quick to construct very real mental pictures of the Masters.

Leadbeater had now created a definite role for himself in the Theosophical Society: he was to be chief regent, entrusted with the education and cultivation of the Lord's chosen one. This was distinct from Besant's role, which was as world proclaimer, the medium whereby populations across the globe would be prepared for His coming. The circumstances in which the whole Adyar community currently found itself were the result of a divine plan, operating in accordance with karmic law. Leadbeater had been chosen to live at this precise moment in history in order to receive the boys and create in one of them a human being of messianic potential. It was a matter of destiny.

His immediate requirement, after having enrolled Krishnamurti, was to educate and mould him. The boy must be taught how to present himself to a western audience and to articulate the profoundest reaches of his spiritual consciousness in clear, eloquent English. This was an artificial demand for one whose young life had displayed such a reluctance to communicate at all, let alone conduct well-reasoned discourses in the best British lecture-hall tradition. The hot-house environment of the Theosophical headquarters was also alien, particularly the regimented lifestyle that had been prescribed for him, and the awesome prospect of the pedestal onto which it was expected he would soon arise. It was to be a programme of strict inculcation for the young brothers over the next decade, and the result, for Krishna, at least, was a gradual division of his life into the public and the private.

His public profile, exposed for the first time when Leadbeater ushered the dazed young Initiate out of Annie Besant's chamber on the morning of 12 January 1910, was to be characterised by a well-polished exterior, a sobriety of purpose, a cosmopolitan outlook and an otherworldly, almost beatific, detachment in his demeanour. All of these can be said to have characterised Krishnamurti's public image to the end of his life. Alongside this exterior there emerged a very different private side, which in the early years he preferred to keep hidden from Leadbeater and Besant for fear of invoking their disapproval. It found expression in bouts of private grief, long periods of dreamy contemplation and minor acts of rebellion. It represents his human personality – an entity Leadbeater found conveniently vacant at the start of their relationship, and attempted to quash on the occasions that it showed itself in the years to come. Krishna, keen to please, the son of an ambitious father who had brought the boy up to obey his seniors without questioning, willingly submitted himself to Leadbeater's demands. But there are signs that from quite early on he neither understood nor empathised with the figure Leadbeater would have him become.

Some observers on the periphery, clearly doubting Leadbeater's integrity, expressed grave concern as to the role being prepared for Krishna. These were summed up by the architect Edwin Lutyens, writing to his wife, Lady Emily, who was to play a pivotal role in the story: 'I do not believe any Christ was ever brought up to be a Christ – as a profession – as one might call it.'[1] The philosopher Ouspensky maintained that Leadbeater had completely invented the spectacular 'aura' vision on the beach, but had been convinced that, given time and proper training, the young candidate would naturally 'develop certain Christ-like qualities'.[2] According to this theory, there was no divine agency involved, nor did the boy display particularly unusual qualities; any empty-headed child would have sufficed, such was the ripeness of Theosophists' expectations. Leadbeater certainly believed children's minds could be shaped to order. Twelve years before meeting Krishna he had written that if any child were given over at birth into the care of an acrobat, its young body could be trained so as to be able to perform gymnastic feats, no matter what its genetic inheritance. Moreover, he wrote, 'If the physical body of a child is thus plastic and readily impressible, his astral and mental vehicles are far more so. They thrill in response to every vibration which they encounter, and are eagerly receptive with regard to all influences ... [children are] as clay in our hands, to mould almost as we will ... it rests with us to awaken the germ of good, to starve out the germ of evil.'[3] This drawing out of the best, the divine, in children was the cornerstone of his educational theory. Krishnamurti may have been no more than pliable clay in the hands of a maverick experimenter.

This does not, however, prove Leadbeater was a fraud and Krishna an impostor. He never claimed that the boy was Christ, but that, given the appropriate preparation and schooling, his body might one day be used as a vehicle for the Christ. A successful outcome would clearly not be apparent to anyone until the experiment had run its course. It is tempting, in the shadow of the controversy that still surrounds Leadbeater, to ridicule the role he played in Krishnamurti's early life, or even to suspect sexual motives. It is not as simple as that. Even the most hardened cynic would have to pause for a moment's sober reflection on just how Leadbeater could have recognised the hidden potential that would one day turn this boy into a teacher of global stature. There is no reason not to believe Leadbeater's personal conviction, especially when one remembers that another candidate, indeed, his own former choice and a much more physically appealing boy, Hubert van Hook, was on his way to assume the role. Heightened, even frenzied, expectations there certainly were in the Theosophical Society, but Leadbeater must be credited for his perspicacity in selecting so unlikely a candidate as the boy Krishna.

One Theosophical observer, who witnessed the results of Leadbeater's educational programmes, wrote that, 'In six months he would transform even an ignorant street boy into a charming well-mannered gentleman. One could see the change almost daily, making the face of an ordinary boy into that of an angel.'[4] In no individual was this transformation more apparent than in Krishnamurti, who in a matter of months had begun to converse intelligently in English, presented himself immaculately, and grew in physical beauty. Photographs taken after his emergence from the Initiation ritual illustrate this change movingly. Less gaunt and fragile in bearing, it is the radiance of his face which most catches the attention. Gone is all trace of disease and degradation. This is now a child in the prime of health, looking to the future with innocent wonder. His eyes seem to marvel and yet there is a vacancy of expression, a complete absence of self-consciousness. It is the very stuff of ideals, and it cannot be wondered at that the world of Theosophy was soon bewitched by so entrancing an image.

Leadbeater's experiment had begun successfully, but his results were not achieved without severity. An intensely industrious and disciplined man himself, he did not believe he was over-stretching his educational principles by insisting on unerring obedience. Fear of any kind he would not tolerate, and subjected his pupils to psychological challenges in order to bolster their confidence. One story has it that Krishna took fright in the sea one day when he looked beneath him and saw, through the water, the cavernous darkness of a sudden deep spot. Leadbeater appeared not to have noticed the boy's fear, but later the same day abruptly announced they would return to the sea, 'and find that hole'.[5] Another technique he employed to fortify children was to tell them gruesome stories in the best gothic horror tradition. Grimly explicit tales of vampires and malign spectres would be spiced by the inclusion of Leadbeater's own swashbuckling participation, thereby adding not only to the stories' feel of authenticity but his own heroism.

Cruelty was not alien to his nature. He was noted for the brutish way he would treat certain people, particularly old ladies or those outside his group of intimates, and he was seen to take warm delight in squashing tropical bugs under the flat of his paper-knife. However, apart from a single incident, when he is said to have slapped Krishnamurti's hanging jaw shut, all reports stress his kindness towards children, most particularly towards the two brothers now so prominent in his plans. Ernest Wood, at times an acid critic of Leadbeater's personality, drew attention to a maternal warmth which he showed his pupils, and added, 'I have often thought what a devoted mother he would have become but for the accident of sex.'[6] The brothers no doubt found Leadbeater's swings of temperament confusing. One moment they would be adored, pampered, idolised, and the next scolded for breaching some piece of esoteric etiquette they did not understand. A letter Krishna wrote to Leadbeater in 1915 gives a rare insight into the resentment he felt at this early time: 'When I was with you I did not appreciate what you did . . . Of course now I know you did what was good for me and I did not see it . . . I hurt you in many ways and now I see it all and I am very sorry. Let us forget the past except the happy bits.'[7]

Paramount amongst Leadbeater's priorities was to maintain Krishna's purity of body and mind while at the same time building up his physical health and intellectual resources. Only the most perfect of bodies would be appropriate to receive the Lord Maitreya, and yet the chosen vehicle would not be able to accomplish his mission unless psychologically equipped to encounter difficulties in the material world. The brothers' grooming programme would therefore have to be styled according to these two principles – protection and selective instruction. The imposition of a strict routine was considered important, so as to repair the damage inflicted by their irregular and disorderly past. A daily balance of classes, meditation, exercise and relaxation was prescribed, together with an insistence on absolute cleanliness and nourishing food. Not unlike the personality of Leadbeater himself, this routine involved the integration of traditional British values and eastern religious ideals.

The boys' day began at 5 a.m., when they performed their orthodox Brahmin ablutions by the well. A meditation session was followed by their morning meeting with Leadbeater at the Octagon Bungalow, during which they received warm milk, prepared, as befitted their caste, by a Brahmin servant. Leadbeater would then enquire about their dreams and fill their minds with descriptions of the astral events they had experienced together the previous night. At 7 a.m. they would depart on a bicycle ride, which was considered an important part of their education, not just to promote physical vigour, but to encourage self-reliance. Leadbeater took great pride in logging the statistics of Krishna's mileometer in his letters to Annie Besant. On one occasion they made it all the way to Chingleput and back, a round trip of sixty-six miles. As soon as he spied the returning cyclists coming across the distant Elphinstone Bridge Leadbeater would run warm baths so as to have everything ready for their arrival. The boys were then dressed in cotton dhotis and shawls before beginning their main schoolwork for the day, with its emphasis on English, Sanskrit, handwriting and basic mathematics. The afternoons saw them out and about once more, either playing tennis, swimming or going on an expedition. A final and thorough bath was the last event of the day administered by Europeans, after which the boys would retire to eat their evening meal in the company of Brahmins. They would usually attend Leadbeater's twilight roof-top meetings, listening to his latest occult discoveries or his mesmerising tales of the Masters, before going to bed. These evening gatherings were an indispensable part of community life at Adyar, and the medium whereby Leadbeater maintained regular contact with all ranks within the Society.

When Annie Besant was resident at the compound she would read books to the brothers and meditate with them in the shrine room. They soon developed a respectful affection for her and habitually addressed her as 'Mother' or 'Amma'. Besant was convinced by the assertions of Leadbeater's *The Lives of Alcyone*, and maintained that her relationship with Krishna was nothing new, but as old as the hills – older, indeed. As she wrote to him, 'I love you, my own dear Krishna . . . I have loved for so many years. How many? I do not know. Since we were leaping animals, and guarded our Masters' hut? Perhaps longer still; perhaps, when we were plants, we put out delicate tendrils to each other in the sunshine and the storm; and perhaps when we were minerals – oh! So very long ago – I was a bit of crystal and you a bit of gold in me.'[8]

The men entrusted with the task of teaching the boys were selected from amongst the younger and academically qualified members of Leadbeater's inner circle, the Englishmen, Dick Balfour-Clarke and Ernest Wood, and a fellow South Indian called Subrahmanyam Aiyar. Krishna did not shine at his studies, often resorting to the question, 'Why do you trouble me with these things? I shall never need them.'[9] Bearing in mind the spiritual throne to which their ward would one day ascend, this was a somewhat knotty question for his teachers to answer. Some skills, however, he did absorb quickly and willingly. His written English, for example, within a few months was clear and articulate, and his handwriting began to show a strong similarity to that of Leadbeater.

On one level it is surprising that Besant, who had done so much to promote public sympathy with Hinduism, should decide to anglicise her two wards to such an extent. Lessons were conducted in English, western eating and sleeping habits adopted, a British education proposed and, before long, a European code of dress and hair-style. Leadbeater's support of these measures was understandable. Although disgraced and unwelcome in his home country, he never thought otherwise than that the British Empire represented the summit of material civilisation. Besant's view was that Krishna should be groomed as a cosmopolitan, or, more precisely, a commonwealth, figure; his British connections would be all-important in gaining him access to a wider stage. The World Teacher could not be exclusively Hindu. It was his role to present the most sacred elements of oriental wisdom on an occidental platform, thereby bridging east and west, Hindu and Christian, as opposed to elevating one to the exclusion of the other.

One area in which his Theosophical education was insufficient was in the provision of child company. Apart from his younger brother, the only other child he was permitted to see on a regular basis was Hubert van Hook, his one-time rival. There can have been little common ground between the Brahmin Alcyone and this precocious young American; and their relations can hardly have been improved after Leadbeater decreed that Hubert should not even touch Krishna's possessions for fear of infecting them with imperfect magnetism. This lack of peer group interaction, and the consequent sobriety which characterised the relationships he was forming with adults, lent disproportionate intensity to his relationship with Nitya, and hindered him developing spontaneity in social relationships later in life. It is difficult to blame the Theosophical Society entirely for his lack of conventional social adjustment. He had been unusually withdrawn and introspective from early childhood; but Leadbeater's insistence that the 'work' and the preparation of his body take precedence above all else, ruled out the possibility of a normal balanced childhood.

The impracticalities, as Leadbeater saw them, presented by a Brahminic way of life, caused him to lose patience, and he began to impose a regime on the boy that gave rise to resentment amongst other Brahmins. The two most burning issues were those of washing and diet. Leadbeater was adamant that the ceremonial daily rinse of the Brahmin, during which the loin cloth was not removed, was insufficient. He prescribed, instead, a vigorous scrub down, with particular emphasis on washing between the legs. The situation was aggravated when it was discovered that the boys had begun to eat their meals in the company of Europeans. Although the food was vegetarian and prepared by Brahmins, this represented a major contravention of Brahminic rules of diet. Narayaniah, spurred on by fellow orthodox Brahmins, began to make complaints, sometimes in the form of embarrassing temperamental outbursts. Leadbeater's way of dealing with the situation was to recite divine sanction – direct messages from the Masters condoning his own methods and advising that the boys be kept apart from the influence of their father. Besant was more diplomatic and managed to placate Narayaniah with promises of a first-class English education for the boys and a glorious future as Theosophists.[10] Fearing a future breakdown in relations, she decided the wisest course was to organise formal guardianship of the boys, and on 6 March 1910 managed to persuade Narayaniah to sign a document to this effect. This was far from the end of the matter, however, and Narayaniah was soon voicing his concern as to the real motives behind Leadbeater's thorough washing regime. He was particularly alarmed by the revelations of Mrs Besant's trusted servant, Lakshman, who claimed to have discovered Krishna naked in Leadbeater's presence, and, on another occasion, Leadbeater himself half-naked, washing Krishna's hair.

The situation between Narayaniah and Leadbeater had become so tense by September 1910 that Annie Besant decided to remove the boys from Adyar for a spell, and take them with her to Benares. She had Theosophical business to attend to, and she dearly wanted to introduce Alcyone to the community at her beloved Central Hindu College. Krishna had already met some staff members, including the principal, a thirty-two-year-old Englishman called George Arundale. Leadbeater had been Arundale's tutor many years previously in London, ever since which he had been groomed for senior office within the Theosophical Society. Arundale and other academics at the Central Hindu College rapidly fell under Krishna's spell. They would sit attentively at his feet, hanging on his every word, reminding a delighted Mrs Besant of the elders who had sat to hear the teachings of the young Jesus in the temple.

E. A. Wodehouse (elder brother of P.G., a professor of English and a noted poet) was impressed:

What struck us particularly was his naturalness . . . He was still of a retiring nature, modest and deferential to his elders and courteous to all. To those whom he liked, moreover, he showed a kind of eager affection, which was singularly attractive. Of his 'occult' position he seemed to be entirely unconscious. He never alluded to it – never, for a single moment, allowed the slightest hint of it to get into his speech or manner . . . One [of his qualities] was a remarkable quickness of sympathy, combined with a kind of simple and direct wisdom which made him very helpful to others. Anybody who took a trouble or a difficulty to Krishnamurti could be certain of advice – advice, too, offered in so modest and almost apologetic a manner that it never conveyed an air of superiority. Another quality was serene unselfishness. He seemed to be not the least preoccupied with himself . . . But what I think was most noticeable to all of us . . . was a certain original quality, the quality of a flower with the morning dew still fresh upon it. This delicacy of purity seemed to go right down through his nature – giving the impression of one absolutely unspotted by the world. It was perhaps this, more than anything, that aroused our instinctive reverence . . . We were no blind devotees, prepared to see in him nothing but perfection. We were older people, educationalists, and with some experience of youth. Had there been a trace in him of conceit or affectation, or any posing as the 'holy child', or of priggish self-consciousness, we would undoubtedly have given an adverse verdict.[11]

Krishna's stature as a spiritual figurehead was fast snow-balling. He used, for his talks at Benares, recollections he had gathered, with Leadbeater's assistance, in the months leading up to his Initiation. They were the result of his morning sessions in the Octagon Bungalow, during which he was encouraged to put into words the core of his previous night's astral instruction. They were therefore understood to be discourses issued direct by the Master Kuthumi. As the appetite of his Benares audience increased, Krishna, feeling the absence of his mentor, needed a textual aid to remind him of the Master's teachings. He therefore wrote to Leadbeater asking him to send the notes, which he immediately did, having first corrected, edited and typed them himself.

These texts, or rather, Leadbeater's edition of them (Krishna's handwritten notes having vanished), enjoyed a long and lucrative history in Theosophical circles. Annie Besant, describing them as Alcyone's 'first gift to the world', had them printed, bound in blue leather and published under the title *At the Feet of the Master*. The title gives quaint reference to the medium of their inspiration (Krishna at the feet of Kuthumi), and the spirit in which they should be read (seekers at the feet of Krishna). The book was promoted as a first, privileged glimpse of what would one day become the World Teacher's saving message, and as such it sold in its thousands. Theosophists were introduced to it formally at the Adyar Convention of December 1910, when 1200 delegates from around the world descended on the now enlarged headquarters compound. During its first year twenty-seven editions were published; by 1925 there were at least forty, and it has continued to be printed ever since.

Leadbeater described the texts in the little book as 'those in which the Master tried to convey the whole essence of the necessary teaching in the simplest and briefest form'.[12] Simple they certainly are, though not platitudinous. It was composed as a handbook of behavioural correctness, full of straightforward common sense, that goes beyond the prescriptions of individual religions but draws on the code of pious morality that underlies them all. Nothing, since Blavatsky, carried the sort of authority soon ascribed to Alcyone's document. That authority, of course, depended entirely on the endorsement it received from Leadbeater and Besant – which was total. Krishna's sentences, they claimed, were just a starting point for profound meditations, and in 1926 they published a huge and burbling commentary to supplement *At the Feet of the Master*, in which every line of Alcyone's original is weighed, analysed, laboriously expanded upon.

As to the authenticity of the book, controversy has raged ever since. It was not so much claimed that the boy had composed the texts so much as brought them through. As the Foreword states, 'These are not my words; they are the words of the Master who taught me.'[13] Leadbeater maintained that his own contribution had been minimal, and that he had, on the instructions of the Master Kuthumi, 'altered a word or two here and there, added some connecting and explanatory notes, and a few other sentences which I remembered having heard Him speak to Mr Krishnamurti'. This version of events was confirmed by two leading Theosophists, Mrs Russak and Dick Balfour-Clarke, both of whom swore that they personally witnessed Krishna writing the texts. Balfour-Clarke was so incensed by the sceptics, he continued to assert his testimony at the age of ninety-one. However, it must be remembered that the handwritten document Balfour-Clarke saw Krishna writing was not necessarily the same in content as the typed and corrected version later taken by Leadbeater to the printing press.

Not unpredictably, one of the first to express disbelief was Narayaniah, who claimed that his son did not have either the command of English nor the intellectual sophistication to pen such a document. The boy's juvenile letters of the period would tend to corroborate Narayaniah's allegation. Asked for his opinion, Ernest Wood braced himself in front of Leadbeater and pointed out that 'there were some sentences which were exactly the same as in a book of his [Leadbeater's] which we had already prepared for the press.'[14] This stylistic similarity was often cited, but Leadbeater dismissed the sceptics with a characteristically unanswerable statement: 'When pupils are taught by the same Master, they are bound to have much the same ideas.'[15] Subrahmanyam Aiyar, one of Krishnamurti's tutors, asked the boy outright, in Telugu, if he had actually written it. Thus cornered, Krishna apparently answered that he had not, and that he could not even understand the book.[16] Subrahmanyam also claimed to have heard Krishna say quietly to his father, 'The book is not mine; they fathered it on me.'[17] Annie Besant was so indignant at this story, she banished Subrahmanyam from Adyar, and he died shortly afterwards.

Krishnamurti in later life neither claimed nor disclaimed authorship of Alcyone's little book. Cynics assert that a child who so recently had been described by several witnesses as mentally deficient could never have so rapidly developed the linguistic and theological skills as to be able to write it. This opens the question of just how retarded Krishna was in 1909, or whether he was in fact a profoundly repressed genius. Philosophical perspicacity, the hallmark of his later career, is a much more difficult talent to discern in a child than, say, musical virtuosity. It is possible, perhaps likely, that Krishna was hiding spiritual gifts that found expression only after Leadbeater discovered him and developed his powers of articulacy. Similar cases have been documented in psychological studies.[18] Krishnamurti's so-called retardedness might be ascribed to emotional deprivation following his mother's death, and a failure to communicate with his over-taxed father. His intelligence lay hidden until the circumstances of his life changed and his confidence began to grow. Under these new and intensely focussed conditions it is quite possible that he could have experienced a sudden rush of intellectual capability. Leadbeater's diatribes probably did take root quickly, and to many observers this may have seemed like divine inspiration. It is conceivable that Krishnamurti did, in all truth, write a large part of *At the Feet of the Master*, enlivened, as he was, by an opportunity to unleash his suppressed talents. But the ability revealed in accomplishing this task was more likely one of remembering Leadbeater's lessons verbatim rather than creating original ideas of his own.

George Arundale was deeply moved by Krishna's teachings, and needed no more convincing. In January 1911 he took it upon himself to form an organisation which could be used both as a channel for converts' devotional urges and as an administrative body to prepare the way for the Coming. He called it the Order of the Rising Sun, and enlisted into its ranks a number of his boys at the Central Hindu College. Badges were worn by members, inscribed with the initials 'JK', revealing how attempts to hide the identity of the 'Vehicle' had by this time largely evaporated. Staff and parents at the Central Hindu College were disturbed at Arundale's zealot stance and questioned the appropriateness of using an educational institution as the organ for a new religious movement. Annie Besant herself, the College's founder and a revered figure amongst educated Hindus, was now publicly criticised for her involvement in Arundale's venture. Sensing a problem, Besant abolished the Order of the Rising Sun, but, irrepressible as ever, immediately replaced it with the Order of the Star in the East, an international organisation. The focus of World Teacher propaganda was now intentionally deflected away from the Central Hindu College and spread to regional centres, each to be managed by a separate national representative.

The OSE, as it came to be known, appealed to her own insatiable appetite for orders, ranks and ceremonial. She appointed Krishna its Head, with herself as Protector and Arundale as Private Secretary to the Head. Membership was freely available on application, whereupon a certificate was issued, in return for which new members were asked to devote themselves to the expectation of the Teacher's imminent Coming. A five-pointed silver star was available to members, who were encouraged to wear it and explain its significance as often as possible. Gold stars were reserved for those in high office. The new Order received its name, Besant wrote, 'because the Star in the East was the sign . . . given in the Gospel story of the birth of the child who was to be the vehicle of the Christ, the body that Christ was to use at the time.' She frequently reiterated her conviction that the forthcoming Teacher had not been seen on earth since the time of Jesus, when He occupied the body of that person for the last three years of his life. This time, she maintained, the Lord's ministry would be very different because the way will have been properly prepared and the world would be ready to receive him.

In January 1912, the new Order was given its mouthpiece in the form of a monthly publication, entitled *Herald of the Star*. Krishna was nominal editor, but in practice it was the brain-child of George Arundale. It had something of the comic book in its appearance, with plentiful colour illustrations, blue print and a lively layout, which broadened the net of its readership, and offered something of a relief from the rather staid presentation employed by most Theosophical publications. After a mere eighteen months the new Order had gained 15,000 members. Fresh life had been breathed into the Theosophical movement, and although a number of older members fell away, they were replaced by new ones in their thousands. By 1911 membership had swollen in four years from 13,000 to 16,000, and by 1920, when interest in the World Teacher project had spread far afield, that figure had increased to over 36,000. By 1928 membership reached its peak of 45,000.

While European interest in Theosophy began to boom, the tidal wave of Indian enthusiasm, originally sparked by Annie Besant's championing of Hindu culture in the 1890s, was now on the decline. Narayaniah's concerns about his sons' caste status had been encouraged by Hindu fundamentalists keen to find any stick with which to beat the Theo-sophical Society. Their quarrel was principally with Annie Besant, but they found more meat for their attacks by focussing on Leadbeater. Besant, they now feared, was at heart just another British imperialist, though her weaponry was religious rather than military or political, and was thus potentially more dangerous and insulting to the already down-trodden Indian nation. They were indignant that she should seek to appropriate Hinduism and bend it in accordance with her own matrix for the future world religion. An influential Madras newspaper, *The Hindu*, became the battleground in a three-year war of attrition fought between the leaders at Adyar and a whole variety of objectors rallying to the flag of Hindu fundamentalism. Narayaniah's growing antipathy was the catalyst required to dredge up the entire Leadbeater scandal of 1906 once again. Other parties gleefully joined in, such as a well-known doctor and social activist, T. M. Nair, who published an article entitled, 'Psycho-pathia Sexualis in a Mahatma'. Katherine Tingley, from the Theosophical splinter group at Point Loma, California, joined the foray, furnishing *The Hindu* with as much incriminating material as she could muster. Even London's *John Bull* made good mileage out of the campaign. One article published in relation to the Jiddu brothers and Leadbeater was entitled 'Deified and defiled. Two boys and a beast'. The Christian missionaries in Madras, as ever ready to storm the Theosophical fortress, took their opportunity to add fuel to the fire. The Anglican Bishop of Madras endorsed a statement which accused the Society of pandering to Annie Besant's pretensions of 'immaculate and transcendent wisdom'.[19]

In the midst of this confusion it was thought best to remove the boys as quickly and as far from their father's orbit as possible. England was the obvious choice of destination, as it offered the best educational prospects. Presenting Krishna on a British platform would also demonstrate the seriousness of Besant's intentions for the boys, and would add spice to the OSE's inauguration in the mother country. George Arundale obtained a leave of absence from the Central Hindu College, so that he could accompany the boys as their private tutor. Krishna and Nitya were forthwith made ready to meet the European public. Their ear lobes, which had been perforated (and the holes stretched) in infancy according to religious custom, were agonisingly sewn up, and they were fitted with western clothes by the finest tailor in Bombay. Nothing less, Annie asserted, would be suitable for a future messiah. Thus attired, the boys cut a curiously exotic profile on the SS *Mantua*, which sailed from Bombay on 22 April 1911. Krishna's centrally parted shoulder-length hair was somewhat incongruous above his Norfolk jacket; and as he and his brother hobbled along the decks in their uncomfortable European shoes, trailing behind the noteworthy figure of Mrs Besant (whose pallor betrayed her loathing of sea travel), they caused more than a few heads to turn.

If the boys were speechless with wonder at the marvels they encountered on the voyage, nothing could prepare them for the culture shock of London. British Theosophists had received advance warning of the arrival of Alcyone, and a large crowd gathered at Charing Cross Station to catch a first glimpse of the famous child.[20] A photograph records the extraordinary event, showing the two timid Indian brothers surrounded by grand Edwardian ladies wearing broad hats. Krishna stands between George Arundale on one side, jealously guarding him with a linked arm, and Annie Besant, conspicuous in her white attire amidst the dark clothes of the crowd.

This was the occasion when Krishna was first seen by Lady Emily Lutyens, wife of the rising star of British architecture, Edwin Lutyens. Writing of the event more than forty years later, she remembered, 'his enormous dark eyes which had a strange, vacant look in them . . . Mrs Besant piloted him along the platform, anxious to keep the crowd from pressing in on him . . . As I left the station I found one of our members in an almost fainting condition. She was somewhat psychic and said that she had been overcome by the glory of Krishna's aura.'[21]

Lady Emily had recently become an active member of Theosophy's

London Lodge, and her social connections had made her a useful asset for the Society. She also had strong Indian links, her father (Robert, first Earl of Lytton) having been Viceroy, and her brother, Victor (the second Earl), who was shortly to be appointed to the Governership of Bengal. She was soon to have a second home in India, as in 1912 her husband was given the commission to design New Delhi, the nation's future capital. As if these connections were not gift enough to the Theosophical Society, her occult family background was also of great interest, as she was the granddaughter of Edward Bulwer-Lytton, one of the formative influences on Madame Blavatsky. Alongside Annie Besant, Lady Emily was to become the major female figure in Krishnamurti's early career. A retiring woman, who shrank from high society life, Lady Emily was by nature inclined to pious devotion, be it Christian (in her early life) or Theosophical. She formed an immediate and strong attachment to the Jiddu brothers and frequently called to visit them at the Kensington and Surrey homes of their hostesses in England, Mrs Jacob Bright (the widow of a senior politician) and her daughter Esther Bright, both committed Theosophists. Annie Besant was impressed with Lady Emily's family background and her level of dedication. Although she had only been a member of the Theosophical Society for one year, she was invited by the President to join the Esoteric Section, and then to become National Representative for the OSE in England.

Besant's launch of the OSE in London had the intended effect and set British Theosophists buzzing with excitement. It is some indication of the difference in the religious climate between England and India that she received active support from Christians in London, who did not consider their belief in a Second Coming as contravening their faith or as disobeying the articles of their Church. Such was the legacy of nineteenth-century religious adventurism – the twentieth century had arrived, and anything was possible, even a Hindu messiah. Besant never lacked for audiences and was in constant demand as a guest speaker. Once again, her subject was the impending arrival of the World Teacher, the history of his previous incarnations, the physical upheavals on the planet which forewarned the arrival of a new Root Race, and the changes each one should make in his or her life to prepare for the Coming. As a notorious and eminent public figure she was welcomed into the company of leading politicians, social reformers, cultural luminaries and scientists. Her old radicalism was also brought to the fore when she participated in a massive demonstration for women's suffrage and addressed an audience of 10,000 at the Albert Hall.

The boys, meanwhile, accompanied her wherever she went, quietly sitting near her on the platform, decorative illustrations of her theme. They suffered somewhat from the cold, and Krishna endured agonies when he was occasionally pressed to deliver a few words. But nothing they experienced weighed more heavily on their persons, literally and metaphorically, than the food they were compelled to eat. Vegetarianism, in Edwardian Britain, was a rarity not accommodated with any degree of culinary imagination. This, together with the traditional English disregard for supplemental flavour in cooking, meant that the Jiddu brothers were compelled to wade their way through mountains of bland vegetable mush. 'I do not think Miss Bright understands how much we like rice,' young Nitya was heard to complain, while the two of them heaped salt and pepper onto their plates in desperate search of flavour.[22] Krishna also suffered terrible indigestion cramps, largely due to the quantity of porridge and dairy products prescribed for him by the distant Leadbeater.

There was plenty of stimulus for them in other areas, during their four-month stay: a trip to Paris (where Besant was lecturing at the Sorbonne), riding lessons and toy boat sailing in Kensington Gardens, the theatre, cricket matches, military galas, fireworks and, above all, the coronation procession of King George V and Queen Mary, which they watched from the privileged heights of Admiralty House. Their only causes for complaint, in matters other than gastronomic, were their uncomfortable shoes, the colour prejudice of the British, and the constant jeers Krishna had to endure because of his hair length. His sponsors decided to do away with this particular eccentricity before his next visit to Europe, and he did not have to suffer the humiliation again. Meanwhile Arundale continued to tutor the boys, as regularly as their busy schedule would allow, and some initial research was undertaken with a view to entering both of them for Oxford, the date being set for their matriculation as October 1914.

Besant and her entourage arrived back in India in early October, allowing Arundale to take up his headmastership again at the beginning of the Central Hindu College's new term. The Theosophical Society

Convention was to take place at the sacred city of Benares that year, and it was there, on 28 December, that an event took place which could be described as the second major piece of theatre in Krishna's Theosophical career, the first having been his Initiation. The difference on this occasion was that it was entirely unrehearsed, and took both Leadbeater and Besant by surprise, which added to its significance in their eyes.

It began with the suggestion that it would be 'a great pleasure' if Krishna himself would hand out certificates to new members at a special gathering. Theosophists laid great emphasis on the quality of magnetism that could be transferred to objects through physical contact, and the touch of Alcyone was, of course, extremely propitious. A meeting was forthwith organised, and existing members even returned their certificates so that they could receive them again from Alcyone's own hand. At six o'clock around 300 Star members, 'men and women of many nations and of many faiths',[23] arrived in the Indian Section Hall and sat down – most cross-legged on the floor, but European ladies could opt for the dignity of benches around the walls. Krishna was placed at one end with his sponsors, under portraits of Blavatsky and Olcott, and members began to form an orderly queue in front of him. Certificates were passed to him, and then handed back to the appropriate member. Thus proceedings began, with the first few members returning contentedly to their seats.

Then, suddenly something happened. One description has it that 'a solemn stillness fell upon the whole assembly ... like love tangible ... [it seemed] that the walls of the building had gone down and that in some mystical fashion the whole world was present.'[24] An Indian member, overwhelmed by devotion, prostrated himself before the smiling Krishna, which led others to follow suit, in a spontaneous tide of passion that reduced many to tears. A British army officer, C. L. Peacocke, reported that it felt as if 'suddenly, from somewhere, there surged through that little hall a mighty wave of spiritual energy.' Leadbeater recalled, 'I have never seen or felt anything in the least like it; it reminded one irresistibly of the rushing, mighty wind, and the outpouring of the Holy Ghost at Pentecost ... It was exactly the kind of thing we read about in the old scriptures, and think exaggerated; but here it was before us in the twentieth century.'[25] The climactic moment was when Nitya, apparently unprompted, slipped from his seat near the President and prostrated himself before his brother. The atmosphere of hushed silence was then relieved in an explosive burst of applause, soon after which Krishna closed the meeting with a blessing, and the members 'came down to the ordinary world again'.[26]

What moved several observers was the mixture of people – gender, age, colour, race and religion – who sank to the floor before Krishna. It was a homogenising experience, a microcosmic illustration of Alcyone's power to induce a spirit of universal brotherhood. As Besant said the following day, 'Those of you who were there yesterday, can no longer have any doubt whose vehicle the Lord will use.'[27] In the weeks that followed, she, Leadbeater and Arundale made known their occult impressions of the event: the spectacular display of bright lights, colours, auras, haloes and stars that had cascaded around Krishna at the time, but to which most observers were blind. From that day onwards, 28 December every year was considered an auspicious date in the OSE calendar.

The power of mass devotion does have dramatic effects on the collective psyche, as can be seen in religious movements the world over. Speaking in tongues, ecstatic trances, glimpses of enlightenment, mass outpourings of the Holy Spirit, once initiated, spread like fire through a crowd of like-minded devotees – and occur as regularly within the Christian Evangelical movement as they ever did in the Theosophical Society. It would appear that much of the fever is induced by the soaring aspirations of the participants rather than the intercession of a divine agent. This is illustrated by the similarity of such incidents, despite the multiplicity of persons or objects venerated. The gods are many, but the experience of religious hysteria is consistent.

The World Teacher project was now well and truly launched; indeed, in the judgment of its leaders, it had already notched at least one, if not more, events of biblical stature. Before their very eyes a gospel story was in the making. One major obstacle, however, still prevailed. Narayaniah had been deeply embarrassed by the 'pentecostal' exhibition on 28 December which, he felt, would attract the scorn of orthodox Hindus. His displeasure reached a high point in January 1912, when he wrote to Annie Besant threatening legal action to regain custody of his boys. His main concern, as ever, was their association with Leadbeater. Annie managed to calm him only with the assurance that the brothers' links with Leadbeater would henceforth be severed. Having obtained another signed document from the father, agreeing that the boys could be taken to England for their education, she departed from India with her wards on 3 February, in full knowledge that they would be reunited with Leadbeater at an as yet unspecified European location. The emergency demanded a degree of duplicity, she believed. Once on the seas she wrote to Narayaniah banishing him from the Adyar compound, an act which was interpreted as a declaration of war. By March the rendezvous with Leadbeater had been arranged in Taormina, on the east coast of Sicily, though this was kept secret for fear that Narayaniah might hatch a plot to kidnap the boys. This anxiety was to continue for the next eighteen months. The brothers often had to be accompanied by bodyguards in Europe, their whereabouts kept hidden, even from trusted Theosophists. In retrospect their fears seem exaggerated, but at the time the mission seemed of such vital significance, no risk could be taken. Their every movement, after all, would be weighed in the pages of future gospels.

Leadbeater, the boys and a handful of Theosophists remained in Taormina for four months. The purpose of their seclusion was to navigate Krishna through the second stage of his Initiation (there being a total of five stages to be achieved before reaching Adepthood). Taormina possessed a high level of occult magnetism, having once been host to Pythagoras and, later, the neo-Pythagorean philosopher, Apollonius of Tyana; there could be no more appropriate location for so important a step. The rites of Initiation were accomplished and Krishna was solemnly accepted into his new rank, before returning to England in late July 1912.

Narayaniah now wrote formally to Annie Besant demanding the return of his boys. His letter, reproduced in *The Hindu*, precipitated a legal battle that was to continue until May 1914. It was to be remembered as one of the most notorious cases in Indian legal history, and attracted a good deal of press coverage in England. Narayaniah's case rested on three issues: first, that his son had been subjected to unnatural sexual relations with Leadbeater, a notorious pervert and paedophile; secondly, that false claims had been made by the Theosophical Society regarding Krishna's authorship of *At the Feet of the Master*, when, in fact, the boy had been scarcely literate at the time; and thirdly, that the deification of Krishna was not just a grand deceit, but would be injurious to his son's future. All in all, he claimed, the boys were in the care of malign parties, out to corrupt

71

their bodies and minds. In today's political climate the force of public opinion would certainly have fallen on Narayaniah's side. His son had been abducted by an occult society, whose leaders had been closely linked to more than one child sex scandal, they had defiled the boy's religion, and had subjected him to a variety of esoteric rituals. But it was not so straight-forward in British India of 1912, especially when the plaintiff was a native and the defendant as eminent a public figure as Mrs Besant.

Annie Besant rose to the occasion and conducted her own defence, virulently, eloquently, and not without a degree of indulgent pugilism. Her principal arguments were the educational opportunities that Krishna would enjoy in her care, and the stigma that would remain with him for life if his father's sexual allegations were upheld. The case began at the High Court of Madras on 20 March 1913, and judgment was delivered on 15 April. Mr Justice Bakewell ruled that the charges of sexual immorality could not be substantiated by concrete evidence, but that Mrs Besant had not kept her agreement with Narayaniah in failing to separate the boys from Leadbeater. Krishna and Nitya were therefore declared wards of court and were to be returned to their father by 26 May 1913. Besant, an experienced and indefatigable campaigner, instantly lodged an appeal and requested a stay of execution. The boys therefore remained with her until the Appeal Court's decision, in August, which did no more than uphold the original verdict. Bristling with indignation, Annie now appealed to the Judicial Committee of the Privy Council, in London. This was the most powerful legal body in the British Empire and consisted of senior Law Lords, several of whom (such as the Lord Chancellor, Lord Haldane) were friends of Besant from her political days. Proceedings at Downing Street, where the case was heard, were relaxed and informal. The final judgment was given on 25 May 1914, and stressed that in both previous hearings, due consideration had not been given to the boys' own wishes, which were clearly that they should remain with Besant. Narayaniah's suit was therefore dismissed, and Annie tasted victory at last. Shortly afterwards, she had the pleasure of seeing the Lord Chancellor, who had chaired the Judicial Committee, at a party hosted by Lady Emily. Krishna, who had consistently sympathised with what Annie was struggling to achieve on his behalf, thanked her for her efforts, and presented her with a pearl brooch to commemorate the triumph.

5

Moulding a Messiah

———— ✳ ————

Krishnamurti did not return to India between January 1912 and December 1921. Such a long absence had not originally been intended, but the guardianship battle and Krishna's academic difficultes had to be overcome if the World Teacher project was to go ahead as scheduled. The arrival of the First World War threw much of the world into a period of uncertainty and changing values, which temporarily derailed the Theosophical Society's plans, and Annie Besant's mission to prepare the world for the arrival of the Lord Maitreya lost some of its momentum. Part of the problem was the impracticality of long-distance travel at the time; but there was also trouble with the Vehicle himself, who was now subject to a whole range of new and fascinating experiences, and had begun to develop along lines his sponsors had not anticipated. Krishna found himself reined in at every turn by Leadbeater – a man living on the other side of the world, whom he was now not even to set eyes on for a decade. A return to England for Leadbeater would have led to a resurrection of the 1906 scandal, perhaps even a police investigation, and he preferred to remain resident at his seat of power, surrounded by disciples, in India (and later Australia), leaving the boys' education in the hands of trusted colleagues. Bereft of his principal mentor, Krishna also had to make do without Annie Besant for nearly five years, and it cannot be wondered at that he occasionally lost sight of, or failed to understand, his prescribed destiny. This period reveals an intimate side of Krishna for the first time, different from the public figure of Alcyone that had so far been paraded before the faithful. Although his life was still circumscribed, he now gained sufficient independence and articulateness to let his personal feelings be known, even if he could not yet act upon them. All too often, those closest to him heard him make the remark that came to characterise his early life – an expression born from personal doubt, confusion, and what seemed like a hopeless struggle to live up to everyone else's expectations: 'Why did they pick me?'

The brothers' lives during their ten years away from India were unsettled. They lived at a variety of homes in the south of England, and under the care of different Theosophical hosts, depending on the state of their studies, the circumstances of the war, and the degree of rivalry that developed between the personalities in their immediate circle. In London, they initially made their home with Esther Bright, at 82 Drayton Gardens, and they were frequent visitors to the Wimbledon house of the American heiress, Mary Dodge, a formidable spinster, crippled with arthritis, who lived with Countess de la Warr, the estranged wife of a British earl. She offered them the use of her chauffeur and a house in the Ashdown Forest, Sussex, where they were accommodated with all the comforts afforded the British landed classes. Miss Dodge also settled private annuities on the brothers, £500 a year for Krishna, and £300 for Nitya. Annie Besant contributed a further £125 a month to Krishna. Miss Dodge's vast fortune kept both the OSE and the Theosophical Society afloat, and without her generosity it is hard to imagine how Annie Besant would have been able to finance her great plan for the future of humanity. Funding was never a problem for Krishnamurti; the prodigious Miss Dodge set a pattern for the type of spontaneous donations that sustained his work throughout and continues to sustain it to this day in the activities of Krishnamurti centres around the world.

Dashing looks, stylish dressing and polished bearing were to become hallmarks of the Jiddu brothers' appearance during this decade in Europe. Leadbeater (under divine sanction) had directed that the boys' bodies must be handled like the most precious of treasures, and this included cladding them in nothing but the finest materials. Their shoes were handmade at Lobb's, their suits tailored by Meyers and Mortimer, their shirts by Beale and Inman, and their ties bought at Liberty's.[1] They were always meticulously scrubbed, and their hair 'smelt of some delicious unguent'. This was in accord with Leadbeater's holistic theory of education: if the body were treated with appropriate veneration it would predispose its inhabitant towards spiritual supremacy. The philosophy clearly took root in Krishnamurti, who could be said to have adhered to it for life. It was also a logical continuation of his Brahminic background, with its emphasis on meticulous purity, exterior and interior. His language and cultural outlook had undergone a metamorphosis, but his standards remained consistently high; polished brogues, brushed woollen blazers and pressed flannels superseded the dictates of the Brahmin rule-book as his priorities were translated into a western context.

The boys' level of income allowed them a very pleasant degree of flexibility, overseas travel, and the occasional luxury, such as a motorcycle for Krishna. Their leisure time thus gave the appearance of respectable affluence. Visits to the theatre were a regular treat, holidays were spent in refined company and there was no lack of material comfort. But the elegant living concealed a rigorous daily routine of dreary studies and grooming, along the same lines as they had already been subject to at Adyar. They also had to endure that degree of spartan discomfort encouraged as healthy and character-forming by the English upper class of the time. As before, the food and the cold were alien hardships they were expected to accept without complaint.

The brothers' schooling during their first four years in England was overseen for the most part by Jinarajadasa, with some early contributions by Balfour-Clarke and the later participation of George Arundale, after he had finally severed links with the Central Hindu College. There was an interesting tension in the relationship between these qualified older men and their pupil, Krishna. In some areas, of course, they had to impose discipline on their charge; on the other hand, they felt keenly the privilege of being entrusted with the Vehicle's education. In evolutionary terms, Krishna was their spiritual superior and a channel for divine wisdom, which they would do well to tap. Balfour-Clarke recalled the cross-country runs at dawn, the cold showers and hefty meals. The naturally studious Nitya would apply himself vigorously to his books, while Krishna relieved his boredom by escaping into a realm of dreams, dallying with Romantic poetry. But, as Jinarajadasa noted (and others were to corroborate), while 'Nitya had the sharper mind, Krishnamurti's mind was the bigger mind. He had a wider grasp of a subject, though he was handicapped by not being able to express his thought readily.'[2] Jinarajadasa, mindful of his great responsibility and frustrated at the rate of progress in his principal pupil, imposed a formal regime that the boys ultimately found intolerable. He may have been trying to follow the example of his own tutor, Leadbeater, whose methods, he recalled, were 'not tender'.[3]

The outbreak of war, in August 1914, disrupted the brothers' concentration, and they hoped that it might offer them an opportunity to strike out on their own, beyond the reach of their sponsors. Despite their peculiar circumstances, they were touched by the popular mood and aspired to the glamour of a uniform. But Krishna's detachment ultimately prevailed over any sense of partisanship or patriotism, and indeed he often reiterated his neutral stance, occasionally speaking up in support of the German troops. His was a lone voice amidst the deluge of anti-German feeling in Britain at the time, though his having been removed from ordinary life insulated him from the repercussions of expressing such unfashionable opinions. The leaders of the Theosophical Society certainly did not share Krishna's moderate stance. Leadbeater maintained that the war was part of a divine plan to destroy the 'Lords of the Dark Face' who currently reigned over Germany, and pronounced with regard to the enemy 'that it is actually a kindness to these ruffians to kill their bodies'.[4] Besant was in a similarly belligerent frame of mind when she declared in 1915 that 'to be neutral under such conditions is to betray humanity'.[5] Neutral Krishna none the less remained and, in a spirit of righteous defiance against his mentors, openly declared that 'there won't be any distinction between the ally and the enemy when the Lord comes & he will have a message for the so-called enemy as well as the ally.'[6]

Annie Besant categorically forbade Krishna to enlist, giving as her principal reason, surprisingly, that she feared in the army he would be compelled to eat meat. The boys were instead enrolled to work at a military hospital in London. Their jobs were menial but they were content just to be involved in some capacity. Theosophists, of course, held to the line that, 'happy the wounded, who are privileged to be ministered to by such hands.'[7] The wounded, however, did not apparently share the sentiment, because, as Krishna wrote to Besant, 'I am an Indian and nobody seems to like them.' The brothers were informed that their services were no longer required at the hospital, and racial prejudice eventually prevented them finding any wartime employment at all. Krishna was compelled to return meekly to his studies in a remote outpost of Cornwall, much to the approval of Besant who had considered the whole idea of war-work to be something of an unnecessary indulgence. His replies to her reprimands reek of guilt and humility: 'I know I have not taken my life seriously so far and I am going to do it from now . . . I know too that I have been thinking about my happiness too much, which is very silly really.'[8]

In June 1916 the brothers were sent to a private tutor who ran a small school at Rochester in Kent, in preparation for their Oxford entrance exams – already two years later than originally scheduled. Their tutor, the Rev. John Sanger, assessed Krishna and declared him to be far from ready for the exam. Krishna's letters from this period are littered with linguistic and spelling mistakes, and the handwriting has deteriorated drastically since 1913. His style also reveals a juvenile sensitivity unsuited to the rigours of university life. The date for the brothers' examination was therefore postponed again while they knuckled down to a period of hard work. Their best intentions, however, were to no avail. New College, Oxford, refused to consider either brother because of the publicity generated by the guardianship case. Christchurch and Balliol followed suit, as did colleges at Cambridge. Neither university was prepared to take on board a would-be messiah, especially one who had been publicly accused of sodomy by his own father. Disappointed after five years of study, the boys then set their sights on London University and studied intensively for the entrance examination in January 1918. The results were acceptance for Nitya but failure for Krishna, who was compelled to return to Rochester for yet more cramming. In September he re-took the exam, but was again to be disappointed. He gave a rare glimpse of his own recollections from the period during a taped interview in 1972. Referring to himself in the third person, Krishnamurti said, 'He did fairly well in school as long as he was left alone, but the moment he had to pass an examination, he couldn't put a thing on paper. He would go to the examination hall and look at the clock and blank. Nothing happened.'[9]

At the time, Krishna felt dejected and guilty that he had disappointed his sponsors. He frequently apologised in his letters for the shortcomings of his brain. Leadbeater replied reassuringly, 'Do not be under the illusion that you have not a good brain; it may not be quite like Nitya's, for he is exceptionally clever, but I assure you it is a capital brain. In your childhood it was for a long time ill-nourished, and so it needs careful exercise to draw out its best qualities.'[10] Hope of entering Krishna for university was now fading. He did attend some lectures at London University for a while, but found the journey from Miss Dodge's house in Wimbledon on public transport too stressful. He had never been robust, but his Theosophical upbringing had encouraged him to believe that his body – not unlike those of the sensitive Masters in Tibet – was rare and unusually refined, certainly not suited to the rigours of life in an overly materialist environment. Cities, crowds and noise apparently weighed more heavily on him than on others, and he frequently fainted when too heavy an assault was put upon his delicate sensibility.

The question of Krishna's academic record was a vexed one. There would be some embarrassing questions to answer from OSE members, both because of the Vehicle's apparent lack of intellect and because the unfolding drama of the Coming had been put on hold. However, a period of global warfare was hardly an appropriate time to trumpet the intentions of an organisation dedicated to universal brotherhood and the dawn of a new age. Despite rumours to the contrary, neither Besant not Leadbeater was concerned about Krishna's failures, at least not to the extent of cancelling the project altogether. Their faith in the Masters' intentions remained absolute. In defence of her protégé, Besant could always point out that the new Californian sub-race, harbinger of the golden era, was to be characterised more by an intuitive faculty rather than book-learning intellect, and in the person of Krishna these properties were illustrated perfectly. Leadbeater had for years been declaring that spiritually superior individuals are 'ever looking upwards' rather than focussing on material achievement. As E. A. Wodehouse had said, when asked how Krishna was progressing with his studies, 'Who can teach Christ anything?'

The World Teacher programme eclipsed any consideration of the boys' happiness, and everyone, with the exception of Lady Emily, was blind to the quiet confusion of Krishna's private world. He was a vulnerable human being faced with gargantuan psychological challenges and possessed very little mental weaponry to help him overcome them. He was an outsider, first and foremost because of his skin colour, which jeers in the street never allowed him to forget. He did not even fit into the standard archetype of an Indian in London society – aristocratic, anglicised, cultivated and well-versed in the niceties of cricket. His English language was far from perfect, his education embarrassingly incomplete, he had no distinguished family history to support his status, and he had emerged from a background of near destitution. Great must have been his confusion when, despite these social handicaps, he found himself cast as the spiritual superior to those possessed of the very attributes he lacked: white men and women, ruling overlords of his own country, affluent intellectuals. He was pitifully ill-equipped to negotiate the subtle chemistry demanded by this situation. He had been severed from his family, culture and caste, only to be enshrined as the leader of a new, non-specific religion in a predominantly Christian, conservative country. The guardianship case and its consequent publicity added fuel to the fire. As he was to write in a letter, 'I am a lusus naturae (freak of nature) and nature enjoys its freak while the freak suffers.'[11]

Annie Besant, who as legal foster-mother was responsible for Krishna's emotional well-being, had fallen out of touch with his needs and did not think to scratch beneath the surface of his letters for any signals of unhappiness. They were regular, short, packed full of endearments, but repetitive and stale. They give no impression of his personality, interests or feelings. His main intent in writing them was to appear grateful for all that had been heaped upon him, and mindful of his responsibilities. Such predictable and formal little notes can have been of little more interest to Besant than as quaint reminders of her own magnanimity. Yet she did care for Krishna and was upset if he failed to write. She was just too busy with her own affairs in India to spare much time agonising over the concealed feelings of a young man who was, after all, in the care of trusted colleagues. She therefore neglected to notice how burdensome Krishna's sense of responsibility had become and how painful his sense of failure. Those within his close circle, however, in particular Lady Emily, observed his quiet anguish, his hatred of publicity, and how he was happiest when he could escape onto the golf course or fiddle with the engine of his motorbike.

Besant also failed to question why her ward did not appear to be growing up, but at the age of twenty was writing letters that could easily have been penned by a twelve-year-old. They do not reveal a person of developing opinions and balanced outlook, but one cringing beneath the sword of his elders' expectations. This suppressed level of maturity was the direct consequence of his hot-house upbringing at the hands of the Theosophists, the limits imposed on his horizons and the degree of protection afforded him. Much power was invested in his future, but at present it was purely nominal, and in practice he was not allowed to make any decisions of his own. This kind of deprivation contributed to his growing sense of resentment and impeded his smooth transition towards independent manhood. Besant perhaps felt she was doing the Vehicle a service in removing, as Blavatsky had prescribed, 'the merely mechanical, material obstacles and difficulties from his path'.[12] This was part of the OSE's mission, she would maintain. But the plain result was a man-child, ill-equipped to face the challenges that his awesome destiny would throw up.

Krishna did have one outlet for his emotional turmoil in the person of Lady Emily Lutyens. His relationship with this woman, twenty years his senior, blossomed of its own accord in spite of the artificial environment imposed on him, and was one of the few natural episodes of his early life. Ironically, there was much about their relationship that was far from natural in other people's eyes. At the time she met Krishna, Lady Emily had recently become a Theosophist and was looking for fresh stimulus in her life. She respected her celebrated husband but shared few of his interests and, while he spent every moment of his spare time craning over the drawing-board, she turned herself, body and soul, to matters religious. She had already committed herself to the OSE on the occasion of Krishna's 1911 London visit; but it was not until 1913 that what had started as affectionate deference for the Vehicle turned into obsessive love. She immediately identified with his inner pain and helplessness, and longed to enfold him into the bosom of her family. 'I was never really happy away from Krishna,' she wrote. 'My husband, my home, my children faded into the background; Krishna became my entire life, and for the next ten years I suffered all the difficulties of trying to sublimate a human love.'[13] In pursuit of this sublimation she imposed a number of strictures on herself, including the renunciation of sexual relations. It is understandable why Edwin Lutyens began to resent the influence of Theosophy and Annie Besant, in particular.[14] His letters beg her to pause and reflect before she is washed away in the tide of religious fanaticism.

The Lutyens family provided both Krishna and Nitya with a flavour of informal domesticity that had been lacking in their lives until now. The children, particularly the four girls, took them to their hearts, their initial nursery games gradually and inevitably maturing into bitter-sweet romances. Mary Lutyens, the youngest of the family, whose early life was dominated by a drawn-out passion for Nitya, remembered Krishna's vivid sense of humour, and the infectious quality of his laughter. Her accounts of the brothers joking, capering around on the floor and relaxing, present a very different picture of the 'holy family' to that relayed by sober Theosophical chronicles of the time. Naturally, there were periods when the Lutyens children resented their mother's love for Krishna, which took precedence over everything, including their own needs.[15] But the Jiddu brothers brought an element of exoticism into their lives and they were inevitably drawn into their inner circle of intimates in the years that followed.

The singular nature of Lady Emily's relationship with Krishna is not just the fact that he was Indian and she an English aristocrat, or that he was the spiritual master and she the doting disciple, old enough to take upon herself the role of his mother. This was enough to label it, in Besant's words, 'a very curious relationship'. There was another dimension, ever-present but difficult in the circumstances to articulate, concerning the foggy area of how this passion was to find consummation. Of course, it was impossible that it ever could in a sexual sense; Krishna was expected to lead a life of pious chastity, and Lady Emily, aside from being restrained by marriage, had also renounced sex. The truth is that their love defied categorisation, and had no distinct goal in sight. They simply filled a gaping vacuum in each other's lives and thereby came to depend on one other. In the eyes of conventional morality their love was beyond reproof and, as such, it stretched on for an agonising decade.

The attitude of the Theosophical Society, however, removed as it was from the world of conventional morality, was far from favourable. As early as 1913, Besant, sensing the possibility of a rival, reprimanded Lady

81

Emily for abandoning her children to be with Krishna, who was not her responsibility. George Arundale also felt piqued that his beloved Alcyone preferred to confide in this outsider rather than himself, and Lady Emily was officially instructed to refrain from showing her affection publicly. Tensions escalated at their Cornwall retreat, in early 1915, when Arundale's jealousy and disapproval led him to the verge of a nervous breakdown. A man of great ambition and energy, he had recently left his busy job at the Hindu Central College and was impatient to accelerate the work of the OSE. His enthusiam for the World Teacher project knew no bounds and he felt that Lady Emily's closeness to Krishna was an unnecessary distraction. He wrote to Besant complaining that Lady Emily had been drawing Krishna away from 'the work', and that under her influence the Vehicle was flagging on a lower plane rather than focussing his aspirations upwards. He also wrote an acid letter to Lady Emily herself, trivialising her feelings and stating, 'You have used Krishna more for your own convenience and satisfaction than for any other purpose . . . you really know very little of Krishna as he really is.'[16] Leadbeater and Besant were incensed at what they considered to be thoroughly unwholesome developments in Krishna's personality, and put the blame squarely on Lady Emily. Krishna himself, caught in the cross-fire of these exchanges, sought in vain to explain to his mentors the pure and beneficial nature of his love, but the wound had been inflicted and it cut deep. Arundale was never to be close to him again, and Lady Emily was penalised by not being advanced a single notch along the Masters' path, the worst possible punishment for someone of her religious sensitivity. It was left to Nitya, in a letter to Besant dated 26 January 1916, to calm the waters: 'Krishna has changed tremendously . . . His love for Lady Emily is no longer an infatuation but a very steady love which I do not think will change for he is not a changeable temperament.'[17]

But Krishna continued to exchange letters with Lady Emily almost daily, and these reached a peak of passion in the early 1920s. They are valuable documents in that they reveal his evolving personality, unlike other pieces written by him at the time, particularly his bland letters to Besant. He comes across as a young man exploring his perspective of the world, often resorting to poetic imagery, bursting with observations and flashes of feeling. He can also be seen finding his voice as a sage, and he drops fragments of spiritual advice, almost patronising in their simplicity but gratefully received. It is clear why the Theosophical Society's leaders disapproved of the relationship. The letters reveal a dependence on Lady Emily, some indulgent over-emotionalism, and a want of backbone, all unbecoming in a future messiah. Yet Lady Emily was his sole source of human succour during these developing years, the only person to whom he did not have to put up a paper-thin façade of spiritual authority. She fulfilled the role of mother to Krishna in a way Annie Besant could not.

Above all, Besant and Leadbeater, thousands of miles away, feared the loss of Krishna's vacant nature, the very quality that made him so ideal a candidate for the Vehicleship. The awakening of his own interests, and certainly the development of emotional attachments, would muddy the waters and might make him lose enthusiasm for his destiny. It was of paramount importance, therefore, to maintain that property of virgin receptiveness in him, and to this end they had taken measures to keep him in an ivory tower. It was an unrealistic plan. Limited though his exposure was, he encountered new and stimulating experiences daily, and his outlook was broadening through his academic studies. He started to form his his own opinions, in defiance, almost, of his tutors, Arundale and Jinarajadasa, whose authority he increasingly began to disrespect. His independence was only checked by the occasional thunderous scolding in the post. This happened for the first time in 1913, when Krishna, exasperated by Jinarajadasa's brittle teaching style, wrote to Leadbeater asking that his tutor should be relieved of his duties. Raising his head above the parapet, he also stated that, 'It is time now that I should take my affairs into my own hands. I feel I could carry out the Master's instructions better if they were not forced upon me and made unpleasant as they have been for some years . . . I know that all has been done for the best but it has not worked.'[18] This kind of fighting talk was not well received by Leadbeater. His response stressed Krishna's selfishness and his lack of gratitude for everything that had been done for him, including his having been rescued from the gutter.

George Arundale saw it as his own special responsibility to encourage Krishna in the work of the OSE which, in practice, meant nagging him at every possible opportunity to bring through messages from the Great

White Brotherhood. Krishna's own perception of the Masters at this point was hazy. He did not go as far as to deny their existence, or his own capacity to engage them, and sometimes he did succeed in delivering messages that he felt had been fed to him by superhuman entities; but, faced with Arundale's insistent pressure, he was increasingly loath to make authoritative statements about the occult world. He fell, instead, into a state of apathy. In February 1915, he wrote to Leadbeater, 'By no means is it easy and I do not know what to do. I know I ought to be interested in the work and all that, but at present moment I am afraid I am not . . . [Arundale] thinks I ought to take the lead but I don't feel like it at all and I want to be quiet.'[19] He continued to express deep fondness for his sponsors, remorse for his mistakes and determination to make good, but he could no longer conceal the fact that he had lost sight of the mission.

The year 1915 marks the beginning of a period of secret doubt, on Leadbeater's and Arundale's parts, as to whether Krishna was, after all, the right choice of Vehicle. It is significant that Leadbeater now chose to leave Adyar and make his home in Australia, to begin a new chapter of his life. The World Teacher project remained important for him, but his confidence in it was bruised.

Despite his misgivings, Krishna continued his work for the OSE, albeit with increasing reluctance. He clearly had little choice. His prospects without the Theosophical Society were grim. There was nowhere else for him to go, especially after the guardianship case. He was also fuelled by the prick of guilt – a sharp knife his sponsors were not averse to twisting on the occasions when he stepped out of line. Much of the work was dreary, such as answering correspondence that arrived from OSE members.

Bored though he was, Krishna could never lapse into total apathy, as there was another dimension to his life, a haunting mystery, indefinable yet immanent, which, by its very nature, set him apart from the confusion he felt all around. At this juncture the only possible explanation he could give for it was that offered by Theosophy: metaphysical entities operating on his psyche from an occult plane. It seemed a satisfactory enough answer to him and, as it pleased the people to whom he owed everything, he was prepared to toe the line. To oppose so mighty a thesis would have been a monstrous undertaking, even for the most resourceful of dissidents, which Krishna clearly was not. None the less, his momentary experiences of insight had a simplicity about them quite different from the baroque extravaganzas of Leadbeater's visions. On one occasion, as he was sitting quietly in the Taormina hotel, he was suddenly aware of a sacred presence which he could describe to his companions in no other terms than, 'The Lord Buddha is here.' The experience was intense but momentary, and his response was to rush from the room.[20] A similar event happened in 1920, when he was talking to his hostess in Paris. He wrote to Lady Emily of his embarrassment at the time, and how he had tried to disguise the moment by saying that the heat had made him light-headed: 'All the same I *felt* really inspired & very strange . . . I had to get up and stand a bit & collect my ideas. I assure you, mother, it was most strange, most strange. Between ourselves *absolutely*, in the Theosophical language, there was someone there but I did not tell her.'[21]

When Annie Besant met Krishna again, on returning to England in June 1919 after an absence of nearly five years, she was pleased by what she found. Her protégé concealed his doubts and performed well for her, presiding over an OSE meeting on 14 June. Looking back on this period three years later, she recalled, approvingly, how much he had developed in her absence: 'He is direct and uncompromising, strikes through all pretences and shams, and with startling insight, pierces to the heart of the subject he deals with. He has developed great literary power, vivid, graphic, and arresting, and now and again reveals depths of understanding and compassion, that come as a surprise from one still boyish in appearance.'[22] Her worst fears during the years of separation were now alleviated.

Seven months after Besant's return Krishna sat the London University entrance examination for the third time and is said not even to have put pen to paper. He had for some time been asking if he could break the impasse in his life with a spell in France and, seeing that there was no future in his academic career, Besant at last agreed. He departed London for Paris on 24 January 1920.

Many Theosophists felt strongly that their President had betrayed her office in taking so dogmatic a line on the World Teacher issue, to the exclusion of the many other philosophies that had traditionally held a place in the Society's multi-faceted constitution. Staff and governors at the Central Hindu College, now to be expanded and elevated as the Benares Hindu University, ostracised Besant to the fringe of power because they disapproved of her missionary style. They were also keenly aware of a tendency within the new Theosophical Society to idolize personalities, and this trait of Besant's leadership, they feared, was beginning to infiltrate the College. As soon as orthodox Hindus gained control of the College's governing body, a directive was issued banning students from joining the OSE. It was a humiliating blow for Besant who treasured the College as her own pet achievement.

One of the most damaging acts of Theosophical dissent to follow in the wake of the World Teacher doctrine came from Germany, under the leadership of Rudolf Steiner. As head of the German section of the Theosophical Society, Steiner had influence over sixty-nine lodges around the country. He had been concerned for some while about Besant's contention that eastern mysticism represented the wisdom tradition most in tune with Theosophical ideals. His own inspiration was grounded in western theology and Greco-Roman philosophy. He also objected to what he saw as Besant's self-glorification, and took particular exception to her relationship with Leadbeater, whom he regarded as a sex-pervert. He found untenable the notion of a Hindu boy being physically prepared for occupancy by the Lord Maitreya, and this representing a contemporary reincarnation of Christ. Not only did Steiner suspect Leadbeater of the worst sexual motives, particularly in the light of the guardianship case, but the theory as a whole went against his understanding of Christ, whose incarnation in the person of Jesus, he maintained, was a unique event. As a result, he ordered that members of the German section of the Society would not be permitted to join the OSE. Besant decided that his action broke the rules of the Society and in 1913 expelled Steiner, closing the German section altogether.[23] It re-opened under new leadership shortly after, but Steiner carried fifty-five of the former lodges with him, and they now made up the membership nucleus of his own Anthroposophical Society.

Other veteran Theosophists were turning against Annie Besant because they took offence at her latest passion which, during the war years, overshadowed even her interest in the World Teacher. This new mission was for Indian Home Rule. Besant reported with some pride how in 1913 she had been summoned in her astral body to meet the Rishi Agastya, the Master responsible for Indian affairs, and commanded to instigate a programme of social reform. She then received what she referred to as her 'marching orders' from the Lord of the World himself, to campaign for the self-government of India. Political confrontation was in her blood and she entered into the fray joyously, convinced, as usual, that she had been selected for the task by divine ordinance. A series of eight lectures entitled 'Wake Up India' kick-started her campaign, but her principal tool was a daily newspaper, *New India*, which she bought in July 1914. Within its first six months the paper's circulation increased from 1000 to 10,000. As usual, she targeted the young and initiated several organisations for Indian youth, whose central tenets were self-sacrificing service and brotherly love.

Conservative Theosophists were horrified that their President should enter so vigorously into a campaign that appeared to have little in common with the aims of the Society. But here they were blind to the scope of Besant's ambitions. Theosophy had by now become inextricably focussed on the establishment of the new world religion led by Krishna-murti, with Indian philosophy at its core. Annie's political ambitions for India were therefore wholly in tune with her Theosophical objectives, and she envisaged Krishna, when the time was right, taking his place at her side in the campaign for Home Rule. 'His will be the hand to restore to India her lofty heritage of spirituality, to arouse her to a sense of sublime mission to the world. Our winning of her political freedom is necessary to prepare her for that greater work, when she shall arise and shine, and the Glory of the Lord shall be revealed in the Sacred Land.'[24]

Crucial to Besant's scheme for India was the preservation of its international links – ties of diplomatic concord that would one day be mirrored at a social level, ushering in an era of philadelphian cooperation around the world. Self-government was important, she maintained, but it must not be achieved by cutting off good relations with countries already connected politically to India; in other words, fellow member states of the British Empire. Britain, with its supreme network of international relations and military muscle, would be the agent whereby her new civilisation could spread round the globe; first, a free India, then a friendly Commonwealth, and ultimately, a world federation of brother states. In pursuit of this goal, she fell foul of Gandhi and other more extreme Home Rule campaigners, who regarded her as too much of a moderate. Her vision of a utopian Commonwealth, they declared, presented a soft deal for Britain. She was, wrote T. M. Nair, in *Justice* magazine, a Pied Piper, luring the youth of India to their doom, a woman who had 'disturbed the ordered political progress of a great country because she was in a hurry in her old age to secure supreme political power to her worshippers in order that she might pose as the liberator of a down-trodden country.'[25]

While Besant was failing to please many Indians, her political campaign also led to her being disowned by the British administration. The outbreak of war in 1914 resulted in a public denunciation of any British citizens who expressed unpatriotic sentiments, and in the summer of 1917 Besant was interned, along with George Arundale at the South Indian hill-station of Ootacamund. It was marvellous publicity for her cause, and her popularity amongst Indians soared once more. After ninety-four days of internment, she was released, and shortly afterwards, at the age of seventy, elected to the Presidency of the Indian National Congress, the most senior political position controlled by Indians. It was the crowning glory of her political career in India, but, inevitably, extremists once again began to disagree with her propositions. The opposition she encountered on both sides of the political debate began to depress even so inveterate a war-horse as herself. In August 1918 she wrote to Esther Bright, 'I am sad, heart weary, and would give anything to be allowed to leave this body ... but I have more pain to bear than I know how to bear ... it is so lonely – so desperately lonely.'[26]

There were, however, positive developments within the World Teacher movement at this time. Dissent in some quarters of the Theosophical Society was amply compensated for by membership gains generated as a result of the OSE's allure. In some territories the activities of the new religious movement extended to more than a fringe of zealous non-conformists. In Costa Rica, for example, the World Teacher project became a political issue. Sidney Field, a friend of Krishnamurti in the 1920s, remembered how his Theosophist father, who had founded Costa Rica's first national bank, caused a political furore when he allowed his portrait, complete with an OSE silver star pinned to his lapel, to be printed on currency banknotes. Grandees of the Catholic Church reacted in horror at this challenge to Christian hegemony. Liberals, in response, used the controversy as a means of discrediting the conservative establishment. The Krishnamurti issue thus became entangled in the question of Costa Rican civil liberty and free speech. Federico Tinoco, a leading statesman and member of the OSE, led a political assault on the President, Gonzalez Flores, and in 1917 seized power, establishing himself as head of state. The OSE now became a fashionable ideology, and some cabinet members joined the Theosophical Society to demonstrate their support of the new President. For two years 'the country basked in an era of reason, open friendship and optimism,' claims Field.[27] The end of this unusual chapter of Costa Rica's history came in 1919, when American opposition to the regime led to economic disaster, and Tinoco, pressed from all sides, became a dictator. After he fled to France, the established Church sharpened its knives and the OSE in Costa Rica fell into disrepute.

While Annie Besant settled into her campaign for Home Rule, and Krishna struggled to reconcile his personal needs with the destiny ordained for him, Leadbeater decided to make a new home for himself in Sydney, Australia. He left Adyar in February 1914 for a prolonged lecture tour which was to include Australia and New Zealand. These territories fascinated him; he admired the pioneering spirit of their population, their youthful vigour and forward-looking optimism. He went as far as to evince the theory that Australia, in addition to California, would give birth to the new sixth sub-race, evidence for which he noted in the physical character of several young people he encountered there. Australian Theosophists received him gladly, and were especially charmed by the way he engaged audiences of children.

The reasons for his departure from Adyar are unknown. His enemies in India claimed he was escaping from imminent arrest; those sceptical of the World Teacher movement maintained he was losing interest in the distant Krishna; others speculated that, as an old Tory, he did not want to be too closely associated with Besant, now that she had turned to anti-establishment politics. All three theories doubtless have an element of truth, but none tells the whole story. He was tired of the endless muck-raking by his opponents in India and longed to establish a new court for himself, where his methods would be accepted without reference to dubious past incidents. He clearly still believed in the new age, and the energetic work he was to take up in Australia was motivated with this end in sight. Everything for him pointed to the dawn of a new age, a new race and a new civilising consciousness; though whether Krishna himself was to have any role in the great plan was now no longer certain.

The most surprising, and at the same time dramatic, change in Leadbeater's life, after his arrival in Australia, was his re-adoption of Christianity. This came about through the influence of a new protagonist on the Theosophical stage: James Ingall Wedgwood, an imposing and good-looking man, descended from the prestigious dynasty of British potters. Wedgwood, who had been General Secretary of the Theosophical Society in England, had a particular love of religious ceremonial. In 1912 he founded the Temple of the Rosy Cross, a devotional body set up to add ritualistic spice to the World Teacher preparations. Lady Emily, an active participant at the time, believed Wedgwood's real intent was to rival the OSE by enticing members into a more scented, ecclesiastical organisation. Members of the Rosy Cross were dressed in long white satin gowns, with chivalric-style head-dresses and swords buckled at the waist. During the ritual 'the lives of successive World Teachers were represented by the lighting of a candle, with appropriate quotations from the religions they had founded. The culmination was the dedication of an unlit candle, intended to represent the coming incarnation of the World Teacher. In the words of the ritual, "That candle must remain unlit till He with His own divine hand shall light it and bring new guidance to our hearts and lives."'[28] 'Solemn liturgy and stately ritual,' Wedgwood claimed, reflected 'lofty purpose . . . They are in truth the very steps by which man climbs to the footstool of God.'[29] He clearly understood the enormous attraction of mystery, and held that a religion could not ignite people's hearts if it remained in the sterile realm of philosophy.

A state of uneasy tension existed between Wedgwood and Leadbeater, who was suspicious of any organisation that did not include himself, until 1915, when they met in Sydney. Wedgwood soon brought his senior partner round to the opinion that ceremony had a valuable role to play in the future of the World Teacher movement, and the two men became close collaborators. They even entertained the notion of dedicating a Church organisation to prepare for the Coming, complete with a hierarchy of clergy and its own special liturgy. In England, Wedgwood had already become affiliated to a branch of the Old Catholic Church – a dissident ecclesiastical body, independent both from Rome and Protestantism – and, after receiving Holy Orders in 1913, was consecrated bishop at a London Co-Masonic temple in February 1916. Returning to Australia, he consequently ordained Leadbeater to the priesthood in July 1916, and later the same month consecrated him too as bishop. Thus it was that, thirty-two years after having abandoned Christianity to follow H. P. Blavatsky, Leadbeater returned to the religion of his native culture, and acknowledged once again the sanctity of all that was contained within the symbol of the cross. The two new bishops were given a completely free hand to 'rectify' the mistakes of traditional Christianity when the Old Catholic Church disassociated itself from the Theosophical Society, and they found themselves at the head of a completely independent organisation. They re-named it the Liberal Catholic Church, composed their own liturgy, and sought 'to offer the movement to the World Teacher as one of the vehicles for His force, and a channel for the preparation of His Coming.' The Lord Maitreya (reported Leadbeater) 'was graciously pleased to accept the offer, and to say that He thought the movement would fill a niche in the scheme and would be useful to Him.'[30]

Leadbeater became a zealous convert. Aside from a personal liking for the trappings of ritual office, such as costume and jewellery, he now agreed that ceremony could tap a source of spiritual energy, thereby facilitating man's perception of God. The incorporation of formalised worship into his religious matrix proved popular with many followers. Traditional Christian symbology offered a powerfully seductive comfort in these uncertain times, even for those westerners who professed disillusionment with their religious heritage. Cultural conditioning ran deep, and the sight of a crucifix represented a beacon of sanity to many. This was entirely legitimate, Leadbeater claimed, because the Lord Maitreya might be about to appear again just as he had 2000 years before, in the person of Jesus. It was appropriate that His former mouthpiece, the Christian Church, should be incorporated into the new movement.

However, by re-embracing Christianity, Leadbeater distanced himself still further from Blavatsky's ideology, and loyal supporters of the founder did not take kindly to this new departure. They grew concerned that the original purpose of the Society was now being manipulated to accommodate an entirely new scheme, favoured by Leadbeater and Besant but inconsistent with the intentions of their beloved founder. Blavatsky had reserved special contempt for the Apostolic succession, which Leadbeater and Wedgwood, by becoming bishops, now claimed to have received, and she had described it as 'a gross and palpable fraud.'[31] Theosophists who held with Blavatsky but did not sympathise with the World Teacher project, the OSE or the Liberal Catholic Church now began to suspect that their interests were no longer represented by the organisation based at Adyar.

The end of the First World War opened practical opportunities to new religious movements in the west. Established Christianity had rested on an uncertain footing in late nineteenth-century Britain, and the war had now dealt a violent blow to its credibility. Mourners questioned how a kind God could have willed the slaughter of so many loved ones. It made a mockery of their devotion, their prayers and their morality. Ideals were running high; people needed positive leadership, spiritual guidance, and some satisfactory explanation as to why a whole generation of young men had suddenly been deprived of life. People also needed fire in their lives, now that the fearsome blaze which had scorched them for four long years had at last been extinguished. The old institutions of authority, including the Church, were thought by many to be inadequate for the task of creating a better new world. Had they not, after all, brought about a cataclysmic destruction of the old?

Annie Besant and the Theosophical Society were well-positioned to answer these needs. They promised the thrilling prospect of a new world order, a messiah for humanity, no less; and in their philosophy of reincarnation, they provided a ready answer for the bereaved. Spiritualism, which was enjoying a revival in the wake of the slaughter, proved ultimately unsatisfactory, as it had been in the previous century. But reincarnation implied rebirth, fresh starts for all, shining wisdom rising out from the ashes of past mistakes. The loved ones who had sacrificed their lives on the battlefield, Besant proclaimed, would soon be reborn 'to lay the foundations of a nobler civilisation'.[32] Her programmes for education and youth movements neatly complemented the 1920s spirit of regeneration. It was the inexorable movement of evolution, nature defining her path towards a perfect world.

6

Cracking the Mould

———— ✳ ————

Annie Besant's positive assessment of the poised and apparently confident young man she re-met on her return to England in June 1919 was
far from well-judged. She had little inkling of the problems and doubts
that haunted Krishna at the time, as he had become expert at concealing
the impurities of his 'lower nature', protecting all who had an interest
in his future from potential disappointment. But still he held to the hope
that something mysterious and revolutionary could perhaps occur: that
he might one day magically mature into the Theosophists' super-man,
or that he might be graced with a mind-shattering spiritual experience,
like St Paul on the road to Damascus. This grain of optimism held him
to the ordained path as the 1920s began.

After arriving in France, in January 1920, the sole outlet for his private
agony was his correspondence with Lady Emily Lutyens. Enough of his
letters of this period remain to show that his infatuation with the older
woman was as desperate as at any time in the past, and her passion
for him burned with an equivalent ferocity. During his first weeks the
descriptions of his daily life in France are peppered with love-sick
laments, together with repeated expressions of misery, loneliness and
boredom. His sense of desolation began to pass, however, as he awoke
to fresh attractions and stimuli. The most important new and cheering
influence in his life was the de Manziarly family, under whose protection
he fell while in Paris. Madame de Manziarly, Russian by birth and a

94

dedicated member of the OSE, introduced him to exciting cultural novelties in the fields of art, drama and literature. Three of her four children
were living in France at the time (two girls, Marcelle and Yolande, and
a boy, Sacha), all of whom now became his great friends and admirers. In
their invigorating company Krishna's confidence soared and his hopeless
obsession with his mother-substitute in England began to dwindle.

Signs that his nascent sexuality was beginning to preoccupy him can
be detected in his references to frequent though innocent, brushes with
unchaperoned women. On a trip to the south of France in February,
he writes to a despairing Lady Emily of girls who approached him,
caught his eye, and on one occasion actually set out to seduce him in a
hotel bedroom. His reaction to these advances was mixed. He was simply
too gauche and frightened of sex at this stage, as well as having been
committed by his elders to a celibate life, to contemplate cultivating a
physical relationship. However, in between expressions of shock at the
quantity of make-up and scent used by French women his reports to
Lady Emily betray a certain mischievous enjoyment. He clearly adored
the de Manziarly girls (aged fifteen and nineteen) and was not above
tickling their young passions with some harmless flirting. On a more
personal note, he confessed the recurrence of erotic dreams, experiences
that caused him a degree of perturbation as they seemed to fly in the
face of his self-enforced purity. It was surprising to no one, except
perhaps Krishna himself, that he proved so irresistible to female admirers.
He had reached a peak of physical beauty – slender, well-proportioned,
with thick black hair, and an aristocratic face of finely chiselled features.
He had also, unconsciously, developed a certain authority, intriguingly
juxtaposed, in his manner, with gentle vulnerability, a mixture of qualities
that was to work like an aphrodisiac on the women he met. Add to this
his exquisite sense of dress, cleanliness, and the atmosphere of hushed
veneration that surrounded his every public appearance, and the combination was devastatingly seductive.

His letters from France reveal a young man closer in mould to the
Great Gatsby than a latter day Jesus. He had more style than money
and his patrician's looks and manner gave the impression of greater
affluence than actually existed. None the less, he undertook very little
work, either academic or missionary, and a 1920 diary of events shows

that his day began in earnest only at lunch time. He had a tendency to loaf around his Paris apartment in a dressing-gown unless called upon to meet someone socially, visit an art gallery or accompany one of his Theosophical friends to the theatre. Holidays were abundant and luxurious. During the summer of 1920 he happily followed the de Manziarly family to Lake Geneva, where he remained in or near their company for two months, living in a hotel, playing tennis, golf, swimming and walking in the mountains. He did not shy from accepting the hospitality of OSE members, who felt blessed just to be in his company, and enjoyed some extravagant entertainment at other people's expense. Their assertions of his spiritual superiority never ceased to astonish him, feeling, as he did at this time, insufficiently gifted for his prescribed role. He noted with bemusement how members of the de Manziarly family would fall 'unto raptures' whenever he dressed himself in Indian clothes, and how they thought him 'God on earth – better than Mrs Besant or CWL'.[1] His repeated assertions that he was not unique, that there were 'thousands of people' just like him, fell on deaf ears.

During his Lake Geneva holiday with the de Manziarlys, and free of Theosophy's hard-liners, he felt happier than at any time in his life. While taking care not to offend his hosts and guardians in France, he confided to Lady Emily that he did not 'care a damn' about the Masters, that Leadbeater might be a complete fraud, and that 'when a most critical moment comes [in life], Theosophy and all its innumerable books don't help'.[2]

Lady Emily, still a devout believer in Theosophy, was not overly disturbed by Krishna's denunciations of her creed, because, as she wrote, 'In his letters came flashes of his spiritual experiences which told me that in spite of his surface doubts there remained the unshakeable belief that the Lord Maitreya was to use his body as His vehicle and that he must make himself worthy of that wonderful destiny.'[3] These 'flashes' occurred despite Krishna's brewing scepticism, and even took himself by surprise at times. On 6 May 1920 he wrote, 'Curiously all day I have been *very* dreamy . . . and in my heart there has been a continual thought of Lord Buddha. I was in such a state that I had to sit down & meditate. Think of me meditating. Extraordinary.' He was further invigorated as he read *The Buddha's Way of Virtue*. One particular excerpt moved him deeply with the quality of spiritual independence it defined, unadulterated by the pressure of outside authority: 'All conquering and all knowing am I, detached, untainted, untrammelled, wholly freed by destruction of desire. Whom shall I call Teacher? Myself found the way.'[4]

While Krishna found a sense of equilibrium, if not peace of mind during the summer of 1920, the fortunes of his brother Nitya, who was universally adored for his charm and compassion, received a succession of blows. Although more academic than his elder brother, reading and studying had always been a great strain for Nitya because he suffered from partial blindness. His condition was alleviated slightly when Krishna performed an act of healing on his eyes (a gift the older brother certainly possessed but was reluctant to engage), but a career involving large amounts of reading would have proved impractical. He sought instead to satisfy his strong business instinct through commercial ventures, and his plans reached a pitch of excitement in early 1920, when a major business opportunity came his way. One account has it that he was about to establish himself as a European agent exporting motor vehicles to India, but a letter of the period hints that his speculations extended to trade in grain foods ('Business is too wonderful for words . . . everything points to our success in rice.').[5] His euphoria was to be cut short, however, after he received a telegram from Annie Besant, who had got wind of the news, forbidding him to proceed any further. He was instructed to remain with or near Krishna, as his prime duty in life was to act as a support to his illustrious brother.

There now began a period of intense frustration and misery for Nitya, who was inclined by nature more towards worldly pragmatism than spirituality. In April he wrote despondently to Madame de Manziarly, 'I've never enjoyed anything for which I've not paid dearly, I think it must be because my enjoyments are among the forbidden ones, and those that are permissible are not enjoyable.'[6] He was also confused as to what his future role entailed. Krishna's path, though awesome in its scope, had definition and purpose. His own was, and always had been, indefinite, but to question this situation would have been considered impertinent by his sponsors. Of what import were the petty desires of an individual ego when set beside the monumental unfolding of evolution's master-plan? Aside from remaining with Krishna in Paris, he was per-

97

mitted only to return to a small flat in London where he was supposed to be studying law. For the ambitious Nitya, the prospect of spending his life in obedient service to his brother, with no hope of ever fulfilling his own potential, was heart-breaking. His morale sank still further in May 1921 when he began to cough blood and a malignant patch was detected on his left lung. Thus began his long struggle against tuberculosis, a condition that made the possibility of his realising a career outside the scope of Theosophy even more remote.

Bolstered by the dynamism of the de Manziarly family, Krishna's confidence began to rise. By the end of his summer holiday he felt bold enough to level some private criticisms against the Theosophical Society – not so much in relation to its fundamental philosophy, but in the way it had taken on the appearance of just another religious sect. His ambition was clearly to precipitate reform within the Society, even if it meant challenging the authority of Leadbeater. He wrote to Lady Emily in the summer of 1920 that he would like to: 'stir up the b— Theosophists! I do hate this mamby-pamby affair we are at present . . . What rot it all is & to think what it might be. We will have to do it. Change it from top to bottom and knock the personal element into thick air . . . <u>Damn!</u> I am really fed up with that crowd but at present it is not my affair. One day, as I am really at the bottom very keen on it all, I shall take it up and do what <u>I</u> think is right and hang everybody who has got any personal element in it. Oh, mother, what rot it is. Don't laugh. <u>Damn!!</u>'[7] He was eager to contribute, to help heal divisions within the ranks and keep the movement on a even keel; but he feared that Leadbeater's latest caprice – his involvement with the Liberal Catholic Church – was a potentially damaging red herring.

Jinarajadasa had recently arrived in London and, as Leadbeater's ever loyal ambassador, proclaimed to members the virtues of introducing a note of ecclesiastical ceremony into their movement. Krishna, objecting to this development and, by now itching to take up leadership of the OSE (that had been nominally his for so long), made his feelings plain to Lady Emily: 'Why not clear up the mess we are in <u>first</u> & then start new things? All this only adds to the existing chaos, making it more cumbersome.'[8]

Despite the anger Krishna felt, he was determined in 1921 to complete his education in preparation for the great work, only this time in Paris, at the Sorbonne. His letters to Annie Besant emphasise this lofty purpose, together with his burning desire to join her for the work in India. Characteristically, there is not the least hint in his tone of the rebellious frame of mind he had revealed to Lady Emily. Besant was to be shielded, as usual, from a true understanding of her protégé's complex predicament. The picture she received was of a young man fast developing the qualities of leadership and intellectual vitality that would admirably complement the innate divinity of his nature.

Leadbeater, though now engaged in different activities, still reserved judgment about Krishna. This he made plain to all by sending to Europe a new discovery, a handsome and academic young Brahmin called D. Rajagopalacharya (known as Rajagopal). Rajagopal's arrival in London with Jinarajadasa immediately fuelled speculation in Theosophical circles that Krishna might be superseded by a rival. The newcomer was enrolled for Cambridge University – into which he passed without difficulty – and, like the Jiddu brothers, was sponsored by the generous Miss Dodge. The one person who did not seem bothered by the arrival of the promising newcomer was Krishna himself, though he makes reference in his letters to other people's concerns. With a flash of cynical apathy, he mentions that he would gladly hand over his role to Rajagopal, only he suspects that the Theosophists would ruin his life.

Leadbeater had spotted his new favourite back in December 1913, at the Kerala Theosophical Conference, when the boy was a mere thirteen years old. Once again, he claimed, it was the child's unique aura that caught his attention; it spoke to him of Rajagopal's extraordinary past lives and sensational future. He doubtless felt bitterly torn at having to leave so promising and attractive a discovery, when he departed for Australia just two months after meeting him; but he left Rajagopal in the doting care of Jinarajadasa who found his new pupil vastly more obliging and promising than the petulant young messiah he had left behind in England.

When Krishna finally met Rajagopal in person in the autumn of 1920, he found him affable and keen to help in the work. They were to become friends and close colleagues for years, though scandal haunted their

99

relationship later in life which, in both men's old age, caused relations between them to break down altogether. However, in the 1920s the issue of rivalry was buried before it ever properly raised its head, as Rajagopal, like so many others, found himself drawn into Krishna's service as if by some magic spell.

The principal tool Krishna used, so as to establish an influence in the direction of the OSE, was the editorial column in the Order's monthly *Herald.* He did not enjoy the burden of having to write these regular Editorial Notes and the texts do not display electrifying insights, let alone the spark of divine revelation. They are filled with generalities and pious platitudes about brotherhood, the avoidance of cruelty, religious tolerance, physical health and the wickedness of vivisection, all well-meant, well-articulated, but sermons to the converted. His tone is reprimanding as he calls on members to wake up and practise the ideals they preached: 'The Order of the Star in the East has been for many years in a state of coma . . . We are like a great power house, but it is to no avail, either to the world or to ourselves, if we do not know how to use our power.' One interesting theme that does come across, however, is his emphasis on a political and international outlook. In the wake of the First World War world attention had been fixed on the establishment of a League of Nations which was intended, through the machinery of diplomacy, to prevent the recurrence of future wars. This brand of idealism was consistent with the Theosophical Society's ambitions for the golden new age. Krishna reflected the spirit of the times when he began to talk of the OSE's role in contributing to the state of world cooperation. The Lord Maitreya's Vehicle, he stressed, would be an international figure, a 'Super-Man', at the centre of religio-political alliance of peoples across the globe.

He had had the opportunity to observe the League of Nations Assembly personally, while in Geneva, and what he witnessed spurred his imagination to conceive an alternative and superior body, that would unite the interests of diplomacy and spirituality. He writes in the Editorial Notes of his observations along these lines, but a more vivid picture of his feelings on the subject is contained in a letter to Lady Emily, where he says of the League, 'They are a lot of insincere and money grubbing lot of people . . . I know how much better we Theosophists could manage the League of Nations for I think we are more disinterested. We must someday have in the TS a true League of Nations which includes *all* nations . . . You wait, when we get going we shall make a hum & beat them all at their own game.'[9]

Encouraged by the positive effect his words appeared to be having on members, Krishna pursued his favourite themes at the first Congress of the OSE, which was held in Paris between 23 and 27 July 1921. The Order now boasted a membership of 30,000, and the Congress was attended by 1400 delegates from thirty-nine different countries. Krishna was determined that the event should not lapse into the mould of a standard Theosophical gathering, complete with self-congratulatory diatribes and sycophantic eulogies. He had been compelled to endure more of these tedious assemblies during his youth than he cared to remember. This Congress, he stressed in advance through the Editorial Notes, was to mark a turning point for the OSE: 'We cannot go on in the lethargic way to which . . . we have been accustomed. If we do not act in a very decisive manner, we shall be swept aside and others will, naturally, take our place . . . The time has come when we, not individually, but as an Order, must set a standard of high practical idealism, according to which our daily lives must be strictly regulated.' The Congress turned out to be a great success, and Krishna's profile as leader was established in a tangible sense. A delighted Annie Besant noted how well her protégé controlled proceedings; she particularly admired his firm hand in deflecting distractions, his frequent quotations of Jesus' words as illustrations of his own points, and his new proficiency as a speaker, not just in English but French as well. She accepted his authoritative condemnation of ritual within the Order and thrilled to hear him rally the troops to action. She was convinced, not just by his performance in the chair but also by his Editorial Notes, that Krishna was now impatient to begin the Work. Besant sensed that his time was near at hand. Her instinct for publicity also told her that the handsome young Indian possessed qualities that would rejuvenate Theosophy and draw ever greater numbers to her cause.

The movement was definitely gathering steam. OSE conferences were scheduled in territories all over the world and chaired by members of the Society's inner core, such as Jinarajadasa, Arundale and Wood. Annie

Besant wrote of her intention to 'Theosophise everywhere: Churches, Schools, Colleges, Universities, Gaols, Reforms, Governments, Politics, Commerce, Trade, Professions, Manual Labour.'[10] The Anglican Church clearly considered the Theosophical Society a formidable enough organisation to warrant discussion at a special conference of bishops, held at Lambeth Palace, in 1920. As a result of this meeting, an ecclesiastical committee was appointed whose purpose was to explore and define the relationship between Christianity and Theosophy, especially with regard to the Liberal Catholic Church.

Another important milestone for the OSE was reached in 1921, when Krishnamurti met a young Dutch aristocrat and Theosophist named Philip van Pallandt. The van Pallandt family had been involved with the Society since the days of Madame Blavatsky[11], and Baron Philip was keen to maintain the connection. He, like so many of his generation, was infected with the post-war mood of idealism, and determined to dedicate his estate at Ommen, near Arnhem, to some positive public cause. He had seen Krishna in London during 1920, but it was only after the Paris Congress of the following year that a friend suggested inviting him to Ommen. Krishna arrived alone at the Baron's house, Castle Eerde, in September 1921, and stayed for two weeks.[12] Krishna warmed to van Pallandt's straightforward affability and simplicity and the two young men struck up an immediate and lasting friendship. They also shared a common interest in cars and motoring. As a result of this encounter, Philip van Pallandt decided to offer Krishna not just the castle, but 5000 acres of fields, lakes and woodland attached to it, as a gift. Krishna had the foresight not to accept the property as his own personal possession, but recommended setting up a Trust that would hold ownership of the estate on behalf of the Order. A European centre was required for the OSE, to complement the Order's activities in India, and establish it as a body independent of the Theosophical Society. Castle Eerde was thenceforth nominated international headquarters of the OSE, and the surrounding land became a venue for mass gatherings. Starting in 1924, thousands of people, mostly young idealists, would descend for the annual summer Star Camps at Ommen, presided over by Krishna and organised meticulously by a team of local administrators. While the huge majority of visitors ate, slept, washed and attended lectures in tents of various dimensions, Krishna and his entourage were accommodated in the castle itself.

Eerde, despite its classification, could only be described as a castle on account of its double moat, which a bridge spanned, leading up to a broad entrance staircase. In every other way it resembled a large early eighteenth-century manor house of considerable elegance. Approached by a long avenue of beech trees, it was flanked by various stables, pavilions and outbuildings, some of which were later converted for comfortable guest accommodation. A full-time staff worked in offices contained in a basement beneath the residential rooms; the main house, with its capacious hall, Louis XIV staircase, antique furniture and tapestries, was ideal for OSE receptions. It also presented Krishna with the opportunity to play host in a setting appropriately stately for one who was destined to mix on equal terms with kings and presidents.

Aside from winning the friendship of Philip van Pallandt, and procuring for his Order a magnificent property, Krishna fell passionately in love during his fortnight at Ommen – this time with someone of his own generation. She was a seventeen-year-old American girl of Dutch extraction, called Helen Knothe. Helen had come to Holland to study the violin, with a view to making a profession out of it, but before taking lessons in Amsterdam, her Theosophist mother had taken her first to the OSE Congress in Paris, and then to Ommen. Helen was an exceptionally spirited and intelligent girl, liberal in outlook and bohemian in inclination. Describing the assembly at Ommen, she wrote, in 1992, 'There were young people from all over Europe gathered on the banks of the river Vecht to voice and practice their ideas, hopes, and plans for a better world. They were early hippies and [I] fitted happily into their group, [my] life opening up to new and important influences.'[13]

She had already seen Krishna from a distance at the Paris Congress, but had not been introduced to him and had no idea of his presence at Ommen until one day the van Pallandt Rolls-Royce pulled up near to the camp area, and he stepped out with Baron Philip. Helen had just run a race against a Swedish girl and she breathlessly asked the dashing young Indian for his autograph. Krishna was instantly attracted to her, and van Pallandt, sensing the chemistry, asked Helen on the spot if she would like to join them at the Castle for a meal. For the remainder of his stay at Ommèn, Krishna was hardly ever out of her company, walking, cycling or driving around the estate in the Baron's car. It was a magical summer week for the couple, removed from the real world, in a rural environment of great beauty. Although painfully shy – so much so that he had to cover his face with a handkerchief before addressing her – Krishna confessed at the end of the week that he was deeply in love, and that she had joined the three people in his life who meant the most to him, Annie Besant, Nitya and Lady Emily. Helen was attracted to him, and felt flattered that so eminent a person should choose her, 'an insignificant schoolgirl of no great distinction or looks', but did not as yet feel consumed by the sort of passion to which he laid claim. Krishna, for the first time in his life at the age of twenty-six, felt the floodgates of legitimate romance open wide.

He knew that the next step in his career was a return to India, and with so little time left in Europe before his scheduled departure, he determined to visit Helen in Holland once again. After spending a final fortnight in England, saying goodbye to friends, he returned to Amsterdam for a few days on the pretext of attending some Theosophical meetings, but made sure to stay near Helen at the Dutch Theosophical headquarters. He arrived laden with presents for her, spent a few days pledging his devotion and, when the time came for him to depart, left a note which ran: 'Darling Helen, I love you with all my heart & soul & shall *always* do so. Bless you. Krishna.'[14] He did not attempt to hide his feelings from Lady Emily, though the frank way he told her the news must have cut her to the quick. Just three days after his note to Helen, he wrote to his old confidante, 'I *am* awfully in love & it is a great sacrifice on my part but *nothing* else can be done. I feel as if I had an awful wound inside me; don't think I am exaggerating. I shall not see Helen for God knows how long & you know, mother dear, what I am . . . I hope you are not jealous, dear old Mum??'[15]

When Krishna told Annie Besant about his love and showed her a photograph of Helen, she did not express any discouragement, and surprisingly offered to have the photograph framed on Krishna's behalf. But this seemingly moderate response was more strategic than honest. She realised that to break Krishna's heart at such a sensitive moment could do untold damage, and it would be best to let him live out his romantic dream until it expired of its own accord. It was in this spirit that she wrote a touchingly maternal letter to Helen from Adyar, soon after Krishna's arrival: 'About Krishna, dear, I know something of the tie between you. He will help you immensely, I know, but the affection may have a good deal of pain in it, from the ordinary standpoint. He has a great work to do and it may keep him much from you physically. For the world needs him and he cannot, as it were, belong to any one of us. Are you big enough and strong enough, I wonder, to help him and not to hinder him?'[16]

The decision to bring the budding World Teacher back to India after an absence of ten years signalled Besant's confidence that her protégé was ready to take the helm – at least partially, and under the watchful eye of his seniors. His arrival in Bombay on 3 December 1921 was a jubilant occasion and she announced to the heaving throng of spectators who had come to witness the historic event, 'The two brothers, who left as boys, have returned as men.' Nitya, still far from healthy, was spared the spotlight and would stand alongside his brother while the doting crowds – infinitely more demonstrative than their counterparts in Europe – looped garlands round their necks and touched their feet. It was felt appropriate, in view of such traditional expressions of greeting and veneration, for the brothers to change out of their suits and into Indian clothes, a custom which Krishna maintained throughout his life on arrival in India, together with adopting local eating habits.

As soon as he was settled, Krishna began to confront the problem of how best to present himself to the community. He dreaded having to endure, and be seen to endorse, Theosophical rhetoric (or 'humbug' as he often called it); and above all he shrank from the idea of meeting scores of expectant disciples, primed by the likes of Jinarajadasa and Arundale, full of admiring smiles and probing questions. As he confided to Helen by letter the day after arriving in India, 'I sat there blushing and feeling stupid ... They expect such a lot of things.'[17] The first opportunity to make his position plain was at a lecture he gave during the Benares Convention of that year. The date was 28 December which, because of the 1911 'pentecostal' incident, was considered particularly auspicious. The excitement of members in anticipation of the talk was matched only by the anxiety of Krishna, as he squirmed at the prospect of facing them. However, as soon as he mounted the podium in the huge marquee, he made it plain in his first sentence that he had no time for hocus-pocus: 'As it is December 28th, you are all probably expecting something miraculous, and I am afraid you will be rather disappointed, because I am a very matter-of-fact person, and I want to present you with a common-sense point of view.'[18] He went on to clear some cobwebs, galvanising his audience to improve themselves, and stressing the importance of positive action over the passivity of meditation and reading. Back at Adyar for the South Indian Convention, Krishna delivered an even more forceful message in a lecture that took him two days of hard work to prepare: 'True spirituality is hard and cruel, and the World-Teacher . . . is not going to be lenient to our weaknesses and our failings . . . He is not going to preach what we want, nor say what we wish, nor give us the sop to our feelings which we all like, but on the contrary He is going to wake us all up whether we like it or not, for we must be able to receive knocks as men.'[19]

The mission ethic that had been drummed into him for the past ten years, was suddenly and dramatically beginning to bear fruit. He had struck the right chord, and in the early weeks of 1922 was much in demand for private interviews. In the circumstances, there was little he needed to do in order to convince Theosophists of his calibre. So much had been invested in him by the Society over the years, he was perceived as the very embodiment of divinity even before he uttered a word. His quiet, self-effacing demeanour was a pleasant change for members used to the vanity and bombastic confidence of Besant. And the fact that he challenged each individual to dig within him or herself in search of the divine, rather than repeating standard Theosophical clichés, came as a welcome surprise.

He was none the less still privately torn, especially when he remembered Helen and the levity of his life in France the previous year. As he wrote to Lady Emily: 'What a life & is it worth it? This striving striving. For what I don't know . . . I dream and dream of a different life . . . there is a rebellion within me, surging quietly but surely. To what purpose I don't know. A continuous fight, fight & then some more fighting.'[20]

Krishna and Nitya had neither seen nor been in touch with their father, Narayaniah, since their last visit to India in 1911, during which time the bitter guardianship feud had driven a wedge between them. The seismic scale of Narayaniah's allegations and his assault on the Theosophical Society's leaders had left deep wounds, but the compassionate Nitya felt that it was only right and proper to visit the old man and attempt to heal the rift. A few weeks before embarking for India, he wrote to Annie Besant, 'Don't you think we ought to go and see our father? ... Don't you think we ought to make an effort to become friends? Of course, this will be as you say, for he has said some unpleasant things about you.'[21]

One account of their subsequent reunion at Narayaniah's house in Madras was, surprisingly, recalled by Krishnamurti himself in 1973. It paints a stark picture in which Narayaniah is hardly able to tolerate the presence of his sons, let alone share food with them, because they had broken caste. This image of the embittered, unforgiving old Brahmin has been contradicted by his daughter-in-law, the wife of Krishna's elder brother, Sivaram, and an eye-witness of the meeting. She describes a deeply moved Narayaniah, in tears as he greeted his sons, being comforted by Krishna. This tendency towards high emotionalism is consistent with earlier descriptions of Narayaniah, and goes some way to explaining Nitya's comment, in a letter to Mar de Manziarly at the time: 'Nous avons vue notre père qui est gaga.'[22] The issue of caste was clearly a problem. When food was offered to the brothers they hesitated, unsure as to what the appropriate response should be. The meeting was nevertheless congenial and was followed by three subsequent visits. After these, for some unspecified reason, Krishna and Nitya did not see their father again, though they were to remain in India for a further two months. Narayaniah died in 1924 and his passing elicited no response from Krishna, hostile or otherwise.

The brothers' meeting with their father paled somewhat beside the prospect of a more awesome reunion, planned for April 1922. They were to travel to Sydney, and there reacquaint themselves with their childhood mentor, Charles Leadbeater, in his new capacity as bishop of the Liberal Catholic Church. The whole idea of it filled Krishna with dread and he was unnerved by the stately expressions of welcome that began to reach him from religious zealots in Australia. 'You don't know how I abhor the whole thing,' he wrote to Lady Emily soon after arriving in Australia, 'all the people coming to meet us, the meetings & the devotional stuff. It all goes against my nature & I am not fit for this job.'[23]

His fears were compounded by rumours of yet another sex scandal brewing for Leadbeater. Key members of the Australian section of the Theosophical Society were up in arms against the bishop, and the atmosphere to which Nitya and Krishna arrived, on 12 April 1922, was one of hot-house intrigue. Leadbeater's reputation was about to sink to its lowest point, but, as usual, he and those nearest to him were deaf to all assaults. The aging patriarch of Theosophy had insulated himself from his detractors by creating a fiefdom in which he held complete authority. Nitya commented in a letter that he found Leadbeater milder but otherwise unchanged: 'Just as in Adyar, he takes everything for granted, never a question of doubt, never a question that anyone else can doubt; he is always sure that everything is as real to everybody as it is to him.'[24] Both brothers warmed to the old man, and for a while forgot their differences, but Krishna felt nothing but scorn for the pomp and ceremony of the Liberal Catholic Church. He attended one service that lasted two and a half hours and nearly fainted with boredom, but decided that it would be tactful to button his lip and refrain from public criticism of the Church. The coals of rebellion were temporarily doused by Leadbeater's magnetic enthusiasm.[25]

Leadbeater had surrounded himself in Sydney with a group of adolescent boys (and, surprisingly, a few girls as well) whose lives were dedicated to finding and advancing along the path of the Masters. He admired these sons and daughters of the pioneering new race in Australia – their physical prowess, vigorous energy and outdoor lifestyle. The long-term aim was that this select group of pupils would inherit his mantle and ensure the continuance of his work in the golden new age to come, perhaps even as forefathers of the new sub-race. They also provided him with a useful pool of altar-boys, who added decorative opulence to his rituals in church. Nitya was scathing about the bishop's boys, finding them both gullible and crude: 'they may have been princes and kings in past lives, but now they unfortunately are Australians.'[26]

It was the combination of Leadbeater's interest in boys and Church ceremony that was at the root of the storm Krishna witnessed during his stay in Australia. The Sydney Lodge of the Theosophical Society was divided between those who supported the Liberal Catholic Church and those who found it an abomination and a scandalous deviation from H. P. Blavatsky's original intentions. The former General Secretary of the Australian Section, and one of its chief financial supporters, T. H. Martyn, had started a Loyalty League, committed to re-evaluating the aims of modern Theosophy in the light both of Blavatsky's work, and the moral character of the Society's current leadership. This League stood opposed to personality cults, Church ceremony and the World Teacher project; but its fiercest vitriol, and Martyn's own offended conscience, was directed at the character of Leadbeater himself, his questionable clairvoyance, and his persistent interest in pubescent boys. The simmering trouble boiled over at a Convention meeting on 19 April, when certain members of the 'Back to Blavatsky' campaign denounced Leadbeater from the floor, hurling abuse, and calling for a vote of confidence.

The New South Wales police, who had investigated Leadbeater's private life without result in 1917, now heard evidence from Martyn and his wife that they had seen him naked with boys on several occasions, either in bed or in the bath. There were also reports that the bishop regularly masturbated his boys; then came the affirmation from Hubert van Hook in America that he had been sexually abused as a child and had been enlisted to gather fake information for *The Lives of Alcyone*. The weight of feeling, if not evidence, turned still further against Leadbeater in the wake of revelations concerning his colleague and fellow bishop, James Ingall Wedgwood. An Australian detective had seen Wedgwood visit eighteen public lavatories in a period of two hours, a practice that led police investigators to the gravest suspicions. In addition, a British Liberal Catholic priest called Reginald Farrer had confessed, in February 1922, to having had sex with Wedgwood and other named clergymen were also said to have been involved. Wedgwood had further enraged Martyn by attempting to seduce his wife while staying as a guest in his house.

A theory was now put forward that Leadbeater leapt on the World Teacher project in the wake of the 1906 scandals, so as to divert attention away from his own misconduct while allowing him to continue his association with adolescent boys. As one modern commentator has put it: 'So the doctrine of the World Teacher and the unique status of Krishnamurti was nothing but a cruel hoax committed by the most despicable of reasons by this *bête noire* of the TS.'[27]

Leadbeater, as usual, remained aloof from all insults, and appeared unmoved by even the most outrageous of assaults. During the Convention uproar, he sat detached for the entire two-and-a-half-hour debate, during which his name was dragged through the mud. At the end he rose to leave but not before blessing the assembly with a sign of the cross. When asked afterwards how he could endure the insults, he replied, 'To tell you the truth I never heard anything they said. I was much too interested in watching what was happening to their solar plexuses.' On another occasion 'two burly men' invaded Leadbeater's church during a service and started a brawl. During this disturbance the bishop sat calmly on his throne, 'with an exceedingly interested look on his face, as if he were observing a new specimen of humanity for the first time'.[28] Annie Besant observed Leadbeater's stoicism with admiration. 'Bishop Leadbeater is so far above them,' she wrote, 'that all their raging cannot touch his exquisite serenity. His is the spirit of the Christ, who prayed: "Father forgive them, for they know not what they do."'[29]

Leadbeater escaped criminal charges. The alleged misdemeanors could not be proved, and it was decided that sharing a bed with a boy (the backbone of the Martyns' testimony) was not in itself a criminal offence. The consequences of the scandal for the Theosophical Society, however, were more damaging. The 'Back to Blavatsky' movement had gathered much support and in July 1923 the Society in Sydney was officially split, with Martyn leading the new Independent Theosophical Society. Other disillusioned members around the world also now broke away from the Adyar Society.

Krishna and Nitya, having both been 'Leadbeater boys', were inevitably drawn into the adverse publicity. Aware that Krishna was his prize asset, Leadbeater may well have insisted on his coming to Australia at this time in order to help defend him. If so, Krishna did his job impeccably. When called before the police investigators and asked explicit questions regarding possible sexual impropriety in his past, he denied everything. Nitya, Jinarajadasa and others said exactly the same, and it was in part thanks to this united defence of their teacher that Leadbeater survived. They had to endure a lampooning in the press, and some cruel insults in public, with newspapers sporting headlines like 'Dandy coloured coons' (referring to the brothers), and 'Leadbeater: a swish bish with the boys.' Krishna was later to tell Philip van Pallandt that the Australian experience was the most awful time of his life.

Nobody knows if Leadbeater forced sexual relations on the Jiddu brothers as boys. Biographers and supporters until now have hotly denied the possibility. Every occasion when Krishna was encouraged to blow the whistle on his former tutor he responded firmly and without hesitation that he had never known or heard of any impropriety. Even in his correspondence to Lady Emily, his usual depository for honest and reproachful sentiments, he never once intimates that Leadbeater might have entertained sexual intentions towards his pupils. Quite the opposite; he continued to admire the old man, despite their philosophical differences, and was genuinely pleased to see him again when he arrived in Australia. Unless Krishna was a clever liar or a disturbed individual who attempted to deny past trauma, one must assume he was telling the truth. Leadbeater appears to have deliberately stopped himself tampering with the Vehicle or his brother, probably because of his own decree that complete physical purity was a necessary requisite for divine habitation. However, his murky record with one pupil after another for nearly half a century points to the likelihood that there were multiple sexual encounters.

Considering the delicacy of his position after recurrent scandals, one must ask the question: why did Leadbeater so frequently jeopardise his life's work? Was it more than mere sexual gratification that drove him to abuse one child after another for nearly half a century, to sleep with naked boys as a matter of course, despite the risks of discovery? Gregory Tillett, in his far-reaching biography of Leadbeater, proposes one possible answer, which places Leadbeater in a long tradition of occult sages dating back to ancient Greece. The theory is that Leadbeater practised masturbation with his young pupils, sometimes in ritual group sessions, in order to glean physical vigour from them. He was trading his own wisdom for their youthful vitality as manifested at the point of orgasm. With practice and proper psychic guidance, Leadbeater claimed that boys could use orgasms to reach subliminal states of spiritual awareness. This would explain his insistence on catching boys early, before they had begun psychologically to associate the sexual impulse too closely with women. In connection with this, he may have been linked to an occult circle of sexual ritualists known as the Ordo Templi Orientis which included Aleister Crowley in its ranks.

The turmoil in Australia took its toll on Nitya's health, and in April 1922 he was diagnosed as having tubercular patches on the right as well as the left lung. His spirits had descended to a low when he wrote to Madame de Manziarly on 22 April, saying Krishna wanted to visit America but that he himself was unsure whether or not to accompany him. Theosophy, public scandal and the prospect of a life spent in reflected glory had combined to grind him down. A few days in the Blue Mountains helped rally him somewhat, after which it was decided that he should return to convalesce in Switzerland. However, the Theosophical Society's General Secretary in America, Albert P. Warrington, suggested both brothers go to California, where the climate would help Nitya's condition, and where they could break the journey before travelling on to Europe later in the year. He knew of a small house they could use in the Ojai Valley, eighty miles from Los Angeles, that would offer them complete privacy and peace. Once all parties had agreed to the plan, the brothers' departure was set for 14 June.

Annie Besant was scheduled to leave for India a fortnight earlier, and she realised that neither she nor Leadbeater might see the brothers again for a very long time. Both leaders had the sense to perceive that the young men's morale was low and that without some refreshing stimulus their enthusiasm for Theosophy might begin to wane. The good influence of Albert Warrington in America would be essential, but Krishna needed a boost, to reignite his spiritual urge. With this end in mind, the leaders engaged Krishna and Nitya in a series of intensive discussions in the days leading up to their departure. The brothers had the opportunity to vent their feelings and discomfiture; and Krishna was graced with a message direct from the Master Kuthumi, via his agent, C. W. Leadbeater. The message maintained that the Masters still had the highest hopes for Krishna, and that a little effort to perfect himself would have the best results. It was a mixture of carrot and stick, and it worked like a charm.

Despite his doubts, his miseries endured in Europe, his brief taste of love and a carefree life, Krishna was still vulnerable to the charisma of his sponsors. Leadbeater had spun his magic once again, demonstrating that his powers were undiminished, despite the recurrence of insalubrious allegations and the gradual erosion of his power base. Krishna was in no doubt at all but that the message had indeed come from the Masters. 'It is just what I wanted,' he wrote to Lady Emily on 2 June; and even two months later he was to write that he thought about the message every day, and used it as a springboard for his meditations. Nitya was also inspired. Having earlier in the year poured scorn on Theosophy and the gullibility of Leadbeater's Australian pupils, he wrote on 2 July, 'I'm beginning to find out my realities . . . I feel we [Krishna and I] could do things if only the enthusiasm would last, and this time I hope it will last.'[30]

It did last, and this was to a large extent due to the fact that for the first time in their lives the boys were granted a spell together, away from the watchful eyes of key Theosophical players. This did not lead them to seek escapes, material pleasures or new interests. Quite the opposite. The taste of freedom inclined both of them to concentrate on tapping their spiritual resources and plan out the roles they were to play in the future of the mission.

Once ashore in the New World, Krishna felt as if he had come to the promised land. Having spent his entire life bedevilled by Anglo-Saxon condescension, he was greatly relieved to find in America 'the air of equality, which is the equality of opportunity and of ability, irrespective of creed, caste or colour'.[31] This was exemplified by the atmosphere at Berkeley's university campus, which he visited during the festivities of Independence Day, 4 July. He regarded it as a model university, a place that he wished he could transplant to India, a place where people spoke plainly and directly, not through lack of courtesy but because they had not been tainted with old world mannerisms and anachronisms.

The Theosophical significance of California would not have escaped him. The territory and its inhabitants had been the subject of many new age diatribes delivered by Annie Besant, and OSE members around the world were eager to know what the Lord's Vehicle would have to say about the new race. His observations in the Editorial Notes were eagerly devoured: 'One can already see that a new mode of thought is coming into being, a new perception of life, a new attitude towards our fellow-beings, and a mind that is willing to experiment with new ideals. In fact, a new race is in the process of being created,' a race defined by 'virility, strength and independence of character.'[32] After his experience of a Europe still reeling from the destruction of war and brooding ominously about the balance of power, he found America enthrallingly refreshing. Everything he saw throbbed with optimism and enterprise: the sky-scrapers, the Golden Gate Bridge, the desert reclamation schemes, the broad avenues and parks, even the soft drinks ('fit for the very gods'). In short, he was seduced by the fabulous economic boom that was setting America at the forefront of the commercial world in the 1920s.

The landscape also made a deep impression on Krishna, its variety and climate, its forests, fruit farms and mountains. In the heart of such glorious scenery, fifteen miles inland, was the Ojai Valley, where the brothers first arrived on 6 July, and which was to provide a home base for Krishna, periodically, for the rest of his life. The Chumash Indians had once found shelter in the valley, and had given it the name Ojai, meaning 'nest'. By the time Krishna arrived there, the valley basin was dedicated to farming apricots and oranges, its seclusion protected by a range of hills rising up on either side. The landscape, the intense daytime heat and the fragrance of wild herbs reminded the brothers strongly of India and they took great pleasure in exploring, either on foot or on horseback. News of their story had blazed a trail in San Francisco even before they docked. As Nitya wrote to Lady Emily: 'We are trying to avoid publicity and notoriety here, but Martyn & co. have telegraphed their people over here so everyone knows.' The reporters who tagged after them were, of course, 'after the Messiah story'.[33] Ojai offered them a refuge, tired as they were of the sensationalism that had dogged their footsteps for so long.

Their benefactor in Ojai was a wealthy Theosophist called Mary Tudor Gray, who owned an estate in the valley. She furnished them with two small cottages, one for the brothers and the other, nearby, for Albert Warrington, whose amiable presence in no way disturbed their peace. A nineteen-year-old girl, with fair hair and striking blue eyes, was enlisted to look after the ailing Nitya. Her name was Rosalind Williams and she

Helena Petrovna Blavatsky.

Charles Webster Leadbeater in 1924.

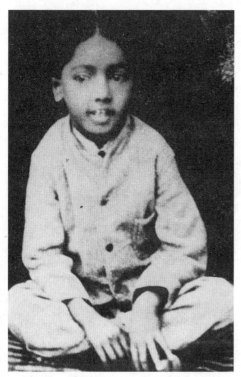

Krishna aged five.

Krishna and Nitya shortly after Krishna emerged from his initiation ritual, January 1910.

Theosophists at Benares, with their prized mascot, 1911. Besant and Leadbeater are seated in the centre. Left of them are Krishna, Arundale and Nitya. Behind Krishna in white, stands Hubert van Hook.

Part of the Theosophical estate at the time of Krishna's first involvement with the Society.

Krishna photographed prematurely in the attire of an MA graduate, 1911. In fact he never even matriculated at any university.

Krishna sports a moustache, 1912.

The sojourn at Old Lodge, Ashdown Forest, 1912. *L to r:* Krishna, Dick Balfour-Clarke, Nitya, Basil Hodgson-Smith (formerly a pupil of Leadbeater's), Jinarajadasa, Harold Baillie-Weaver.

Taormina, 15 September 1912. *Standing:* Arundale and Jinarajadasa;
seated: Krishna, Besant and Leadbeater; *cross-legged:* Nitya.

Taormina, January 1914. *Standing, l to r:* Arundale, Dr Mary Rocke and Nitya;
seated, l to r: Lady Emily Lutyens, Krishna and Francesca Arundale.

Bishops Wedgwood and Leadbeater
in Sydney, 1920.

Castle Eerde, when it was headquarters of the OSE.

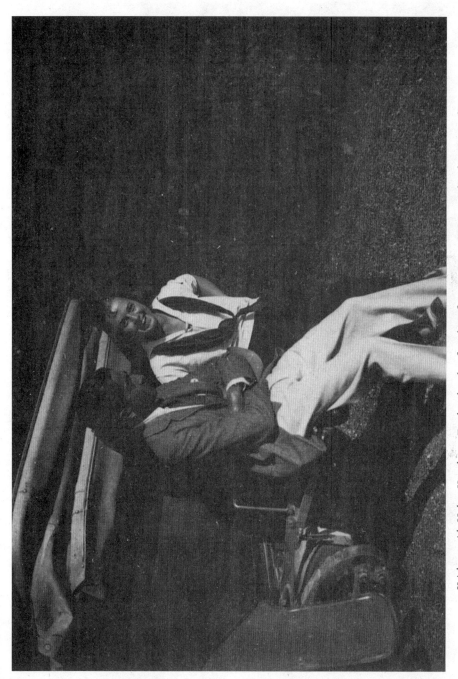

Krishna with Helen Knothe at Eerde, shortly after their first meeting, 1921. Her bright personality outshone all the other women who competed for his attention in the early 1920s.

Eerde, summer 1924. *Standing, l to r*: Betty Lutyens, Mary Lutyens, Helen Knothe, Lady Emily, Ruth Roberts, unknown, Harold Baillie-Weaver, Rajagopal, Nitya; *seated*: Krishna, Koos van der Leeuw, unknown.

was the younger sister of a devout Theosophist, one of Mrs Gray's local friends. Rosalind immediately established a strong bond with Nitya. Their chemistry appeared almost pre-ordained, when Nitya, on first touching her hand, exclaimed in surprise that he surely knew her already. She was perfectly cast in the role of nurse — naturally maternal, spirited and practical. Krishna noted with some relief that his brother acquiesced willingly to Rosalind's demands, whereas when he himself had asked the patient to observe the same sensible measures, Nitya had been quick to snap at him. Within a short time a romance developed between Nitya and Rosalind, which left Krishna to his own devices, though there is no evidence to suggest that he resented this exclusion. He was enjoying the sense of well-being and peace at Ojai. His original resolve, to spend this time completing his academic education, had now paled beside his more pressing pre-occupation with spiritual matters.

The Masters, the Lord Maitreya, his own role as Vehicle, the new Californian sub-race bursting with energy — these were his principal obsessions. In the course of the previous three years he had sunk to the depths of the Theosophical mire, with its over-worked philosophy, its petty intrigues and scandals, its rules, rituals and dogmas; and now he had surfaced, mature, at the head of his own branch movement, the OSE, feeling his way towards a role in public life. His star was on the rise. The influence of his aging sponsors was still present, but distant and not overbearing as it had been in the past. The fruit was ripe and the harvest near. In such an atmosphere of heightened expectancy and introspection a dramatic turn of events was somehow inevitable.

7

In the Presence of the Mighty Ones

———— ✳ ————

An extraordinary chain of experiences began for Krishna in August 1922 that was to transform his life for ever. It was as if the blinding light he had so longed for, the revelation that would sweep aside all doubts and distractions, was suddenly granted, but in a most unlikely manner. He could never have anticipated the physical and psychological trauma that was to accompany his awakening. It was as if he were required to endure a transfusion of his very life-blood before laying claim to divine enlightenment.[1]

On the evening of Sunday 20 August 1922, five exhausted people were assembled on the verandah of the brothers' small cottage at Ojai. Albert Warrington, General Secretary of the Theosophical Society in America, and Bishop Walton, Vicar General of the Liberal Catholic Church in America, sat on a bench opposite Rosalind Williams and Nitya. This little group gazed wordlessly at the hills as the dusk cast its shady haze over the surrounding valley. Krishna was slumped on a cushion some yards away from the others. This was the third day since his illness had begun, and his principal carers, Rosalind and Nitya, were at a loss what to do next. It had started on the Thursday with a pain in the back of his neck and a swelling like a hard ball. The following day Krishna had seemed to be in the grip of a bad fever, eyes rolling sightlessly, complaining one moment of intense heat, the next shivering as though naked in a cold wind. Nitya had wondered if it was influenza or even a recurrence of the malaria they had both suffered as children. Then Warrington, who had come across symptoms such as these before, suggested solemnly that Krishna might be entering a metaphysical process, a notion that sent something of a chill through the young, uninitiated Rosalind.

Krishna ate a little lunch but was sick soon after, and did not attempt to take any other food for the next three days. He was in a state of high sensitivity; any physical contact brought a sharp reaction, as though he were both pained and polluted by touch; distant sounds would make him jump with shock, and even the silent attendance of his helpers was an intolerable disruption of the peace. Rosalind and Nitya tried to keep their thoughts and feelings calm as they sat near him, so as not to upset his sensibility, unconscious though he seemed to be.

Krishna was, in fact, not unconscious at all, but had ascended to a different psychic plane, one in which he felt mysteriously spellbound by his surroundings:

There was a man mending the road; that man was myself; the pickaxe he held was myself; the very stone which he was breaking up was a part of me; the tender blade of grass was my very being, and the tree beside the man was myself. I almost could feel and think like the roadmender, and I could feel the wind passing through the tree, and the little ant on the blade of grass I could feel. The buds, the dust, and the very noise were a part of me. Just then there was a car passing by at some distance; I was the driver, the engine, and the tyres; as the car went further away from me, I was going away from myself. I was in everything, or rather everything was in me, inanimate and animate, the mountain, the worm, and all breathing things.[2]

On the morning of the third day, the physical symptoms seemed to have worsened. In his delirium Krishna kept longing for Adyar, and the presence of his companions now filled him with revulsion. He thought his bedding was filthy beyond imagining, even though Albert Warrington affirmed that the linen had been changed that very day. Rosalind and Nitya had no option but to leave him sitting alone in a dark corner of his room. They went out on to the verandah to sit with the other two, seriously concerned, but also excited, as if fate had chosen them to be witnesses to an extraordinary event that they all felt to be imminent. Thus assembled in the fading twilight, they were joined after a while by Krishna, who meandered across to the far side of the verandah and collapsed on a cushion, mumbling incoherently.

There they remained for a while, until Warrington, sensing Krishna's need for solitude, suggested that he go and sit under a young pepper tree situated some yards away in the garden. Tired and faint from three days of suffering and no food, Krishna reluctantly shuffled over to the tree, and sat against its trunk, facing east. Then he began to chant, in a pathetic ethereal voice, the same mantra that was traditionally sung in the evenings at Adyar. The effect of this sound on the four people observing, against the peaceful backcloth of the Ojai evening, was electrifying; and the sight of Krishna under the tree brought to mind images of the Buddha himself, who had received enlightenment sitting beneath the Bodhi, or Bo tree (the tree of wisdom). Nitya's description of what happened next reveals that he and the others were drawn into a meditative trance of their own:

> now there was perfect silence, and as we looked I saw suddenly for a moment a great Star shining above the tree, and I knew that Krishna's body was being prepared for the Great One ... The place seemed to be filled with a Great Presence and a great longing came upon me to go on my knees and adore, for I knew that the Great Lord of all our hearts had come Himself; and though we saw Him not, yet we all felt the splendor of His presence.[3]

At this point Rosalind Williams experienced a vision exclusive to herself, though the others participated completely in the magical atmosphere of the moment. She looked up above the tree and beheld a splendour beyond all words. 'Do you see Him, do you see Him?' she called out, which the others took to be a reference to the Lord Maitreya descending into his Vehicle, Krishna. Her wondrous expression left a profound impression on Nitya and was vision enough to persuade him of the authenticity of her experience. It revealed 'the rapture of her heart, for the innermost part of her being was ablaze with His presence'.

This ecstatic condition then spread to the other three observers as they distinctly heard strains of divine music played by the Gandharvas, etheric angels.[4] Warrington later described the music as a single, sustained and resonant chord. Rosalind now entered into a dialogue with the fabulous presence she alone could define, pledging, 'I will, I will,' and repeating to her companions, 'Do you hear the music? Look, do you see?' After half an hour thus spellbound, Krishna returned from the shadows of the garden and at the sight of him Rosalind fainted clean away. She later remembered nothing of the experience except the music, a fact that has caused some sceptics, including her own daughter, to doubt the authenticity of Nitya's account or, at least, his interpretation of the incident.

Krishna's own description of the event omits the atmosphere of majesty that left such an impact on Nitya. He stresses instead a sense of unutterable peace, 'the calmness of the bottom of a deep unfathomable lake'. He describes the sensation of leaving his physical body and being transported into a mighty presence. The star overhead and the names Maitreya and Kuthumi are mentioned almost in passing, as if he felt obliged to pay lip service to the appropriate Theosophical iconology; but the heart of his experience is contained in a concluding paragraph:

> I was supremely happy, for I had seen. Nothing could ever be the same. I have drunk at the clear and pure waters at the source of the fountain of life and my thirst was appeased. Never more could I be thirsty, never more could I be in utter darkness; I have seen the Light. I have touched compassion which heals all sorrow and suffering; it is not for myself, but for the world. I have stood on the mountain top and gazed at the mighty Beings. Never can I be in utter darkness; I have seen the glorious and healing Light. The fountain of Truth has been revealed to me and the darkness has been dispersed. Love in all its glory has intoxicated my heart; my heart can never be closed. I have drunk at the fountain of Joy and eternal Beauty. I am God-intoxicated.[5]

The purple tinge to Krishna's literary style and the romantic imagery of his public pronouncements at this stage of life are purely superficial. The essence of his experience under the pepper tree is communicated in equally vivid though less formal terms in his subsequent correspondence to friends. To Leadbeater he confesses having previously lost sight of his mission, but affirms that he has now 'changed considerably', and that his 'whole life, now, is, consciously, on the physical plane, devoted to the work'. To Lady Emily he writes, 'I am happy beyond human happiness. I feel & live in exaltation ... All that I have written is absolutely genuine & profound. I can never be the same ... there is nothing for me but the work.'[6]

Both brothers felt contrite about having strayed from the path in the past, even to the point of having doubted Leadbeater and his Masters altogether. In the euphoria of those early days they were quite happy to interpret the illuminating event under the pepper tree as a validation of Leadbeater and everything he had upheld. What they did not anticipate was that this incident was merely the bottle unstopped. The consequences were to be infinitely more devastating – spiritually and physically – as the tide of Krishna's awakening began to gather momentum.

Immediately after the pepper tree incident there was a period of calm and Rosalind went to visit her mother for a few days in Santa Barbara. After her return, however, on 3 September, Krishna's symptoms began to recur.[7] Nitya recalled how he and Albert Warrington were unsure whether to view the unfolding drama from the perspective of scientific experiment or sacred revelation. Were they laboratory assistants or temple acolytes? Would their accomplishments be judged by Darwinian evolutionists or future congregations? Nitya believed his own role was that of custodian and chronicler and took care to note down every detail of the events.

Krishnamurti's symptoms that returned in early September were discomfort in the spine, an intolerable sensation of heat, and a feeling of revulsion towards the physically invasive. This extended to touch, light, noise and human company, each of which, even in its mildest form, could cause him agonising pain. It was as if the Brahminic puritanism of his family and childhood had returned to haunt him in a monstrous, mutant guise. He also suffered from light-headedness, and frequently lost consciousness altogether, so that he had to be accompanied everywhere in case of accident.

Although spinal and neck pain was the most consistent symptom, it was the sensation of burning that was to cause him the most suffering.

Nitya maintained that it was worse than childbirth, and that his brother was suffering the agonies of a man burnt alive. In the depths of this torment Krishna would occasionally have a fit and attempt to run off, sometimes in the direction of the river, so that he could jump in and cool himself. His carers had to restrain him and, as touch was almost impossible, they were compelled to leave him writhing and twisting on a floor mattress. The symptoms intensified during the course of September, reaching a high point in the middle of October. Nitya later described the condition in a letter to Leadbeater as introactive and therefore frustratingly difficult to alleviate: 'It is not ordinary pain as from a cut or a wound, but a sense of intolerable congestion, which would be easier to bear if something within burst.'[8]

Nitya noticed that the burning shifted to different parts of the body and surmised that his brother was being subjected to a process of gradual purgation that would eventually leave his entire constitution cleansed. This explanation was endorsed by the regularity and punctuality of the daily sessions, as if the whole operation were being enacted according to a planned schedule, its nameless administrator mysteriously bridging the temporal and spiritual worlds. Krishna had fallen victim to a gruesome but consistent routine, according to which a certain measured amount of work had to be accomplished, limb by limb and organ by organ, every evening. If for some reason the usual time span of the 'process' (as Krishnamurti's ordeal has since become known) were interrupted, the shortfall was made up by an appropriate period of extra time at the end. By the same token, every evening's session was halted at precisely the same time, 7.30, when Krishna would recover from his delirium for a short rest, after which he was returned to a different brand of torture.

All parties involved in this bizarre process were convinced that an outside 'presence', was overseeing and directing its progress. This invisible being (sometimes more than one) was felt as a vibrant energy within the house, and Nitya described its daily arrival as like giant engines starting up. The precise nature of the entity was identifiable to no one except Krishna, and then only during his trances. At these times he seemed to be participating in a dialogue, which Nitya recalled was like hearing one side of a telephone conversation. He noted how Krishna was sometimes allowed a pause from the agony, when he would recover a little and occasionally burst out laughing, as if his invisible companion had cracked a joke. He did not seem to resent what was being done to him; quite the opposite, he would frequently apologise to the entity for the way his body was reacting to the pain. At other times he would be aware of a less congenial being in the house, like some harmless but uninvited voyeur. Krishna would firmly order it off the premises, muttering, 'The impudence of these fellows.' When he recovered from the sessions and returned to normal consciousness, he could remember neither the pain nor the unseen beings, and was fascinated to hear a blow by blow account from those who had sat with him.

A fundamental characteristic of the process witnessed by Nitya, Rosalind and Warrington, was the division of Krishna into two separate personalities during his experience, each represented by a different voice. There was the voice of a mature, responsible Krishna who talked to the hidden beings, and who frequently urged them to continue their process no matter how he might complain at the pain; and there was the voice of the other, the bodily shell, or 'elemental', as it became known, that was left behind to suffer the physical consequences of Krishna's metaphysical intercourse. When the agony became quite unbearable, this 'elemental' would scream for Krishna to return, and beg for the process to pause. At these times his real voice would take over, as if it had been forced to come back against its will and better judgment, typically apologising to the unseen powers for the interruption, and answering their unheard questions with remarks like, 'Rather! I can withstand a lot more.' If Nitya or the others felt that the suffering had become too intense, they would forcibly bring the 'elemental' back to consciousness, to be greeted by an irritated Krishna telling them not to interfere.

His out-of-body experiences took on another peculiar quality when the physical 'elemental' began to talk in the manner of a four-year-old infant. This immature voice proceeded to reminisce about Krishna's childhood, as if the very depths of his psyche were being dredged. Many of the revelations came as a surprise to Nitya, who had never heard the stories, nor did he know that Krishna could remember such details. Every evening, for about an hour, he would talk non-stop, giving graphic and dramatic reconstructions of events such as his mother giving birth, his lying ill with malaria, his fear of school, and his mother's death. Less serious anecdotes and juvenile confessions also surfaced, some of which had his companions in stitches of laughter. '[He] says some screamingly funny things,' Nitya wrote to Lady Emily. 'only one can't put 'em on paper for everyone to read ... Even as a boy he must have made "the end of the corridor" jokes. Rosalind is very easily shocked and I've had most fun out of it.'[9]

Rosalind was probably the first woman for nearly twenty years to have offered Krishna intimate physical comfort, and it is therefore not surprising that he should turn to her as a mother-substitute at such a moment of crisis. It became clear that his agonising process could not go ahead in her absence, and whenever Rosalind departed from Ojai the symptoms, both physical and metaphysical, would begin to recede. This left an enormous responsibility on the young girl's shoulders, but she was resilient and accepted Nitya's word as to the great significance of the process. Nitya worried privately about how Leadbeater would respond to the news of Rosalind's pivotal role. As he wrote, echoing the misogynist sentiments of his mentor, 'The feminine influence is, as a general rule, not considered advantageous.' None the less, Krishna's needs were para-mount, and Rosalind's care was especially vital when undergoing his out-of-body sessions. 'Mother, will you look after me, I'm going a long way off?' he murmured to Rosalind before leaving the physical elemental to its routine torture, and then turned to the invisible entity and said, 'It's all right, she'll look after me.'

On 2 October the suffering began to reach a climax, and such was the sanctity of the phase into which Krishna was apparently now entering, there were times when no one, not even Rosalind, was permitted to attend him. He was to face whatever had been promised him alone. The pain was intensified to an insufferable degree, and this time focussed on his face and eyes. He described the sensation to Nitya as like being pinned down in the desert and being forced to face the sun 'with one's eyelids cut off'. Krishna assumed that his sight was being purged in preparation for coming face to face with a Lord high up in the divine hierarchy, perhaps the Buddha himself. On 5 October Krishna warned Nitya, Rosalind and Warrington that a Great Visitor would be coming to the house that evening, and they were to remain outside while he closed himself within the 'inky black' room. Listening anxiously at the door, Nitya heard Krishna's screams and cries, snippets of his one-sided conversations, promises of secrecy, apologies for the clumsiness of his body, and assurances that he would remain absolutely still for the momentous presentation that was about to begin. Later, Nitya became aware of an awesome presence filling the house, quite different from the theatrically supernatural atmosphere they had grown accustomed to during previous sessions.[10] When he and Rosalind reentered the room, the 'Holy Ceremony' had been completed successfully and Krishna seemed transfigured. He was talking to what appeared to be a room full of invisible people congratulating him on having accomplished some monumental task. 'There's nothing to congratulate me about,' he said, self-deprecatingly, 'you'd have done the same yourself.'

Krishna must now have felt his trial was over. He relaxed and addressed his dead mother through Rosalind: 'Everything will be different now, life will never be the same for any of us after this . . . I've seen Him, Mother, and nothing matters now.' The pain did not, in fact, cease until a fortnight later, and even this was only a temporary respite. 1923 was to bring fresh suffering, as he travelled deeper into his mystic adventure, leaving himself and his friends more and more baffled as to what it could all mean. One matter they all eventually agreed on: that the mysterious process was primarily spiritual, the physical symptoms being unfortunate side-effects. It was divinely ordained – part of the preparations for the Coming of the Lord Maitreya – and they therefore need not be concerned on medical grounds. Krishna's life was not at risk.

Nitya concluded his account of the Ojai process in a deliberately biblical style: '[we] have lived through days of marvellous holiness, we have lived in the presence of the Mighty Ones, we have even received Their benediction. The Lord comes into the world after many centuries, and we have had the truly amazing privilege of being near, when the body was being prepared for Him. We have now but one thought, that soon the Beloved of the World will be among us.'

What are we to make of this process that was to mark such a decisive change in Krishna's life and outlook? As the weeks of pain progressed, the brothers toyed with various theories but, as Krishna stated more than once in his letters, he simply did not know what was happening, nor why, and he longed for Leadbeater to come up with the answers. The puzzled bishop did not reply for some time, a delay that caused the brothers to reflect deeply about themselves and the whole incident.

The most obvious solution, they decided, was that the process must have something to do with the rising of Krishna's Kundalini energy. The Hindu theory of Kundalini dates back in one guise or another to pre-dynastic Egypt, 5000 BC, and would have been familiar to the brothers both from their Theosophical education and Brahminic heritage. It relies on the principle of *prana*, the creative energy of the universe. *Prana* invests all organisms with life, and binds together all matter, animate and inanimate, in a dynamic, interactive relationship. It would not be far-fetched to liken *prana* to the Christian concept of the Holy Spirit, the mystical intermediary, property both of the material and divine worlds at the same time. According to the tantric Hindu tradition, cosmic prana comes to rest at the physical level (matter) and lies dormant as a potential energy called Kundalini. In this rested form Kundalini is represented through Hindu religious imagery as a coiled up snake, located at the base of the spine behind the sex organs. Awakening Kundalini from this dormant state is considered a sure route to divine realisation, but is also a destabilising and dangerous undertaking. It involves inverting the generative potential of prana away from the reproductive system (the sex organs), and channelling it upwards along the spine in a stream of powerful energy that passes through six stages, or *chakras*, before reaching sublimation and release through the cranium – the final step that frees the experiencer from the bondage of material reality. The spiritual result of awakened Kundalini is a vast increase in mental capacity and creativity, leading to absolute enlightenment. The method prescribed by age-old Hindu tradition for setting this process in motion is yoga and meditation. But students are warned by their guru to expect demonic obstacles on the path, sometimes resulting in madness, sometimes in agonising pain, especially burning along the course of the spine.

Krishna might have expected to go through an awakening of Kundalini as part of his preparation for receiving the Lord Maitreya. The symptoms and the results of his Ojai experience appeared to be consistent with the Kundalini explanation. His celibacy to date was, of course, a vital prerequisite for the attainment of such an awakening. The sexual tension that underlay his relationships with certain women, particularly Helen Knothe, had remained as yet untapped. A tantric interpretation of events would maintain that in 1922 Krishna, already predisposed to spirituality, had sublimated his procreative urge through meditation. His preparation and attainment were in accordance with classic guidelines recommended by yogis since the distant days of the Indus Valley civilisation.[11]

A modest library could be assembled on the theology of suffering and the association of religion with pain. In the case of Kundalini, a degree of physical suffering is integral to the spiritual result, a condition sometimes referred to as the 'Kundalini injury'. Nitya tells us that Albert Warrington immediately recognised Krishna's plight, because he had witnessed five previous cases in which similar symptoms had been displayed. Psychosomatic injury induced by religious practice is today a syndrome recognised within the field of academic bio-chemistry, and theses have been postulated that attempt to draw empirical conclusions about the neurology of Kundalini.[12] Most confirm that the result is a form of psychic revelation, experienced as increased intelligence, and that the route to this illumination is consistently accompanied by physical discomfort, particularly the sensation of intense heat. There is a possible link here between the cleansing principle of Kundalini and the Christian notion of purgatory, or even baptism by fire. Nitya's account of his brother's plight tends to corroborate such an analogy.[13]

The Ojai process seems to gain credibility when it is stripped of its Theosophical terminology and placed in the context of other religious experiences. In the fever of messianic expectation, Nitya and other interested parties failed to recognise the universal nature of Krishna's experience. Indeed, there is a strong case for saying that Kundalini is a neuro-physiological event common to many races and religions. It reflects the potentiality of the human organism, regardless of cultural origin, to aspire to a higher sphere of knowledge, one that brings about a sense of union with the ground of its being. The Old Testament is littered with references to encounters with God that entail physical hardship and result in spiritual rebirth, not least that of Jacob wrestling with the angel. Jacob endures physical agony, participates in a dialogue with the nameless presence, and afterwards, convinced of God's benediction, embarks on life with a new name.[14] A brief look at shamanism around the world also reveals how 'out of body' religious trances involving suffering similar to Krishnamurti's are routine occurrences in many cultures.

There is, of course, a sceptical angle from which to view the incident, and Krishna's state of mind in the months and years leading up to the Ojai process necessitates a mention of it. His personal doubts about the destiny prescribed for him reached a crisis point in 1922, in the wake of meeting Helen Knothe and the stress of Leadbeater's scandal in Sydney. It is not inconceivable, in the light of this, that his suffering and awakening at Ojai were symptoms of a nervous stress disorder. There are reports that the previous December (1921), in the build up to his much-awaited talk at Benares, Krishna was seen 'lying for two days . . . in a sort of trance, twitching and gasping in his throat, so that people were afraid for his health.'[15] Modern psychoanalysis often prescribes an artificially induced state of trance or hypnosis as a way of disgorging repressed emotion. It is possible that the child persona who surfaced during Krishna's Ojai process was an involuntary symptom of just such repression. In primitive communities, or in centuries past, these types of personal revelation might have been viewed as a form of religious experience; but in western secular society it is to psychology that victims of such symptoms more often turn, rather than theology.

Rosalind Williams' daughter, Radha Sloss, wrote a book in which she attempts to discredit many aspects of Krisnamurti's reputation. On the subject of the Ojai process, she hints that Krishna may have acted out the whole drama, consciously or otherwise, in order to gain sexual intimacy with Rosalind – in a bizarre inversion of his need for maternal succour. Sloss then cites other occasions in his life when the process recurred, and claims (incorrectly, as it happens) that he needed the company of women to help him endure the symptoms, thereby attaining a physical closeness with those women that would otherwise not have been permissible. This theory does not stand up to scrutiny. When viewed together, the accounts of Krishnamurti's processes over the years are astonishing not for the character or gender of the people that attended him, but for the staggering consistency of his symptoms, and that *despite* the many differences of attitude and terminology he adopted after 1922. The proximity of feminine care at Ojai and later was not so unusual. Most sick people the world over are attended by women, either as nurses, friends or family; and Krishna's need for very close attention during the process can be connected to a long tradition with regard to Indian holy men. Whilst enduring the awakening of Kundalini, the sage is invariably tended, and his body protected, by disciples or close associates. The same sort of protection for Krishnamurti was to be insisted upon by Besant, after the events at Ojai.

Another attempt to define Krishna's process in terms of conventional psychology has been put forward in the *Harvard Theological Review*.[16] This theory seeks to prove that extreme bereavement in childhood can induce a sense of divine union later in life, and that the 'beloved' thought to be God is, in actuality, merely the subject's own projection of the deceased. In Krishna's case, the deep grief that surfaced during the 1922 process, the theory maintains, was centred on his mother, hence the reversion of his personality to infancy, his misidentification of Rosalind for Sanjeevamma, and the reminiscences of his mother's death. His 'delayed grief' was cured, or at least compensated for, by the sense of union he experienced as a result of the process. This is not unrelated to Freud's interpretation of the mystical state, which he associated with 'oceanic' consciousness, a condition derived from the sense of unity experienced in the womb. Seen in this light, a mystical experience might be no more than the psyche retreating to the safety and integrity of the pre-nascent state.

Purely physical explanations of the process have included malaria (which he suffered as a child), recurrent migraines, malnutrition, vitamin deficiency, schizophrenia or even epilepsy, a condition which Radha Sloss claims he may have inherited from his mother. Yet even if any of these hypotheses were correct, it would not detract from the mystical nature of his experience. Physical trauma, whether it is induced by disease, accident, self-deprivation, malnutrition, or old age, can bring about a change of consciousness very much akin to that traditionally described as religious; this goes some way to explaining the prevalence of mystical experiences amongst ascetics and the impoverished, or in victims of the near-death-experience.

The temptation for Krishna to view his experience as the apotheosis of Theosophy's master-plan was insuperable. At first he was unsure to what degree the Masters themselves had been involved in the process, but their role became more defined in recollection, as the allure of winning his sponsors' approbation began to influence his interpretation of the event. His references to the process in later life were few and evasive. The notion of coming face to face with an entity identifiable as one of Theosophy's Masters, as we shall see, he later denounced as auto-suggestion. Masters, or personified gods, he would maintain, were projections of one's own ideals, and the result of an individual's past experience. They were the children of conditioned knowledge, spectres formed by thought structures, and therefore had no relevance or substance in the organic world. Real divinity – such as he knew he had encountered at Ojai – was beyond the measurement of thought or language. But in 1922 he was required to account for his experience in words, and such were his own ideals and those of the people closest to him at the time, the words he chose were Theosophical. Later recurrences of the process were very similar in essence to the first, and there is no question that he understood and trusted the experiences to be genuine, but he never felt the need to interpret them as he had in 1922. The particular imagery associated with the first process, with its Masters, stars, angels, and music, he was subsequently to discard as illusory.

Nitya clearly believed that something of major historical consequence had taken place at Ojai. The conclusion of his written account would have us believe that the Coming had actually occurred, the Lord Maitreya had taken the body of Krishna, and Christ was once again among men – for the first time since the Crucifixion. Parallels with the Gospel story of Jesus were inevitable. Was it not possible, they asked, that Krishna's process was the symbolic equivalent of Christ's trial in the wilderness? Even the timespan of the two incidents was approximately the same. It was an irresistibly attractive idea, and Christological comparisons inspired nothing short of the noblest ambitions in those who conceived them.

Everything, of course, depended on what Leadbeater would have to say on the subject, and the brothers waited eagerly for a reply to their accounts. The patriarch in Sydney, blustering onwards with his work despite recent assaults on his reputation, hesitated before committing himself on the subject. He and Besant decided between themselves, before writing to the brothers, that the pepper tree incident must have been Krishna's Third Initiation, a major step up in his occult status. But Leadbeater was flummoxed as to why such a degree of physical suffering had had to be involved.[17] He could not shake off the grain of doubt as to whether everything was going according to plan. The process might be either a giant leap forward in the World Teacher project or its death blow. If the matter turned out to be nothing more than a young man's fantasy, the very survival of the Theosophical Society might be at risk.

His first response is dated 14 November 1922, nearly six weeks after both Krishna and Nitya had written to him. He congratulates Krishna for the experience and confesses relief that his occult life is progressing, because at one stage he had begun to have 'a little anxiety' about his protégé. Leadbeater grew more perplexed when he heard about the second stage of the process, and started to hint at nameless sins in Krishna's past as being the cause. Scenting guilt from across the Pacific, he was not averse to twisting the knife in this particular wound. There is a hint of accusation in his tone when writing to Nitya, 'There was nothing of all this in the future that stretched itself before us in those happy days at Adyar so long ago. The body then needed preparation indeed, but not *this* kind of preparation; what has been done to it since that has made all this necessary?'[18] Leadbeater had gone to great lengths in the past to protect the boy from contamination and unwholesome influences, even confining him to his own private railway compartment on train journeys. Nitya replied to Leadbeater with shame that he himself had done 'idiotic & stupid things and some harmful things' to his body, but that Krishna had always remained spotlessly pure.

Leadbeater's hesitancy made the brothers doubt their own diagnosis of the situation. In 1923, exhausted and unsettled, they begged Leadbeater to come over to Ojai so that he could witness and mastermind proceedings. He did not oblige, and began to voice his concerns in stronger language to Besant: 'I am very much troubled about the whole affair, for I have never met with anything in the least like it, and I cannot feel sure that it is right or necessary . . . all this is so utterly opposed to what I myself have been taught.'[19] He was also, of course, somewhat peeved that his juniors should claim encounters with the Masters while he remained completely in the dark. Not since the death of Blavatsky had anyone claimed a more direct wavelength with the Masters than he, and yet here, apparently, was a landmark event in the occult world about which he had been given not the slightest forewarning.

As time went by, he distanced himself from the whole business and avoided mentioning it. He consistently refused the mantle of responsibility that the brothers so wanted him to take on their behalf, and this doubtless severed an umbilical tie between Krishna and the mother organisation that had nurtured him. Leadbeater remained quietly unconvinced that his beloved Masters had played any part in Krishna's experience, and this led him to consider the possibility that less benign entities had been at work on the young man. The brothers sensed the bishop's unstated scepticism, and it left them feeling somewhat disoriented. Nitya voiced a rare note of reproach, writing that he found Leadbeater's attitude 'a little disquieting . . . [it] gave me a queer feeling – as a matter of fact, I had a sick feeling in my stomach.'

Later in life, and despite his dismissal of the Masters theory, Krishna did repeatedly refer to the intervention of an outside agency in his life, the same power that first revealed itself during the Ojai process, protecting and guiding him. In old age, he attempted to reconcile his knowledge of this immense power with the influences that had ruled his interpretation of the process at Ojai. 'I think there is a force which the Theosophists had touched but tried to make into something concrete. But, there was something they had touched and then tried to translate into their own symbols and vocabulary, and so lost it. This feeling has been going on all through my life.'[20]

The process at Ojai, whatever its cause or validity, was a cataclysmic milestone for Krishna. Up until this time his spiritual progress, chequered though it might have been, had been planned with solemn deliberation by Theosophy's grandees. There had been magical moments, dramas, traumas, and even a few minor crises, but the project had lumbered forward within the confines of the structure originally set up for its accommodation. Something new had now occurred for which Krishna's training had not entirely prepared him. On a personal level he felt for the first time a reconciliation between his private searching self and his public Theosophical profile. A burden was lifted from his conscience and he took his first step towards becoming an individual (in a literal sense: an undivided entity). In terms of his future role as a teacher, the process was his bedrock. He felt utterly certain that he had crossed a threshold, that areas of mental activity previously dormant and ignored had awoken within him. He did not know in the 1920s what it meant or where it would lead, but it was a real, dynamic experience of his own, not a dogma, not a sacred text, nor a tale spun on the rooftops of Adyar. It had come to him alone and had not been planted in him by his mentors, a fact that caused Leadbeater a degree of alarm, as we have seen. It provided Krishna with the soil in which his newfound spirit of confidence and independence could take root. It was fertile soil, and weathered many changing seasons in the future, bearing abundant fruit in sixty-four years of teachings.

The mysterious and traumatic events of 1922 had sapped Krishna's enthusiasm for academic study and, though he still felt pitifully equipped in an intellectual sense for his life's work, he opted to dedicate his working hours at Ojai to the Order of the Star in the East. His Editorial Notes and lectures of the time called for immediate action. There was no time to be lost; his time was near at hand. Nitya shared his resolve, and felt physically stronger, impatient to change the world. When the process resumed its relentless routine in January 1923, he was reconciled to the fact that the Coming had not yet fully happened and Krishna clearly had to undergo a lengthier transfiguration before he could ascend to the throne that was Christ's.

Acting on his own initiative, Krishna planned ways to reinvigorate the OSE so that it would be ready, as an effective administrative and international body, to receive the World Teacher when He arrived. If Krishna was to wield influence in public affairs in the world at large (which he viewed as the mere start of his mission) he would have to be supported by a committed and well-qualified army of workers, the movement's infra-structure. To this end, he set up 'self-preparation groups', consisting of truly dedicated OSE members, to whom he would address a monthly newsletter. The encouragement of these groups, first in America and then worldwide, was to become a core element of his work and teaching in the next few years. He also continued to write his Editorial Notes, struggling to present an air of equanimity despite the turbulent adventure taking place in his personal life.

He did not exercise quite so much restraint in a 12,000–word moral fantasy, composed during the period when he was undergoing the process in late 1922. It was later published in the *Herald* and entitled *The Path*. Conceived on a lyrically epic scale, it rambles, in sumptuous prose, through a myriad of emotions and atmospheres, searching for the elusive thread of divinity. It reads at times like a self-conscious attempt to give literary sanctity to the process of his awakening, although it does not describe particular events but resounds with the agony and ecstasy of the experience.

> Like the smile of a sweet spring morn the path beckons me to walk on it, and like the angry and treacherous ocean it cheats me of my momentary happiness. It holds me as I fall, in blissful embrace, making me forget the sorrow and suffering of the past, kissing me with the kiss of a tender mother whose only thought is to protect, and when I am in complete oblivion and ecstasy as that of a man who has drunk deep at the fountain of supreme happiness, it wakes me with a rude shock from my happy and ephemeral dream and pushes me roughly to my aching feet.

Had Theosophy triumphed, and Krishnamurti become the founder of a new world religion, it is very probable that *The Path* would have been enshrined as a sacred text. The predominant emotion, the voice of the poet-author, is lonely grief. Disillusioned by every pleasure the world has to offer, he returns to the bitter path of spirituality with its relentless pain. He is enslaved by his 'lover' (Truth, God), and is spared no misery on his quest for union. There is a sensuous underpull in the prose, wholly tied up with his longing for divinity, that betrays the sexual preoccupations of its author, both procreative and subliminal, thus adding weight to the Kundalini explanation of the process. The conclusion is victorious and sacerdotal, as befits a would-be messiah, reading like a prayer, and finishing with a simple declaration of pantheistic immanence: 'I am the lover and the very love itself. I am the saint, the adorer, the worshipper and the follower. I am God.'

In May 1923, as part of his new resolve to work, Krishna set out on a tour of ten American cities, accompanied by Nitya. At most destinations he gave three lectures, attended parties in his honour, and went about raising funds for education projects in India, a cause that was to absorb so much of his energy in later life. The tour culminated in Chicago, where the brothers attended the annual Theosophical Society Convention. Nitya wrote to Annie Besant that 'everyone in America whom [Krishna has met] is in love with him', that his talks were inspired, and that 'he more than came up to everyone's expectations . . . like one who has found his goal.'[21] Krishna painted a rather different picture in a letter to George Arundale, written on the same day as Nitya's. 'I am not a good speaker and it is perfect hades for me to speak.'[22] The tour was nevertheless deemed a success, and the brothers progressed to Europe. They were welcomed on their arrival at Plymouth on 11 June by the devoted Lady Emily.

Their stay in England was a brief stop-off before going on to Vienna, where the Theosophical and Star congresses were due to be held in July. They stayed at Wimbledon as guests of the formidable Miss Dodge and Lady de la Warr, whose house on West Side Common was of course very familiar territory to the brothers from boyhood. They were given interconnecting bedrooms and Mary Lutyens, who, as an adolescent girl, still viewed the fabulous brothers with a mixture of worship and desire, remembered looking inside the wardrobes to see 'their neat suits and rows of brown shoes polished like horse-chestnuts, and stacks of fine shirts and handkerchiefs'. She noticed that Krishna was now regarded with more reverence by those around him, word of the Ojai process having presumably spread to a selected few within the inner circle; but to her 'he seemed just the same, though more beautiful than ever'.[23] She admired the princely glamour of both young men, and noted how it infected those close to them, seducing them like an irresistible spell.

Lady Emily was naturally eager to hear more about the process, but found Krishna frustratingly evasive on the subject. It had been decided that the incident should be talked about as little as possible, and was too sensitive to publicise beyond the immediate inner family of Star activists. When Lady Emily asked him a direct question about his experience, Krishna would simply faint. Nevertheless, she was aware of subtle changes, not so much in his outer appearance, but from deep within: 'a controlled but immense concentrated power flowing from him'.[24] This was particularly apparent when he took the stand and spoke at Theosophical or Star meetings, now fluently and without notes. His message at these talks was not noticeably different from when she had last heard him, except he now seemed satisfied that his call to arms within the movement had been heeded. The emphasis was on members preparing themselves, not waiting for a central authority to goad them into action. There was nothing worse, he argued, than the armchair religious theoriser, all pompous lethargy and no action.

On 18 July the Theosophical Congress began in Vienna, followed by the Star Congress, which Krishna had to supervise almost unaided. To his great disappointment, Annie Besant had been unable to come, as she was recovering in India from a scorpion's sting. On a personal level, however, his stay in the Austrian capital was thrilling as it brought him together once more with Helen Knothe. Though separated for nearly twenty-one months, their fascination with each other had remained undimmed, and Helen, studying the violin in Amsterdam, had lived for the regular letters that had arrived from her exotic friend far away. By chance, she had moved to Vienna in February 1923, in order to study with a new teacher, and was very much present when Krishna arrived in July. When the congresses were over, it was arranged that Krishna and Nitya should take a holiday in the Austrian Tyrol, accompanied by an entourage that included Helen, Lady Emily, Mary and Betty Lutyens, Rajagopal (on vacation from Cambridge), Marcelle de Manziarly, Ruth Roberts (who had intrigued Krishna the previous year in Sydney), an Indian couple, and the Star representative for Austria, John Cordes.

They took two chalets in the village of Ehrwald, near Innsbruck, where, it was believed, the summer weather and mountain air would help Nitya's health and provide Krishna the right degree of tranquillity to recover from his ordeals of the previous year. Neither goal would be achieved, although much else took place, which led to Ehrwald having its name etched in the pages of OSE history as a sacred site.

After their arrival, on 30 July, members of the party spent a fortnight walking the hills, playing rounders and reflecting on their progress along the spiritual path. The mixture of fun and sobriety was exemplified in the person of Krishna, who was both amiable friend and inscrutable teacher. The five unmarried women in the company, all of whom competed for his attention and approval, playfully called themselves Krishna's gopis, using the term applied to the milkmaids who attended Lord Krishna in Hindu mythology. Despite their lofty spiritual aspirations, the gopis were subject to the same romantic dreams and sexual tensions that would haunt any other young girl, and petty rivalries, though carefully concealed, were abundant.[25] The prime target of their disaffection was, of course, Helen, with whom Krishna was completely and openly enthralled. None of them could help liking her, despite themselves, because of her intelligence and vivacity, but took consolation in telling each other that she was not particularly pretty.

So powerful was the atmosphere of veneration that surrounded Krishna at this time, his companions were prepared to suffer humiliating blows to their morale, all in the cause of self-improvement. The gopis would seek out private interviews with him, during which he mercilessly tore down their defences and laid naked their faults, invariably ending with the girls crying their hearts out, but feeling it must be for the best. Unlike his soft-hearted brother, Krishna could be uncompromisingly frank. If he could induce a state of inner crisis in those he talked to, he believed it would prompt growth and change. Elizabeth (Betty) Lutyens looked back on the experience with humour but no little bitterness. She found the self-conscious piousness of Krishna's circle 'hypnotically overpowering', but 'redolent of of spiritual snobbery'. There was no benefit in confessing all to the young guru, she would maintain; 'these supposedly privileged and beneficial sessions consisted of Krishna repeatedly pointing out well-known faults and picking on everything detrimental and sapping one's confidence.'[26]

Krishna did not think he was being unkind. He was undergoing his own intensely arduous awakening, and believed that everything should take second place to the mission – personality, feelings, likes, dislikes and talents. This presented a problem for Helen, who was faced with the prospect of a first-class career as a violinist. Krishna persuaded her that the world was full of professional violinists, but the role that was hers to play in the Coming would be unique. Some matriarchal advice, by letter, from Annie Besant ('Do you care enough for the spiritual life and for the helping of humanity to give up everything else for that aim?'[27]) compounded Helen's resolve, and she prepared to dedicate her life to the Star. Betty Lutyens, who later matured into one of Britain's most distinguished composers, resented being made to feel that her musical talent was 'frowned upon', and that it was her 'bounden duty to attempt to suppress it'.[28] But Betty did not enjoy the prominent role in Krishna's life that was to be cast for Helen as the month of August began to unfold.

Despite their passion, there was never any question of a physical relationship between Helen and Krishna, and to this extent their involvement was restrained by modern standards. But by the middle of the month Krishna began to show symptoms of his process once again, and before long Helen had been sucked into the maelstrom. For she was now required to assume the role previously taken by Rosalind Williams: nurse, mother, amanuensis and, along with Nitya, chief collaborator in the mystical experiment. The symptoms, which occurred every evening for a month, were similar to before: torturous pain in the neck and spine, particular agony in the top of his head, where he felt the 'powers' had opened up a hole, together with fainting, nausea and weight loss.[29] He also had an aversion, bordering on terror, to light and invasive noises – particularly the church bells that were rung daily in the village. So frightful were the screams coming from Krishna's room, John Cordes felt bound to explain to the farmers, living downstairs, that their friend was the victim of epileptic attacks.

Once again, Krishna experienced a departure from his 'elemental' body, leaving a childlike shell to suffer the pain, and it was at this point that Helen's maternal comfort was most needed. She grew fond of the vulnerable infant personality and worked hard to do what was expected of her; but she did not have Rosalind's stamina, and found her task at times unbearable. She was horrified at Krishna's suffering (like 'hot pokers in an open wound'[30]) and mystified by the implications of it all; but it drew her ever closer to her beloved, and at peaceful moments he would vow eternal love to her. She could not resist feeling flattered. Above any woman in the world, she had been selected to play what she was now convinced was an indispensable part in the new messiah's life. The influence of Theosophical thinking weighed deep on her, not just because of the company at Ehrwald, but through her family, several of whom, including her parents in America and an aunt in Holland, were committed Theosophists (though her father thoroughly disapproved of Leadbeater).

Krishna started to 'bring through' messages from the Masters, culminating with a formal congratulation to all on the evening of 20 September. The household was thanked, the brothers were warned that the ordeal was far from complete in the long term, and the building in which they had been staying, the Villa Sonnblick, was declared sacred.[31] This message marked the end of the Ehrwald process, and the band of Theosophists departed two days later. Helen returned to Vienna to pack and bid her teacher farewell, resolved to face the wrath of her father who by no means approved of her abandoning a musical career. She joined the brothers at Castle Eerde, for the occasion when Philip van Pallandt formally handed over his estate to the OSE, and they then travelled to England before sailing across to New York. The brothers were destined for another spell at Ojai, while a timorous Helen was due to be reunited with her family at Ridgewood, New Jersey. Her farewell from Krishna, which they both thought would be temporary, as she was expected to follow them later to Ojai, was misery for her. Krishna, with typical severity, but certainly not callousness, remarked that the unhappiness would be good for her. Suffering had to be faced in order to be understood.

The brothers, together with Rajagopal and a Dutch Theosophist, Koos van de Leeuw, travelled across America to California by train. Rajagopal had taken a year out of Cambridge in order to participate in what Krishna and Nitya were convinced would be a new and climactic chapter of the process when they arrived at Ojai. Nitya wrote to Annie Besant en route that they were keen now for the 'training' to be completed so that they could come out to India and begin their great work in earnest. They arrived in the valley on 8 November 1923, no longer guests, but owners, in all but name. They were principal trustees of the Brothers Association, a body that had been set up to own property on behalf of the OSE, and one of their first purchases was the cottage at Ojai, naturally deemed another sacred site after the events of 1922, together with a neighbouring house and some land. Once again, it was in all likelihood the beneficence of Miss Dodge that made this acquisition possible. The cottage where the brothers had stayed and experienced the first process was given the name Pine Cottage, while the other, larger house, into which they now moved, was called Arya Vihara, meaning noble monastery.

Rosalind Williams stayed at Pine Cottage with her sister, and the romance with Nitya soon began to blossom once again. Nitya brought up the question of marriage – rather prematurely, as Rosalind had just begun to study for college and was in no mind to take such a decision. Krishna was always against the institution of marriage, believing that it restricted individual freedom and stultified relationships. He frequently berated his friends for allowing themselves to be seduced by the illusory security of wedlock, and news that Nitya might be considering such a move elicited his contempt.

A matter of days after they had settled in at Arya Vihara, as they had all expected, the process began. The symptoms this time were worse and more complicated than at any time in the past, so much so that Nitya began, for the first time, to have serious concerns for his brother's health. He wrote in desperation to Leadbeater asking if there were any evidence that 'the Master Jesus' had had to endure trials of this sort when his body had been purified. An impatient Leadbeater passed the problem over to Annie Besant, who assured him, and thus the brothers, that everything they were experiencing was for the best. The situation cannot have been eased by Krishna's surprising rejection of Rosalind. Pining for Helen, he found the ministrations of his former nurse an irritation, and refused to have her near. Helen, meanwhile had been absolutely forbidden by her father from travelling to Ojai, and had to satisfy herself by giving uncommitted violin performances in local New Jersey churches. Her dream of going to Australia to study with Leadbeater, and thus improve herself, was out of the question.

Krishna felt lonely, irascible and unhappy. The process seemed interminable, and the atmosphere at Ojai had turned sour. Bored and claustrophobic, the group of participants began to irritate each other. As Nitya wrote to Besant on 7 February 1924, 'We've had so far 76 nights of Krishna's process . . . The evening business is more of a strain than it has ever been, now all the excitement and fun, if ever it was fun, have gone ... Krishna, I think has almost forgotten how to smile ... now he wakes up with it [the pain] and goes to bed with it ... The body itself, though it is absolutely sick with weariness, seems to prefer to go on, rather than take a holiday.'[32]

A fitting climax was reached on the night of 11 April, when the three young Indian men at their Californian outpost felt the presence of the Lord Buddha tangibly in their midst. It was a thrilling experience for them all, jaded as they were from weeks of tedious routine and frayed tempers. The marvellous evening culminated in a lengthy message, supposedly from the Lord Maitreya, brought through by Krishna and enthusiastically transcribed by Nitya.[33] Once again, it congratulates the brothers for their endurance, assures them that everything so far has been accomplished successfully, apologises for the pain, and gives advice on how to look after themselves in the immediate future. Conveniently for Krishna, the Master's words echoed his own innermost longing with the statement, 'The body cannot be relaxed properly until it gets a little time with its supposed mother [Helen]. If it has an opportunity, let it see her.' Thus sanctioned by a will none of them dared to contradict, plans were formulated for a European summer holiday together along the same lines as the previous year's sojourn in Austria. Helen failed to win her father's approval, but as an independent and strong-minded young woman decided to be mistress of her own destiny and left anyway. She parted from her father without a word of goodbye and they were not to be reunited until years later, when the brokenhearted Frank Knothe wrote saying he could no longer bear the separation.

8

Journey to the Heart of Loneliness

———— ❋ ————

Krishnamurti emerged in the mid-1920s a confident and independent individual. Gone were the days of black despair, of longing for a different destiny, of cringing beneath the weight of his sponsors' expectations. Although he had as yet only apprehended, rather than comprehended, the immeasurable mystery that underlay his spiritual experiences, he had touched the ground on which his future teaching was to be built. Henceforward the kaleidoscopic theorems of Theosophy were for him as arid and flighty as sand in a desert wind.

Along with his new groundedness came a shift in his personal manner. Many of those who spent time with him during these years write of his playful sense of humour, his infectious fits of giggles, and his partiality to practical jokes. He shocked some followers with his unashamed mischievousness – such as on the occasion when he delighted in squeezing toothpaste out of an upstairs window at Eerde Castle onto the bald and cerebral head of Koos van der Leeuw beneath. Others were surprised by his growing passion for fast American cars and his choice of reading material – the popular detective stories of Edgar Wallace rather than landmarks of religious philosophy. But the light-hearted Krishnamurti would recede as the teacher within him came to the fore. The shifts were both sudden and deep-seated, and members of his inner circle never ceased to wonder how the flippant jokester they laughed with at breakfast could shortly afterwards have them hang their heads with shame at their own superficiality. He himself acknowledged the dichotomy of his personality and would frequently refer to his body, with its needs, delights and caprices, in the third person, while his true self, the teacher, the entity that departed his shell during the 'process', remained free from the influence of material things. The body (which he would often henceforth refer to simply as 'K'), he explained in 1926, 'though it has its cravings, its desires to wander forth and to live and enjoy separately for itself, does not in any way interfere with the true Self.'[1]

When the ineffable teacher withdrew, the personality left behind felt as nervous as ever about how to satisfy the demands of his followers. Publicity was still an ordeal, and even informal socialising, as long as it was within the Theosophical sphere, presented a problem. Shyness, on a personal level, was to continue to be a major stumbling block thoughout his life, so long as people expected some satisfaction in return for their projected image of him. His reticence in small-talk would evaporate, however, as soon as he slipped into the role of teacher. His modesty would be replaced by a communicative style awesome in its authority and dignity. Audiences frequently noted the switch occur. He would sit before them for a few minutes, until the silence became awkward and then, as if from nowhere, a new energy appeared to possess him, filling his delicate frame with poise and confidence. He assumed focus, attention and sensitivity, though not necessarily of the gentle sort.

In the early summer of 1924 the little community at Ojai split into two groups; each departed for different destinations and what was to be the next chapter in the World Teacher project. Rosalind Williams, having abandoned her plans of a college education, travelled to Sydney, along with Koos van der Leeuw, to be helped along the Masters' path by Leadbeater. Krishna, Nitya and Rajagopal went to New York, where they were joined by Helen Knothe, before crossing to Europe. There Krishna was reunited with Annie Besant for the first time in two years, and he joined with her in various celebrations to mark the fiftieth anniversary of her entry into public work. The three Indian men and Helen then proceeded to Ommen where they attended the first Star Camp in the woodland near Castle Eerde.

These Star Camps, at Ommen and elsewhere, were to become one of Krishnamurti's principal means of disseminating his teachings to a wider (and not necessarily Theosophical) audience, although in 1924 only around 250 people attended, and their accommodation, which in later years was to become highly organised, was at this stage experimental, to say the least. The attractions of outdoor camping had caught the young public's imagination since the inception of the British Boy Scout movement, which formed its first international links in 1920. It was an invigorating, egalitarian and inexpensive hobby, and as such was favoured by practical idealists of the post-First World War era, many of whom were now being attracted to the teachings of Krishnamurti. Encouraged by humanitarian visionaries like Fridtjof Nansen, socialist politicians like George Lansbury, philosophers like Hermann Keyserling and literary figures like Anatole France, they had come to believe that the world community was on the verge of dramatic transformation; and they found in the young Indian teacher a spiritual message on which to hang their hopes of a better future. It was in many ways a parallel movement to that which occurred during the 1960s. Krishnamurti enjoyed the spontaneity of this new breed of audience, and found it refreshing after the turgid intractability of Theosophists.

After the Ommen camp, Krishna and a party of close friends, consisting for the most part of those who had been with him at Ehrwald the previous year, went to Pergine, in the Italian Dolomites. They stayed at the Hotel Castello, a converted eleventh-century castle, perched on a rocky hilltop. The main purpose of the holiday, apart from allowing Krishna to relax in the company of friends, was to prepare the gopis (Mary and Betty Lutyens, Ruth Roberts and Helen) for training under Leadbeater in Sydney. To this end, a daily routine was instituted at Pergine, consisting of meditation, readings from the Gospel of Buddha, a little outdoor play in the field beneath the castle, and a series of talks by Krishna. In addition they were each to have private sessions with him, which, again, though uplifting, usually resulted in a massive outpouring of emotion and no little shedding of tears.

Betty Lutyens remembered the atmosphere at Pergine as 'even more hushed and holy than at Ehrwald. One felt that even the mountains held their breath waiting for Krishna to speak.'[2] The air of sanctity was enhanced when Krishna began to enter once more into his process, and a strict regime had to be respected to allow him peace, quiet and isolation at the appropriate times. Despite the high spiritual plane Krishna occupied most of the time, he still managed during his secular moments to upset some with his risqué humour, which one witness described as unprintable and Lady Emily considered 'the most terrible sacrilege'.

Most of the party who had enjoyed the spell at Pergine reassembled in November to sail to India. It was on this voyage that Nitya and the sixteen-year-old Mary Lutyens, overwhelmed by a healthy romantic urge, declared their love for each other, resting against the ship's rail at sunset. It was the happiest moment in young Mary's life, as she had worshipped Nitya from a safe distance for years. Their innocent idyll was marred by a serious recurrence of Nitya's tuberculosis, and by the time the group arrived at Bombay he was coughing blood and had begun to decline rapidly. Shortly after their arrival at Adyar, it was thought best for Nitya to go and recuperate at the hill-station of Ootacamund. The gopis, meanwhile concentrated their energies on improving themselves in anticipation of meeting the legendary Leadbeater.[3] Krishna encouraged them wholeheartedly and, rather surprisingly in view of the line he was shortly to take, showed not the slightest hesitancy in recommending his former mentor as the best possible guardian of their spiritual welfare. He actively discouraged Mary Lutyens from studying in preparation for Cambridge University and stressed that the only work worth doing was that which increased her chance of being accepted as a pupil of the Masters. Helen had travelled on to Sydney almost immediately (joining Rosalind who had been there since the previous June), and Nitya was absent in the hills, which meant that Krishna now had to endure the agonies of his process unaided by those who had stood by his side in the past.

The most important result of this visit to Adyar was the acquisition, by a Trust similar to that responsible for the Eerde estate, of 300 acres for the establishment of an educational institution. It had been Krishna's vision, ever since visiting Berkeley, to found his own university in India, and in this he had the full support of Besant's Theosophical movement. It was hoped that this first enterprise might be the founding of a university at his birth place, Madanapalle (considered by Theosophists a sacred heartland, a Bethlehem of the future), and to this end, Krishna set off in January 1925 prospecting for a suitable location. By 1 February he wrote to Nitya that he had found a beautiful site a few miles from

Madanapalle, about 2500 feet above sea level, set beneath the sacred mountain, Rishi Conda. It was given the name Rishi Valley and the following year a school, rather than a university, was founded. It exists to this day and is one of the most prestigious in the subcontinent. In 1928, the Rishi Valley Trust, as it was to be called, succeeded with painstaking insistence in persuading the British military authorities at Benares to sell a further 375 acres on which the second Krishnamurti-inspired school took root. The Rajghat School, as it is known, which was not opened until 1934, also flourishes today, and is of special significance because of its location on the banks of the sacred River Ganges.

Elsewhere in the world at this time moves were afoot to acquire land and buildings in the name of the coming World Teacher. In the suburbs of Sydney, perched spectacularly on the cliffs above the harbour, a Greek amphitheatre was all but complete, from which, it was maintained, the new messiah would proclaim his mission to the world. Much of the cost was to be met by individual subscriptions for twenty-five year leases on each seat. The *Herald of the Star* wrote that the theatre was 'as prominent a feature of Sydney Harbour as the Statue of Liberty in New York', and the Perth *Call* described its appearance as 'the most picturesque event in the history of religion in Australia'.[4] Deliberately imitative of Pythagoras' theatre at Taormina, which had impressed Leadbeater so much in 1912, the Sydney bowl was constructed from reinforced concrete and provided seating for up to 3000. In addition, there was a restaurant pavilion, library, chapel, and cinema projection room. Leadbeater turned the first sod on the site on 28 June 1923, in full episcopal regalia and to the accompaniment of formal occult rituals. Krishna, by contrast, when he visited the incomplete theatre in 1925, surprised many by beginning his talk with the words, 'I am not going to tell you any occult stuff, so don't get frightened.'[5] His informal manner was a far cry from the messianic splendour some disciples had come to expect, especially those who spread the rumour that he would arrive at the theatre walking in glory across the waters of Sydney Harbour.[6]

Krishna, Nitya and the Lutyens family arrived in Sydney on 3 April 1925 and were met at the docks by an ebullient Leadbeater, accompanied by his favourite boy of the moment – who was known to share the bishop's bedroom. While the Jiddu brothers stayed with Rosalind at the home of a Mr Mackay, the Lutyens were accommodated in a community of over fifty people, Helen amongst them, at Leadbeater's headquarters, a huge rambling house overlooking the harbour, called The Manor.[7] The irrepressible Leadbeater was surrounded as ever by disciples who hung on his every passionate assertion, his lurid tales and eloquent diatribes. He still cultivated an atmosphere of heated spiritual ambitiousness, with every member of his community vying with one another to ascend the Path of Discipleship and prove their spiritual distinction.

Very shortly after he arrived, it became clear to Krishna that his own path was diverging from that of Leadbeater more rapidly than he had realised. Sometimes he was plainly amused by the antics of his old master, particularly during pompous ceremonies at the Liberal Catholic Cathedral; at other times he was simply appalled by the blind submission of Leadbeater's disciples to the dictates of the old man's fantasies. Some of the gopis whom he had encouraged to visit Sydney, now felt ashamed with themselves for falling under the bishop's spell, especially when it was so clear to everyone that their true guru, the radiant young Krishna, was so far removed from the whole Theosophical edifice. As Mary Lutyens noted, 'He was like a perfect rose ... growing in a beautiful garden, whereas we at best were paper imitations, without scent or colour, manufactured inside stuffy rooms by hands practised to turn out these shoddy counterfeits by the dozen.'[8] Helen Knothe did not entirely share this opinion and entered into the spirit of her adventure enthusiastically. She enjoyed making music in the cathedral and felt comfortable pursuing the course Krishna had previously recommended. It was his change of attitude rather than her own which now precipitated a slight cooling of relations between them.

In the light of his new-found perspicacity, Krishna viewed the preoccupations and schemes of Leadbeater and Besant as childish delusions. It was difficult for him to share his feelings with anyone in his circle at the time, including Nitya, who considered his derision of the Society disloyal; but Nitya and the others had not experienced Krishna's enlightenment, which, whether one believes in it or not, left him feeling that he had to make a simple choice between Truth and un-Truth. Krishna, unlike Nitya, was faced with a future at the very spearhead of the movement, with thousands looking to him for spiritual leadership. With this extraordinary destiny before him there was no choice to be made. Truth, immeasurable, eternal and divine, must take precedence over notions of temporal loyalty. He would compensate by dropping as many favourable public remarks about the Society and its leaders as his conscience allowed. But as the latter half of the decade progressed, his continuing 'process', with its sensation of cleansing, of wiping out the burden of past conditioning, led him into ever greater contradiction of his sponsors' orthodoxy.

He was clear, however, about his mission as World Teacher, and for most of 1925 still believed that he was in tune with the wishes of the great Brotherhood of Masters. This is revealed in his correspondence with Nitya while the latter was convalescing at Ootacamund. On 4 February he wrote to describe meetings he had had on the astral plane with the Lord Maitreya and an even greater power in the hierarchy, the Mahachohan. Krishna declared at the meetings that he 'would sacrifice anything and everything' for Nitya's recovery. The Mahachohan replied to this request with solemn dignity and certainty: 'He will be well.'[9] Krishna went on to write that his younger brother had been granted a 'last chance' to prove his faith in, and dedicate his life to, the mission. He explained that the illness had been meted out by the Masters as a warning, to make Nitya change his ways before it was too late. It was now a matter of life or death. 'You *weren't* sure of all these things; you had a vague kind of belief in all this but *not* a strong conviction. So again you are ill.'[10]

In the face of Krishna's affirmations, Nitya's continued decline carried with it depressing spiritual connotations as well as physical. Just before leaving for Sydney, in March 1925, ailing and emaciated, he wrote to Leadbeater that, in the light of Krishna's words, he could only blame himself for his latest relapse: 'So I have failed, in many ways.'[11] Less than a week after his arrival in Sydney, Nitya was examined by a specialist, pronounced dangerously sick, and instructed to retire immediately to the mountains, where he would benefit from the cooler air. He was accommodated, along with a few friends, in a comfortable log cabin, and remained there, nursed by Rosalind (much to the chagrin of a love-sick Mary Lutyens), until the following June, when he was declared safe to travel. He then departed for Ojai, with Krishna and Rosalind, where his condition began to stabilise. During August he suffered two more haemorrhages and lay immobile, in a critical condition for most of the autumn. Although Krishna was deeply concerned for his brother, and closer to him than at any time in the past, he still felt confident of his recovery, having been assured of such by a higher authority. He even considered the illness might be a 'process' of sorts for Nitya, and that he might emerge a stronger, purer servant of the mission.

The tenuous link between Krishna and his parent organisation was put under further strain during the summer of 1925, by the activities of George Arundale, who now emerged as his chief antagonist. Krishna had decided to cancel that year's gathering at Ommen because Nitya's dangerous condition would have prevented him attending. George Arundale, however, would have none of it, and published an appeal in the *Herald* calling all Star members to show their loyalty and proceed to Ommen with or without the presence of their leader. He was joined in this venture by a new and firm ally, Bishop Wedgwood.

The pair arrived in Holland in July, accompanied by Arundale's teen-aged wife, the meek ingénue, Rukmini, and a young Norwegian Liberal Catholic priest, Oscar Köllerström. They went straight to Huizen, near Ommen, where a neighbour of Phillip van Pallandt had made over some land to the Liberal Catholic Church. As if to rival the Star headquarters at Eerde, Wedgwood had established an LCC centre at Huizen, complete with its own church, St Michael's. It was here, days before the Ommen gathering commenced, that strange and dramatic occult events began to occur with startling rapidity. On 26 July Arundale was ordained priest by Wedgwood, and a week later consecrated bishop. He also claimed to have been bombarded with messages from the Masters, most of which announced stupendous occult advancements for him and the others at Huizen. On 1 August, Arundale and Wedgwood were said to have taken their Third Initiation, a great honour which ranked them alongside Krishna. Young Rukmini meanwhile had ascended to her Second, having achieved her First a few days previously. Annie Besant was impressed by Arundale's descriptions of these events, which to her signalled that the great engines of her messianic revolution were on the grind. She decided to cancel an important string of London lectures, and travelled to Holland to be with the excited group of Theosophists.

Arundale, from his new position of ecclesiastical and occult authority, now began to dole out instructions from the Masters, some rather eccentric, such as the requirement for LCC clergymen to wear silk underwear. Then the Initiations began to tumble down with ever greater momentum. On 7 August Arundale announced that he, Wedgwood, Krishna (travelling astrally from Ojai) and Jinarajadasa (from India) had taken their Fourth Initiation, and were therefore Arhats, on a level with Besant and Leadbeater. On the night of 12 August, Rukmini, who had been declared 'without fault', took her Third and Fourth Initiations, a wholly unprecedented dash to Arhatship. And Arundale's grand climax came the following night, during which it was claimed, he, Krishna, Jinarajadasa, Leadbeater, Wedgwood and Besant had taken their Fifth and final Initiation; Rukmini was later to be added to this list, having achieved a rise from plain disciple to Adept, the highest spiritual status obtainable for mortals, in little over a fortnight. How this must have struck the dedicated Lady Emily, who had struggled to improve herself for fifteen years only to be rewarded with a First Initiation (for which she was joyously grateful) is not on record. It was generally considered, until this point, that for ordinary people a lifetime of effort was required to ascend one, or at best two steps up the occult hierarchy.

Arundale's revelations did not stop at occult advancements. He announced to Annie Besant at the Ommen gathering on 10 August that the names of Twelve Apostles for the World Teacher had been revealed to him by the Lord Maitreya. Besant trumpeted this good news at a public talk the following day, proclaiming the names of six of the Twelve: herself, Leadbeater, Arundale, Jinarajadasa, Rukmini and Köllerström. In the heat of the moment she forgot to mention Wedgwood and accidentally included Krishna, the one ordained to take the role of Christ. She felt that a landmark had been reached. She went on publicly to announce the foundation of a World Religion and a World University, both of which involved Arundale as principal agent. Her description of the World Religion was a 'fellowship of faiths' which would involve no loss of autonomy for individual religions representing different cultures. As ever, her ambition was for brotherhood through federalism, although in practice she was in fact promoting the interests of her own organisation as the keystone for the new civilisation.

One can sense almost tangibly through all this the machinations of Arundale. He had always been ambitious and was now using the occasion of Krishna's absence to recommend himself as Besant's natural heir. As clairvoyant 'mystic' and administrative leader of Theosophy's grandiose new projects, he was carving for himself a profile that combined the powers of both Besant and Leadbeater. But for the thorny problem of Krishna, he might yet rise to a position stronger and more authoritative than either of the Society's present elders.

Annie Besant, trusting as ever the integrity of her friends, was naively carried along by the excitement. She was also keen to see the World Teacher's mission materialise within her own lifetime, and at seventy-eight may have begun to feel that time was against her. Another nagging concern was the threat of war. Economic hardship, resulting in the rise of threatening political spectres, especially communism and fascism, fuelled her sense of urgency. She must do everything in her power to clear the way for Christ's immediate and glorious return.

Leadbeater refrained from making any public criticism of the bizarre events at Huizen, but privately fumed. He felt distant and frustratingly powerless to influence developments. As presiding bishop of the Liberal Catholic Church, his approval should have been sought before Arundale's consecration. When he heard news of the proposed move, he telegraphed to register his disapproval, but was too late; the ceremony had gone ahead regardless. Leadbeater wrote to Krishna 'as one of the innermost circle,' that there had been 'some misunderstandings and exaggerations' at Huizen; and to Ernest Wood he privately berated Besant's pronouncements, saying, 'I hope she will not wreck the Society.'

Krishna, observing from Ojai, was in a difficult position. He felt utterly repelled by reports of what had occurred at Huizen and Ommen, but had to contain his derision or risk splitting the Society, which would disable his mission as World Teacher before it had even begun. It is no wonder he let loose 'an avalanche of sarcasm' when he met Lady Emily the following October.[12] The doctors had assured him that his brother was out of immediate danger and Krishna felt it was safe to travel over to Europe. He was due to meet Besant in London and he hoped while there to salvage what he could from the wreckage of Arundale's fiasco. The multiple Initiations, he felt, had trivialised and profaned a sacred mystery; and the matter of Apostles selected for his service was simply farcical.[13] Their appointment was intended, of course, to endorse the coming World Teacher's credibility by creating yet another parallel with Jesus of the Gospels. The obvious difference in this case was that the Teacher himself, in the body of Krishna, was to have no part in the matter of selection.

Faced with her idol's obvious unhappiness, Lady Emily now began to suspect that Besant had been misled, perhaps even hypnotised by Arundale, and asked Krishna why he did not speak out. 'He said it would be no use – all they would say would be that he had failed or was under the influence of the Dark Powers.'[14] The only way open to him was to win over Besant by explaining his own scepticism and hope that she would stand by him rather than uphold the assertions she had made in Holland under the influence of Arundale. He attempted to talk to Besant several times in London, but she would not 'take it in'. Although they were staying under the same roof in Wimbledon, Besant was always up and away on some mission, and they never had sufficient quiet time alone together for the sort of conversation Krishna wanted.

Krishna only remained in England for a fortnight before setting off for India along with Rajagopal, Rosalind, and the chief protagonists of the Huizen drama – Besant, Wedgwood, Arundale and Rukmini. Although their differences had not been made public, the atmosphere on the voyage was far from comfortable and there were electric moments when Krishna felt sharply the two bishops' disapproval. They were on the way to Adyar, as had been planned for some while, to attend Theosophy's Golden Jubilee Convention, fifty years having elapsed since Blavatsky and Olcott had joined forces to found the Society.

The party paused en route in Rome, where Arundale and Wedgwood paraded themselves at the Vatican and elsewhere as venerable churchmen, robed in purple, with heavy crosses hanging around their necks. Krishna was disgusted at having to associate with them. Their behaviour and ecclesiastical pomposity insulted the divinity that he felt he had touched. Arundale intimated that unless Krishna fell into line, he would find himself ostracised and might thereby be the cause of his own ruin. There was even talk of the Masters punishing Nitya because of Krishna's obstreperousness. On hearing the news, via telegram, that Nitya was ill with influenza, Arundale mellowed somewhat, and reported that he had been assured personally by the Masters that they had great plans for the young man's future. Krishna still shared this conviction. The benign Masters, who guided his every foot-step and blazed like a lamp to light his path, would surely never have allowed him to leave Ojai if his brother now faced death.

Late in the evening of 11 November, while their ship was docked at Port Said, a telegram arrived for Krishna saying, 'Flu little more serious. Pray for me. Nitya.' It had been sent the same day at 9.50 a.m., although Krishna does not appear to have received it personally until returning from an outing to the port, the following evening. On the night of 13 November another telegram was transmitted, but a storm interfered with the ship's reception, so it was not until the morning of 14 November that Krishna, breakfasting alone in his cabin, was visited by Annie Besant and told the news that Nitya had died the previous day.

This tragedy shattered Krishnamurti. For ten days he was completely disoriented, at times dazed with disbelief, at others venting his fury in fits of bitter crying. His brother was dead and the Masters had done nothing to prevent it. The ideological edifice in which he had come to believe so passionately and with such certainty now began to crumble. On a personal level, he had been deprived of the last surviving link to his family and childhood. More than that – he had lost the only person to whom he could talk openly, his best friend and companion; he had lost a well-spring of optimism and generosity, whose consistent ebullience had kept him afloat during the bleak days of their Theosophical training, whose street-wise common sense had compensated for his own vague meanderings since before he could remember, and whose pragmatism had proved so indis-pensable in the organisation of their current work. Helen Knothe, looking back after more than six decades, recalled their relationship as 'as close and as warm and as sweet and as dear as can be. I think Nitya was the closest person to [Krishna] in the world . . . he was just part of him, and Nitya's influence on him was very good.'[15]

Krishna now entered a pit of solitude into which none of his com-panions on the ship, no matter how affectionately they felt, was able to intrude. As the days progressed, he reasoned with his grief, meeting it face on, as his own philosophy demanded, working his way through it to the transcendental void that lay beyond all suffering of the material world. This journey to the heart of loneliness, in which the mind is stilled and relieved of its excess baggage, was to act like an open window for him, now and at other times in the future. He discovered, at the root of sorrow, an emptiness that could not be touched by hurt, because it was the property of an altogether more sublime kingdom, unnameable, immeasurable. This was literally the sublimation of his suffering.

Such was the strength of his conviction that by the time he reached Adyar, Krishna appeared balanced and at peace. As a public figure he was obliged to make public his grief, and did so in various talks and writings, most notably the editorial of the *Herald*'s January 1926 issue. Here, in lyrical prose, he celebrates his friendship with Nitya while acknowledging their differences of temperament. He attempts to explain the sublimation of his grief, that new life has been born out of the ashes, life strengthened by metaphysical union: 'An old dream is dead and a new one is being born, as a flower that pushes through the solid earth ... As Krishnamurti, I have now greater zeal, greater faith, greater sympathy and greater love, for there is also in me the essence of being Nityananda. Sorrow is wonderful if you can taste it in the Divine cup. I am happy; not that I do not miss my friend and brother, but because I have drunk at the fountain of human sorrow and suffering, from which I have derived strength.'[16] He had found, through and with Nitya, union with an entity beyond the reach of human thought, a godhead that he was soon to describe as his 'Beloved'. As he wrote in his poem, 'The Song of Life,' referring to the period after Nitya's death:

> *I worshipped,*
> *I prayed,*
> *But the gods were silent.*
> *I could weep no more.*
> *I sought him in all things,*
> *In every clime.*
> *... And then,*
> *In my search,*
> *I beheld Thee,*
> *O Lord of my heart;*
> *In thee alone*
> *I saw the face of my brother.*[17]

This revelation offered him consolation and immense strength.

On a physical level, Krishna derived comfort from Helen, who arrived with Leadbeater and a party of seventy, including Rosalind, from Sydney. Helen wrote that he 'arrived in Adyar a changed person – older, colder, more restrained. The boy in him was gone . . . the loss of his brother killed something in him . . . Something inside him turned to steel.'[18] It was the beginning of the end of their relationship. Whether it was Nitya's death, Krishna's new spiritual life, with its disdain of possessive love, or Helen's recent passion for socialism (which entailed a disapproval for the extravagance of Krishna's lifestyle), they were never to be close again. She returned, for a spell, to Australia and her own new interests, he to his role as budding World Teacher, and within a few years the letters between them dried up. Helen later married the American socialist, writer and environmentalist, Scott Nearing, and lived happily with him for fifty-three years until his death at the age of a hundred. She herself, like Krishnamurti, lived to be ninety-one, finally dying in a car accident in 1995.

Nitya's death affected everyone closely involved with the World Teacher project. Some thought he had possessed characteristics better suited to the messianic role than his older brother: bookish intellect, an awareness of current affairs, humanity, immediate charm, wit and warmth. Krishna's airy spirituality was charismatic on one level, but for some followers he lacked the requisite definition and grounding that his global role might demand. From his fortress of high, uncompromising standards, he placed little value on the type of diplomatic sensitivity so well displayed by his younger brother. Helen described Nitya as 'the finest second fiddle who ever played'.

After the experience of Sydney, earlier in the year, followed by the events at Huizen and Ommen, Krishna's belief in the standard rhetoric of Theosophy was bruised, to say the least. Nitya's death now caused him to re-evaluate his attitude towards the Society's principal tenet: that the world and its events were goverened by a hierarchy of semi-divine Masters. The result of his discovery was that he felt suddenly and joyously released from an absurd illusion. His total *volte face* was to cause obvious difficulties for Theosophists who, up until now, had been encouraged, or even compelled, to accept the occult teachings of Leadbeater. Were they now to believe that this had all been a grand deceit, and that the Masters were merely figments of Leadbeater's imagination?

It would be a mistake to leap to the conclusion that the old bishop was a deliberate liar, and that what he maintained had no substance. One of the basic principles of esotericism is the role of mediation between the human and divine worlds, effected by angels, spirits, or, in Theosophy's case, Masters. Leading on from this, it is characteristic for esoteric systems to lay emphasis on the power of imagination to bring about mental dialogue with these mediators. The mind works to build physical images of what are essentially metaphysical entities, and in this process of imagination lies the mystery of transcendental intercourse. The imagination is a hazardous playground, and it is likely that, as the years progressed and his bombastic confidence soared, Leadbeater confused the receptive quality of his psychic intuition with something altogether more manufactured. The result was an occult matrix of Lords, angels and spirits moulded to fit Leadbeater's own perception; his Masters were his own thought-creations, their reality amplified by repeated recollection.[19] If devotional practice within the Christian tradition can bring about physical symptoms as extreme as stigmata, then why not visions of Masters in the Theosophical? The spiritual atmosphere around Leadbeater, at Adyar and elsewhere, was intense, with all members of his community longing more than anything to be favoured with a visitation from the Masters. In such conditions it was undoubtedly possible that individuals' visions of etheric bodies, though powerfully real at the time, were nothing more than personal wish-fulfilments.

Krishnamurti, as Leadbeater's impressionable protégé, had been subjected to the full passion of his mentor's opinions. His imagination was cultured and moulded more forcefully than any other in the Society, young, vacant-minded experiment that he was. It was only after the death of Nitya that he understood fully, for the first time, the hollowness of all such manufactured imagery. And it was only then that he realised that the 'Lord of his heart', was ineffable and quite beyond the reach of word or image. At this point, the Masters evaporated for Krishnamurti.[20]

His attitude to the Masters in later life was clear and consistent: they are an irrelevance, nothing more than a toy to serious seekers of Truth; they are shaped by the experiencer's own perception and are therefore limited to that individual's past thinking. Appeals to such projected deities are as flawed as the whole notion of prayer. 'When the mind is made quiet through prayer, the unconscious, which is the residue of your own satisfactory conclusions, projects itself into the conscious mind, and therefore your prayer is answered. So when you pray, you are seeking an escape, happiness; and the outside agency which answers you is your own gratification.'[21] This is as true for the man in the street, and for Leadbeater, as for himself before 1925. It was self-gratification, rather than the voice of a Master, that had answered his prayers for Nitya's life. And now Nitya was dead.

Krishna was therefore on the cusp of change as he took his seat at the opening of Theosophy's Jubilee Convention in December 1925. It was to be a much publicised event, and newspapermen from around the globe had gathered to observe the hordes of delegates as they arrived. Film clips of the Convention show linen-suited Europeans mixing freely with the teeming multitude of Indians in their freshly ironed white dhotis. The entire crowd would gather under Adyar's vast Banyan tree for lectures, with Leadbeater and Besant installed in comfortable thrones, shaded from the occasional intrusive sunbeam by a collection of parasols, framing their heads behind. Theosophical and media representatives alike were excited by the auspiciousness of the occasion, and the rumour spread that great revelations were to be expected – perhaps even a personal visit from the Masters. Much attention, of course, was focussed on the figure of Krishnamurti, and the press were hungry for juicy snippets about the coming messiah. These were teasingly released to them by a hyperbolic Besant.

Much to everybody's disappointment, the Convention closed without any great supernatural extravaganza having occurred, though the sheeting rain and wind was drama enough for many of the 3000 strong crowd who, now damp and deflated, began to pack their bags. The following day, however, marked the opening of the Star Congress; it was also 28 December which, as any who recalled the 'pentecostal' incident of 1911 would endorse, was the most likely date in the Theosophical calender for wonders to manifest themselves. Star members were not to be disappointed, because there followed what was to be the latest in Krishna's string of theatrical revelations and, to many, the most exciting yet. It occurred soon after 8 a.m., at the end of Krishna's opening talk under the banyan tree. The amplified public address system – the first ever to be used in India – had been switched off, and dark rain-clouds tumbled across the sky. The slender young leader was addressing his people in an 'exquisitely sweet yet powerful tone',[22] about the World Teacher and his intentions for the planet. 'He comes only to those who want, who desire, who long,' he said. Then he appeared to pause, as if taken by some new inspiration, before continuing with a completely different vocal timbre, more resonant and deliberate. 'And I come for those who want sympathy, who want happiness, who are longing to be released, who are longing to find happiness in all things. I come to reform and not to tear down, I come not to destroy but to build.' Most critically, he had switched from speaking in the third person to the first. After these two concluding sentences, he returned to his seat in silence.

Many witnesses at the time felt a thrilling shiver, not just at the change of tone, but at what seemed to be a sudden magic in the air, much as had occurred in 1911. Balfour-Clarke still swore by the event at the age of ninety-one, as did Mary Lutyens. Others spoke of a holy presence descending upon Krishna, and a radiant, universal love shining from his eyes. Wedgwood and Arundale, claimed to notice no change at all and said they thought Krishna had merely been quoting scripture. The newspaper reporters also failed to notice the divine descent, though, when later informed of it by Besant, were quick to give it their full attention.

Annie was in no doubt as to what had occurred: 'that event marked the definite consecration of the chosen vehicle ... the coming has begun.'[23] On other occasions she spoke repeatedly of 'the voice', not heard in this world for 2000 years, now ringing out once more to the ears of mankind. Her enthusiasm knew no bounds, nor did Lady Emily's, who wrote, 'The world has changed for us since the morning of 28 of December. For us a new Christmas Day has dawned ... The night of the world is over, the new and glorious Day of the Lord has dawned.'[24] This was music to the ears of millenarian optimists and all those who dreamt of a glorious new age.

Leadbeater, though moved to concur with Besant that Krishna had been overshadowed briefly by a celestial entity, urged caution. He was not of a mind to tolerate the hysterical pronouncements of elderly ladies. There had been no great drama, he wrote, no opening of the heavens and no Day of Judgment. The Lord Maitreya was 'a very busy person' and could only afford to enter Krishnaji infrequently and for short spells, as he had, admittedly, on 28 December, both in 1925 and 1911. But, Leadbeater was firm in pointing out, this did not mean that everything Krishna now said was to be interpreted as the Word of the Lord. At all events 'rabid sensationalism' should be avoided, and if asked whether the Christ has come, members would be best advised to answer, 'Not in the sense in which you now mean.'[25]

Krishna himself believed he had entered into a new dimension that morning. Immediately after taking his seat he was questioned by Besant, and replied that he remembered nothing of what he had said, but felt dizzy, as if having woken from a dream. Later, he felt more certain that he had been divinely inspired and told people both publicly and privately that his personality seemed to have been cleaned out of him, so that he felt like a shell, or a vase – or, perhaps, a Vehicle. But, like Leadbeater, he steered away from extravagant pronouncements and did not use the incident to stir up wild expectations.

Rosalind Williams' daughter claims that her mother was told by Krishna, before going out to give the talk, 'You watch! I'm going to show them something.'[26] This would imply that the whole incident was manufactured for effect. Krishna was, perhaps, fired by the auspiciousness of the date and the anticipation of his audience; but he was also riding high on a wave of new insight since the death of Nitya. Perhaps a combination of the two led to his adoption of the messianic style that morning. It was certainly not a pose he was to maintain for long, as his oracular manner of speaking was soon to be replaced by a more down-to-earth form of teaching. He was to abandon biblical parables and verses in favour of straightforward prose, stripped of artificial solemnity.

While Krishna grew ever more divine in the eyes of ordinary Theosophists, and was thus elevated onto a pedestal, the senior management of the Society that upheld him grew infested with jealousy, doubt and conspiracy. Adyar at the time of the Jubilee Convention was hotbed of power lust and personal schisms. The most clearly-defined feud was that between Leadbeater on the one hand, and Bishops Arundale and Wedgwood on the other. Leadbeater had been seething ever since the pronouncements at the summer camp, because his advice had not been sought in advance either by the errant bishops or his old ally, Besant, and he now chose to sulk in haughty nonchalance. There was also tension between the three Liberal Catholic bishops and Krishna, whose recent growth in stature had threatened to throw them all in the shadow. In her heyday, Annie Besant might have risen to the occasion and been able to reconcile the warring parties, but she was beginning to lose her lust for battle. She did make one attempt to draw everyone together, inviting Krishna to join her, Leadbeater and the participants in the events at Huizen, for a meeting in her rooms. There she asked Krishna straight if he would accept the assembled company as his disciples. He replied flatly that he would not, with the exception, perhaps, of Annie herself. The dilemma she now faced ate at her metal, and she seriously considered resigning her presidency to retire and follow Krishna as an ordinary disciple. Leadbeater managed to dissuade her, although Arundale said the Masters would approve her resignation so long as she appointed himself as the new President. The audacity of this piece of self-advancement infuriated Krishna.

Another blow to Besant came in 1925, when the Czech section of the Theosophical Society defected in protest at the apparent chaos of the Adyar leadership. In fairness to Besant, her attention at this time was distracted by other pressing business, most importantly her work for Indian Home Rule. She had been in constant touch with Indian leaders and British cabinet ministers in order to put together a constitution for the subcontinent that would be acceptable to London. The result was her Commonwealth of India Bill, which she presented to the British Labour Party with limited success. The plan fell foul of Gandhi, however, who now contended that a free India should not be subject to British sovereignty, and Besant's grand scheme for India floundered. The residue of her political influence was fast draining away.

Her closing years can hardly be described as restful. The laurels she received, both for public and Theosophical work, were paper thin, and reflected no concrete achievement of her cherished ambitions. To the end she was dogged by controversy, surrounded by factionism, and faced with one insoluble challenge after another. Perhaps this was the fate she carved for herself; and, if people are the guiding force of their own destinies, the ultimate fate of Annie Besant might tell us more about her true nature than the scores of articulate volumes that issued from her pen.

9

Fires in the Forest

———————— ✳ ————————

Krishna's inner circle had long considered him as perfect a specimen of mortal man as ever breathed, but their own humble judgment, after the morning of 28 December 1925, appeared to have been endorsed by a higher authority. Krishna had at last been appointed the Lord's mouthpiece, his words no longer mere intimations of a greater Truth, but that very Truth itself. His inner development, in their eyes, was matched only by his outer beauty and poise. He was the very picture of a spiritual leader, every inch the young prophet-prince, and the Indian silks he would sometimes don for private talks were not far removed, in their eyes, from the oriental attire they associated with the apotheosised Christ, as glorified in stained glass windows throughout the western world.

Krishna was wary of the glamorous image that was suddenly his for the taking, and realised that a personality cult was developing around him. His initial response was to want to withdraw from the world altogether, and become a renunciate along the lines of the traditional Hindu sannyasi. But he was also developing a taste for the speaker's platform and a compulsion to share his vision.

The summer following his dramatic speech at Adyar he gathered with his friends once again at Castle Eerde for a private retreat before the onset of the 1926 Ommen camp. Baron van Pallandt's antiquated former home was fast being modernised into a suitable headquarters for the World Teacher, with new plumbing, electricity and proper sanitary facilities – an improvement on the previous toilets that opened straight down into the surrounding moat. Major conversions of the outbuildings were also under way so as to provide more accommodation, while the palatial ambience of the main house was left intact.

Krishna and his select group enjoyed an idyllic fortnight of warm summer weather and spiritual well-being at Eerde. Although he was recovering from a severe chest infection, he gave daily talks which stunned even his long-time admirers by their insight and authority. Their message was that the attainment of the 'Kingdom' (heaven, enlightenment) was not dependent on a prescribed path, was not in Tibet or some far off celestial land, but was immediately perceptible within each individual, here and now.[1] Several of those attending wrote in letters and diaries of how Krishna appeared to be mysteriously imbued with divinity when he talked, so that he spoke not for himself but for, and as, Christ. Lady Emily went so far as to write rapturously to Jinarajadasa, that 'Krishna has become the Lord.'[2]

Annie Besant arrived with Wedgwood in time for the official opening of the Ommen gathering on 23 July, and therefore did not witness Krishna's inspiring prelude at Eerde. Her absence allowed him greater freedom of expression, as Annie was the one person within the Theosophical movement Krishna still shied from upsetting. He had great affection and respect for her, and could not shake off his childhood habit of wanting to please her at all costs.

The administrative arrangements at Ommen had changed beyond recognition since the small gathering in 1924, when Krishna had last attended. Two thousand visitors 'of every conceivable nationality'[3] were now expected, and extra ferries had to be scheduled from the British Isles to the Hook of Holland to accommodate the influx. The pilgrims were to be greeted by 'a model camp city in the midst of uninhabited forests and fields'.[4] Lines of tents and marquees were marshalled along a grid of avenues that struck some as resembling a modern American metropolis, rather than an experiment in close-to-nature living. It was a model of good organisation, with a range of sleeping accommodation, dining areas, vast lecture tents, kitchens, wash-rooms, a post office, shop, medical hut and information bureau. Photographs of the event reveal the extent of work undertaken in advance of the opening: huge cooking boilers were flanked by trolleys, operated on a rail network that linked them direct to every service point in the dining marquees. Purpose-built brick pathways ensured that the mud would not overwhelm pedestrian traffic, and hot water pipes, connected to the bathrooms, were embedded in trenches eight foot deep. The smooth running of the event was safeguarded by a published set of camp rules, and aided by the sense of goodwill that pervaded the whole scene, with everyone helping each other, offering to interpret on behalf of the linguistically challenged, or guide the geographically baffled.

The highlight of every day was the evening talk given by Krishna in a circular amphitheatre built out of pine logs. A huge bonfire was constructed in the centre, around which everyone would assemble at least an hour before the talk, entertaining themselves with folk songs. Krishna would then arrive with Annie Besant, and ceremoniously light the fire, before taking the stand. Aside from transporting his followers into a meditative frame of mind, the bonfire ambience appeared to suit Krishna's temperament as a speaker, and he never talked better than at these gatherings. At the end of the evening, as the great fire lay in a heap of embers, he would chant Sanskrit verses, cutting an exotic figure in his tailored akhan, before returning to his star-shaped log throne for a final few minutes of silent contemplation. The whole camp-fire ritual was very effective and much enjoyed by the crowd for the atmosphere it created, though it could be said that Krishna's adherence to it, now and in future years, contradicted his own firm denigration of religious ceremony.

Expectations were high at Ommen for new manifestations of the Lord's voice, and the general mood of piousness encouraged participants to feel that they were living on a privileged spiritual plane. One slightly sceptical visitor at Ommen described the reverential atmosphere and the behaviour it engendered, observing people 'discussing under old trees the deepest problems of life, and greeting one another with smiles of forgiveness and looks of understanding ... They seemed incapable of saying any but the holiest of things ... They look deep into your eyes when they talk to you; they have a weakness for sandals, for clothes without any particular distinction of shape, for the rougher kind of textiles ... The men affect long hair, while the women keep theirs short

... They did their best to copy Krishnamurti, to be kind and sincere or to make jokes and show how jolly they were.'[5]

In such surroundings, Krishna had no difficulty commanding the total attention of his listeners, although he was aware of the danger that his message might leave less of an imprint than the hypnotising effect of his presence. He warned his audience not to mould an artificial World Teacher out of their aspirations, and begged them to open their minds to a new understanding, to be prepared for the unexpected. But the highly lyrical style he adopted probably had the opposite effect. The audience were entranced by his poetic imagery, by his calls for them to join him in his garden, his kingdom, to unite with him, to become, each in themselves, the 'Redeemer of Mankind', the 'World Lover'.[6] They swooned at his descriptions of the source, the Truth that he had touched, the beauty, perfection and liberation. Best of all were the moments when he was apparently transfigured, and stepped unmistakably into the role of World Teacher, along the same lines as at Adyar on 28 December. At these points, usually towards the end of a talk, his language took on a hieratic quality, resembling familiar sacred utterances, such as the Beatitudes of Jesus:

And if you would walk, you must walk with me.
If you would understand, you must look through my mind.
If you would feel, you must look through my heart.
And because I really love, I want you to love.
Because I really feel, I want you to feel.
Because I hold everything dear, I want you to hold all things dear.
Because I want to protect, you should protect.
And this is the only life worth living, and the only Happiness worth
  possessing.[7]

Only Wedgwood remained unimpressed by Krishna's performance at Ommen, and attempted to persuade Annie Besant that the so-called divine inspiration of her protégé was nothing more than the clever work of a 'black' magician operating on the astral plane. His attempts to woo the President over to his and Arundale's camp were doomed to fail, as he had underestimated her loyalty to Krishna. It also later emerged that he had very few grounds on which to rest his pontifications, and that if anyone was hiding shady secrets, it was himself. In 1922, in the midst of a storm of homosexual allegations, Wedgwood had fled England and settled in Paris, abandoning his ecclesiastical position temporarily to pursue a life of sexual excess. There he fell victim to a cocaine addiction, also supplying his boyfriends with the drug, and took to smuggling it past the authorities inside his crozier.[8]

Annie accompanied Krishna to the United States in 1926, partly to proclaim her glorious message in the country she had not visited since the year her protégé had been 'discovered', and also to survey the Ojai valley, about which she heard so much. She remained in California with Krishna between October 1926, after completing her tour of lectures, and April 1927. Although the accommodation at Arya Vihara was still rather spartan, it was an idyllic, peaceful spell for both of them, and they were joined by members of the Lutyens family, together with Rajagopal and Rosalind Williams.

When Krishna arrived in New York with Annie Besant on 26 August 1926 he was all but overwhelmed at the docks by an army of journalists, eager to catch his first words. There was even speculation as to how the Customs authorities should handle the entry of this allegedly divine visitor. Was it appropriate, it was asked, to examine his luggage, like that of an ordinary human? Reporters were subsequently impressed by Krishna's calm and intelligent responses at news conferences, gracefully deflecting their attempts to ensnare him with difficult questions, and confirming their assessment that he bore the classic attributes of an anglicised Indian aristocrat. At all times Krishna behaved with poise and sobriety, and there were no signs of his being overwhelmed by a powerful supernatural force, much to the disappointment of those hoping for a scoop. But his handsome dignity concealed feelings of distaste at the level of sensationalism afforded him; and chores, such as laying the foundation stone of a new $250,000 Theosophical building near Chicago, he found acutely embarrassing.

The press, in America and elsewhere, were equally interested in Annie Besant, who for so long had provided rip-roaring fodder for their columns.

All her religious lectures were now dedicated to the World Teacher issue, her words carrying greater certainty than ever before. The fulfilment of her prophecy and labours was at hand, she believed; it was also the logical culmination of Madame Blavatsky's endeavours, and the achievement of Theosophy's long-term goal which, as Blavatsky had disclosed in *The Key to Theosophy*, was that 'earth will be a heaven in the twenty-first century.' The Wisdom of God (literally 'theosophy') had been retrieved and under the keystone leadership of the divine representative, Krishnamurti, it was once again to be revealed to the world. Her bold declarations about the coming civilisation and the emergence of a new race type gave rise to newspaper articles that teetered uncomfortably between wry sarcasm at her madness, and serious consideration of a compelling new theory. Despite her age, peculiar oriental attire and decades of adverse publicity, it was impossible to write Annie Besant off as a crackpot.

The United States was enjoying a decade of meteoric careers and news sensations and Krishna, the would-be messiah, cut exactly the right profile to ensure himself a place in the nation's hall of stardom. His filmstar looks, 'Bond Street clothes and Valentino hair-cut' added more spice to the story, as image merchants had begun to recognise the selling power of a handsome public face. Californian girls, or 'flappers', flocked to him, and he was frequently showered with flowers, or dragged, gauche and unwilling, onto the dance floor.

From this time onwards, well-known celebrities were drawn into Krishna's circle, adding to his allure and public credibility. Montgomery Flagg, the popular American painter, announced his conversion, while the philosophical essayist Kahlil Gibran stated that when he first met Krishna in 1927 he said to himself, 'Surely the Lord of Love has come.'[9] The film actor John Barrymore, who had an interest in Buddhism, took Krishna to the major Hollywood studios, introducing him to directors and movie stars. It was even suggested that he might take a role in an epic movie, perhaps acting the part of the Buddha. George Bernard Shaw said that Krishna was not only the most beautiful man he had ever seen, but 'a religious teacher of the greatest distinction, who is listened to with profit and assent by members of all churches and sects'.[10] And this from the same man who had poured scorn on Annie Besant's conversion to Theosophy four decades previously.

By the autumn of 1926 Krishna made it clear to Annie Besant that a metamorphosis had taken place. His former personality had been stripped away, leaving him in a state of constant and irreversible union with the godhead. The time for intermittent dramas and sensational revelations was passed. Henceforth he would be, in his every word, act and breath, an incarnation of the divinity he had come to realise at the very depths of his being – his 'Beloved'. As he was to say in an interview, 'Krishnamurti as such no longer exists. As the river enters the sea and loses itself in the sea, so Krishnamurti has entered into that Life which is represented by some as The Christ, by others as The Buddha, by others still, as the Lord Maitreya. Hence Krishnamurti as an entity fully developed has entered into that Sea of Life and is the Teacher.'[11]

George Arundale fumed but kept his silence to protect the Society from adverse publicity. Jinarajadasa also had doubts, but was torn by a deep personal affection for Krishna. Annie Besant, however, stood by her boy, and open-heartedly entered into the spirit of his claim. The time was ripe, she considered, to broadcast the good news officially to the world, and on 14 January 1927 she made a sensational announcement to the Associated Press of America, a statement that was to receive widespread media attention: 'The Divine Spirit has descended once more on a man, Krishnamurti, one who in his life is literally perfect, as those who know him can testify . . . The World Teacher is here.'[12]

The claim that he had achieved union with his Beloved was, from this time, the principle upon which Krishnamurti's authority as a teacher rested. Over the years his terminology would change, and the word 'Beloved' would be replaced by other descriptions, all of them approximations. The philosophical notion of temporal man blending his consciousness with that of a mystical entity, portrayed in the language of physical love, is common to religious cultures around the world and through the ages.[13] On a certain level, becoming one with his Beloved meant simply, to some followers, that Krishnamurti had become Christ, the Buddha, the Lord Maitreya, or whatever name one chose to give the Saviour of mankind. Theosophists who still held to the notion of a personal god now assumed he had ascended to his throne, thus neatly fulfilling their leaders' prophecies.

Krishna did not entirely dispute this interpretation, though he baffled his idolisers by telling them that the same union could be achieved by themselves and everyone else. Divinity was the birthright of all people, the goal of spiritual life which, when attained, would transform them too into Christ, into World Teachers. The Beloved was not so much a named entity, to be worshipped, prayed to, or meditated upon. It was a spiritual state, a condition of man made perfect, to which one should aspire; and the attainment of this condition would dissolve the personal longings of the aspirant; his consciousness would be fully merged with life itself, impersonal and universal. This was Krishna's Kingdom of Happiness, his garden, and his World Teacher. 'It is no good asking me who is the Beloved. Of what use is explanation? For you will not understand the Beloved until you are able to see Him in every animal, in every blade of grass, in every person that is suffering, in every individual.'[14] Having achieved the state himself, he felt that he had, literally, become Christ, the Buddha, the World Teacher. This line of thought was in accordance with traditional Hindu teaching, one of the central tenets of which is summarised in the statement, 'Thou art That,' meaning that within every individual there exists an impersonal self that is one with God and all creation. 'Thou art That' is the essence of Krishna's message at this time: the godhead, the Beloved *is* the impersonal you – the perfect and incorruptible element of life within you. As he was to say at a lecture in 1927, 'There is no God except a man purified, and there is no Power exterior to himself. There is no heaven or hell, good or evil, except that which he creates himself, and hence man is solely responsible to himself and to no one else.'[15]

A Seattle poster of this period describes Krishnamurti as 'Poet, Philosopher and Friend', which indicates that he felt poetry was to become an important medium for his teachings. The winter months at Ojai, 1926–7, were a fruitful period for his poetic output, and the relative calm of his surroundings allowed him the space to contemplate how best to translate the enormity of his realisation into language. Over the next four years he was to write a good deal of poetry, finally abandoning it as a medium in 1931. Most of his work was published in Theosophical magazines, and is tailored for a readership of disciples. His principal poems, each ultimately published as a volume in its own right (*The Search*, *The Immortal Friend*, and *The Song of Life*), are full of romantic enthusiasm for their subject (the Beloved), and rely heavily on metaphors from nature. He had a good command of language and his use of imagery is heartfelt, if a little simplistic, yet one cannot describe him as a significant poet, as there is lacking that subtle connection of sound, language and imagery so necessary for poetry's effect. The impulse behind them is sincere, and the imagination fertile; but there is a sense that no amount of eulogising can ever do justice to his vision, and so the poems ramble on and on, to the extent that they become vapid and repetitive. At times, the influence of *The Song of Solomon*, his favourite biblical text, is impossible to ignore, and one feels that he is trying too hard to fill the role of mystic poet, in the same genre as Kahlil Gibran, whose *The Prophet* was first published in 1926.

As in his earlier lyrical prose, he employs sensuous terms in his attempts to define spiritual ecstasy:

> *My soul grasped the infinite simplicity*
> *Of Truth.*
> *I lost myself in that happiness.*
> *Thou art the Truth,*
> *Thou art the Law,*
> *Thou art the Refuge,*
> *Thou art the Guide,*
> *The Companion and the Beloved.*
> *Thou hast ravished my heart,*
> *Thou hast conquered my soul,*
> *In Thee have I found my comfort,*
> *In Thee is my truth established.*
> . . .
> *I saw Him look at me,*
> *And my vision became vast.*
> *My eyes saw and my mind understood.*
> *My heart embraced all things,*
> *For a new love was born unto me.*
> *A new glory thrilled my being,*
> *For he walked before me, and I followed, my head high.*
> . . .

Oh! The sea
Has entered my heart.
In a day,
I am living a hundred summers.
O friend,
I behold my face in thee,
The face of my well-Beloved.
This is the song of my love.[16]

Annie was entranced by Ojai, and decided to go public in her pro-motion of it as the cradle of a new civilisation, the sixth sub-race. The most important first step was to raise money to purchase more land, and to this end she started the Happy Valley Foundation. The aim was to buy 465 acres in the Upper Valley, near to Krishna's home, and a further 300 at the lower end. These plots would serve a new colony of residents and would allow for an annual Star Camp, to complement the summer gatherings at Ommen. Settlers sympathetic to the project were now called upon to consider emigration. Her plan for the colonisers, she wrote, was that their 'bodies, emotions and minds shall be trained and disciplined in daily life into health, poise and high intelligence, fit dwellings for the Divine Life, developing the spirit of Brotherhood practically in everyday arrangements and methods of living'.[17] This extended to a new form of education – a notion close to Krishna's own heart – and a socialist style of economics, based on cooperation rather than private enterprise. Her model citizen for this new state bore all the hallmarks of an ancient Greek polymath: democratic, physically tuned, intellectually cultivated and humanistic.

Following the acquisition of land, she planned to begin a massive building project that would include a school, college, library, social club, temple, art centre, Co-Masonic Lodge, theatre and playground, as well as dwellings. It was an overly ambitious project for a Society that had already sucked its members dry for funds to pay for other projects. Nevertheless, it might well have succeeded had it not been for the seismic events of 1929, the rumblings of which were as yet beyond the horizon. As it was, the money required to purchase the Happy Valley outright was not fully obtained until twenty years later, by which time Annie

Besant's dream, and the great woman herself, had passed into history.

Financial and administrative matters within the Order of the Star in the East were now the domain of Rajagopal, who had taken on the role of organising secretary since the death of Nitya. It was a sound appointment, as he possessed both an instinct for business and an eye for detail. Indeed, the smooth running of the Star Camps, the lecture tours, together with the production and sales of Krishna's published books, were the responsibility of Rajagopal. He was a close friend and a dedicated worker, but his passion for order and planning led him to be intolerant of others less organised than himself. As the years went by he developed an obsessive need to control Krishnamurti's affairs, a compulsion that others in the circle found too forceful and overbearing. What had started out as an arrangement to protect Krishna from too much personal involvement in material and financial affairs, ultimately led to an ugly situation whereby Krishnamurti had to risk quarrelling with Rajagopal in order to determine his own freedom of movement.

But Krishna's relationship with Rajagopal was complicated by another factor. Rajagopal had fallen in love with Rosalind Williams and, although she had warm feelings for him, in no sense did she reciprocate his love, finding him too earnest and scrupulous. Meanwhile, she continued to enjoy a close relationship with Krishna, forming part of his inner circle, especially in America, where rumours soon began to spread about the pretty blonde at the messiah's side. Rosalind was almost certainly encouraged by Annie Besant to accept a proposal of marriage from Rajagopal in order to scotch these speculations. Annie was fully aware of how well Krishna had been cared for by Rosalind and Nitya, and hoped that the threesome might continue with Rajagopal taking Nitya's place, as he had in other departments of OSE work. The marriage would serve Krishna, remove the element of scandal, and make Rajagopal the happiest of men. Rosalind's doubts were the only complication, but somehow she was persuaded to agree to the proposal – either by the force of Annie's personality, the allure of a life spent near Krishna, or a moment of extreme fondness for Rajagopal. They were legally married at a London registry office on 3 October 1927, and subsequently blessed in a Liberal Catholic Church, surrounded by all the trappings of a traditional white wedding. Krishna, who had so often expressed his distaste for the institution of marriage, and had nothing but scorn for LCC ceremonies, did not attend. And so, for one day, at least, Rajagopal's star shone. But he was all too soon to be eclipsed once again, and this time the love of Rosalind was at stake. Theirs was not to be a happy marriage, and they were to spend long periods apart, because of the demands of Rajagopal's work, from the very start of their life together.

In June 1927, Krishna gathered once again at Castle Eerde, this time with a larger circle of friends, for a period of teaching and reflection before the main Ommen camp commenced. Annie Besant had pointedly been asked not to attend, as Krishna wanted to speak freely about the issue of liberation, particularly with regard to his own release from bondage, and not be dragged into stale discussions about Root Races or the fulfilment of old prophecies. By excluding Annie he broke her heart, but felt it was a necessary measure in order to give himself a clear field. The time had come for a watershed.

A sense of great expectation pervaded the scene around the huge forest bonfire this year. Several witnesses recalled the reverential hush as Krishna took the stand, not surprisingly, as many believed they were about to hear the words of God, a contemporary re-enactment of legendary events on a par with the Sermon on the Mount. Krishna was straightforward and confident. He told his audience to reject spiritual authorities, including himself. If he were to perform miracles in their presence, then they would believe; but believe what? In the divinity of the man Krishnamurti? The consequences of such a belief were plain to him, and he repeated them again and again to audiences for the rest of his life, as his disciples struggled to reconcile their admiration for the teacher with their desire to follow his teaching. 'When Krishnamurti dies, which is inevitable, you will make a religion, you will set about forming rules in your minds, because the individual, Krishnamurti, has represented to you the Truth. So you will build a temple, you will then begin to have ceremonies, to invent phrases, dogmas, systems of belief, creeds, and to create philosophies. If you build great foundations upon me, the individual, you will be caught in that house, in that temple, and so you will have to have another Teacher come and extricate you from that temple, pull you out of that narrowness in order to liberate you. But the human mind is such that you will build another temple round Him, and so it will go on and on.'[18]

Dogmas, ceremonies and rule-books must be renounced, as must priests and gods. They are a false comfort, a crutch, a 'spiritual drug store', and they have dislocated man from the ground of his being. The way to shed these impediments, Krishna maintained, was to invite doubt. 'I hold that doubt is essential for the discovering and the understanding of the Truth ... examine yourselves by that and scrutinize the very knowledge which you are supposed to have gained. For I tell you that orthodoxy is set up when the mind and the heart are in decay ... But when you invite doubt, it is as the rain that washes away the dust of tradition, which is the dust of the ages, the dust of belief, and leaves you certain of those things which are essential.'[19] It was only through doubting that he himself had shed the bondage of his training and expectations. Liberation, was a perpetual and incorruptible state which could be attained only by peeling back the layers of acquired knowledge, by continual questioning, doubting.

The only qualification he claimed, in being able to address people in this way, was as witness to an altogether different consciousness. He explained repeatedly how he had merged with his Beloved and entered 'into the flame', often resorting to the same sort of terminology he used in his ecstatic poems of the time. There was nothing special about himself, he maintained, except that he had already arrived, and could therefore play the agent who would raise the rest of mankind to divinity. As such, he had no hesitation in assuming the title World Teacher. As he put it, in all frankness: 'I could not have said last year, as I can say now, that I am the Teacher, for had I said it then it would not have been sincere, it would have been untrue ... But now I can say it. I have become one with the Beloved. I have been made simple. I have become glorified because of Him ... My purpose is ... to give waters that shall wash away your sorrows, your petty tyrannies, your limitations, so that you will be free, so that you will eventually join that ocean where there is no limitation, where there is the Beloved.'[20]

The Theosophical Society's old guard was much disturbed by the line being taken by their star mascot. The years of lectures and scores of Society publications had left them philosophically rigid, entrenched in a dogmatic matrix of their own creation. Krishna was rejecting the arduous Path of Discipleship, stating that to focus on the Masters was an irrelevant distraction, and he poured scorn on the notion that there were prizes to be gained along the spiritual path, like a schoolboy's rewards for good behaviour. Senior Theosophists felt they were being rendered obsolete, and even ridiculed. They could not understand why Krishna insisted on stepping out of the current, when so perfect a platform had been prepared for him.

A frequent criticism levelled at him was that he failed to take into account the wounded feelings of those who had looked after him for so many years and, indeed, those who had been swept along by the movement he had, until recently, advocated. He was incompassionate, many complained, and he refused to understand that not all people could achieve the giant leap of faith he described, but needed help, guidance, and role-models to set them on their way. This complaint was to surface regularly in Krishnamurti's question and answer sessions for the next five decades. In 1927 he chose to rebuff the accusations with a medical metaphor: 'A surgeon who sees a disease that is eating up a man, says, In order to cure him, I must operate. Another less experienced doctor comes, feeds him and lulls him to sleep. Which would you call the more compassionate? You want comfort, that comfort which is born of decay.'[21] At times, however, his surgeon's knife cut too deep, and injured even his most loyal supporters, such as Annie Besant. Immediately after the Ommen camp, in 1927, he addressed a gathering of camp workers, who had been prevented from attending the main event. There is no record of the precise text because it was most likely withdrawn from the printing press by the President. But there are reports from eye-witnesses, who say that Krishna openly questioned the existence of the Masters, joked that he had never been able to read a Theosophical book, and could not understand the Society's 'jargon' anyway.[22]

It was the flippancy of his remarks that hurt Annie more than the point he was trying to make. She also feared that Krishna was now only interested in addressing young people and disillusioned Theosophists. She had some grounds, but only in so far as Krishna was tired of Theosophists' persistent expectations and predictable questions. He felt trapped by their idolisation and the way they twisted his words to fit their perspective. They did not want to reject him, while at the same time they refused to listen to his new message. The result was a form of spiritual deal – they attempted to haggle with him, accepting morsels of his teachings, if he would accept portions of their ideology. Even his open revolt against their orthodoxy was interpreted by some as saintly, a parallel of Christ's rage in the temple. Krishna thought they were the blind seeking ever deeper blindness. He certainly preferred talking to the young and those not affiliated to religious organisations. They were more accepting and less bound by preconceptions. Unlike Theosophists, they did not believe that they were a specially chosen band, deserving droplets of wisdom that were to be denied spiritual commoners. He could relax with them and adopt a less formal speaking manner.

Annie's indignance was compounded by the hurt Krishna caused by not inviting her to Eerde, especially as she had for some while thought that some tremendous 'climax' was going to be revealed at this gathering: 'Silly of me, perhaps, but I did so want to be there. I don't think you know how much I love you, dear, because I don't hang around you and fuss. So I have done my little weeps all by myself over my bad karma. You didn't know I was such a goose, did you.'[23] It was not long before rumours began to circulate about a breach between the Order of the Star in the East and the Theosophical Society, which meant between the Vehicle and the President. Arundale and Wedgwood quietly encouraged the split by passing messages to Annie from the Masters, saying that someone else would have to be found if Krishna did not mend his ways, and that Nitya would certainly have lived had it not been for his elder brother's disbelief.[24]

It was symptomatic of the level of pressure put on Besant by the anti-Krishna element, that on 25 March 1928 she publicly announced the launch of a new mission, that of the World Mother. This celestial female entity, who had at one time been the Virgin Mary, was now said to have descended into the body of none other than Rukmini Arundale, the young wife of Krishna's bitter opponent, who had risen so rapidly to occult stardom. The project was intended to divert interest away from the World Teacher and provide a reserve Vehicle should Krishna continue on his maverick course. The notion of a sacred maternal entity also fitted neatly into traditional Hindu philosophy, which held that the

Divine Mother was a manifestation of Shakti, the female energy respon-sible for dynamic life. It was declared that the World Mother would act in association with the World Teacher, her feminine energy complement-ing his masculine, true to the classical model of Shiva and Shakti, whose mystical blending was the principle on which all creation rested. Krishna ridiculed the whole idea, and the press was similarly dismissive, deriding Besant for having stretched their imagination with one sensation too many. Consequently, the World Mother project slid into obscurity, and in later years Rukmini referred to the whole incident as an embarrassing mistake.

Krishna's enthusiasm to embrace a new outlook and be rid of past spectres was carried through into the administrative set-up of his Order. It was no longer to be called the Order of the Star in the East, which inferred an imminent dawn and an oriental core, but renamed the Order of the Star, now that the star had truly risen and shone on west and east alike. Similarly, the *Herald of the Star* was given the new title, the *Star Review*. The changes were outlined in an article (anonymous, but probably penned by Rajagopal) entitled 'Ring out the Old, Ring in the New'.[25] The aims of the new magazine were stated, alongside a brief and rather dismissive history of the old. The emphasis on ceremonial was to be withdrawn, as were grades, badges, ribbons and other 'non-essentials'.

Leadbeater, typically, took a diplomatic stance in public and attempted to smooth over differences between Krishna and Theosophy's leaders by maintaining that there were 'twin paths' to 'the glory of the mountain-top', one for the mystic and one for the occultist, neither better than the other, and both leading to the same end.[26] But privately he confided to a Liberal Catholic bishop that 'the Coming has gone wrong'.[27] One therefore wonders how sincere he was being in 1928, when he gave the impression to Krishnamurti that he agreed with the latter's teachings 'to an astonishing extent'.[28] It would not be the first time Leadbeater had slipped like an eel beneath the moving waters of Theosophy.

During the winter of 1927–8 Krishna was in India, where he undertook a punishing tour of lectures and attended various Theosophical and Star conventions. He then returned to Europe before progressing to Cali-fornia for the first Ojai Star Camp. He had settled comfortably into his role as a public speaker, actively enjoying the media interviews he had previously dreaded, referring to them as 'having buckets let down into [his] well'.[29] Before the beginning of the Ojai camp he addressed an audience of 16,000 at the Hollywood Bowl and a month later, in Paris, spoke in fluent French on the radio to around 2 million listeners. The Ojai gathering was successful, all the administrative difficulties having been ironed out efficiently by Rajagopal, and as at Ommen, the camp-fire ritual was used to enhance the atmosphere and a sense of unity. Every word Krishna uttered, either in talks, interviews or formalised conversations, was now recorded by professional stenographers, and later rendered into print before being sold to a burgeoning mass of followers. The organisation responsible for the distribution of most of this material was the Star Publishing Trust, based at Eerde.

During July 1928, in the weeks building up to the next Ommen gathering, Annie Besant collapsed and was pronounced unfit to continue her work or attend Theosophical meetings for the foreseeable future. There were fears for the old lady's life. The reason given was a severe cold, which was true, but her condition was exacerbated by stress. She was worn out by the rifts within her Society, and realised that the World Mother project had served only to cause further divisions of loyalty. Her understanding of Krishna had also reached a low-point. He had attempted to communicate his feelings to her at various times, and she had attended enough of his talks to gather the gist of his new direction, but it was only now that the crucial implication of his message finally hit home. He was rejecting the role of an enthroned messiah, together with the organisation she had spent the last thirty years constructing. The shock of this realisation affected her mind, and for several days she apparently recognised no one and could hardly string a sentence together. Wedgwood presided in her place at the European Congress held in Brussels on 27 July, and arrangements were made to hold the Ommen gathering without her participation.

When Krishna therefore spoke to his audiences at Eerde and Ommen in 1928, he did so free from the restraint of her presence, and there were dark fears in orthodox circles as to what he might say. The rumblings of discord within the Society's ranks were echoed by rain-clouds and thunder above the tents and marquees at Ommen that year. Three thousand people had journeyed to Holland, their number swelled by prominent public figures, such as the conductor Leopold Stokowski, with whom Krishna had a formal dialogue on the nature of inspiration, Sir Roderick Jones, the head of Reuters, and several British members of parliament. Inevitably, much of what Krishna said at his talks was a repetition of the previous year's material, but delivered with greater force and articulateness. His question and answer sessions were particularly hard-hitting, leaving little room for compromise. Lady Emily noted with personal sympathy that his words left many followers 'naked and alone, their foundations shattered'.[30] By contrast, his camp-fire talks were more poetic and drew on a rich tapestry of metaphors. One legacy of his messianic training had been a mastering of the art of parable composition, and his use of illustrative imagery, though repetitive, was effective. Some dissenting listeners found his metaphors too misty and thought that he took refuge in allegorical gibberish when cornered by unanswerable questions. Others did not even need to understand, but enjoyed the mesmeric atmosphere that his poetic prose and handsome profile engendered on those summer evenings.

In response to queries about differences of opinion between the leaders of the Theosophical Society, he claimed that there had been no quarrelling, but bluntly asserted that those who opposed his views had 'stepped down the Truth' – a frequent metaphor of his, referring to the difference between electricity generated by the power station and that 'stepped down' for safe domestic use. For all their learning, compassion and their spiritual aspirations, he intimated, Theosophists were bound in a cage of their own making. 'Because I have been entangled in complexities, because I have been held in bondage, I urge you to escape into freedom. Because I have found a simple and direct path, I would tell you of it.'[31]

When pinned down, once again, to state categorically whether or not he was the Christ, he answered his questioner, 'Friend, if I say to you that I am, and another says to you that I am not the Christ – where will you be? Put aside the label, for that has no value. Drink the water if the water is clean. I say to you that I have that clean water.'[32] The great spiritual teachers of the past, he said, had not come to found religions but to free people from them. He was doing precisely the same. The Order of the Star was of no use if it became an end in itself, if it labelled itself as the organisation of Truth. The Order should only continue so long as it served as a bridge to 'help people cross the difficult stream of life'.[33] One can sense Krishna now finding himself in a doctrinal cul de sac so long as the Order of the Star continued its existence. Truth and organisation, according to his system, were incompatible bedmates.

By the autumn of 1928 Annie Besant had recovered her health and senses (although those opposed to Krishna maintained that her descent into senility had now begun), and was in a position to take whatever action her conscience as President, and as a devotee of Krishna, demanded. She outlined her most dramatic measure in a letter to Krishna, dated 30 October 1928: 'I am sure that it is better that all our students should devote themselves to the study of your works and ideals, and leave all the older teachings aside for the present. So I am suspending the ES [the Esoteric Section] altogether, indefinitely, leaving all teaching to you.' In the same vein, she banned the use of ceremonial at the Benares Convention in December, a move that pleased Krishna, while infuriating the Liberal Catholic element in the Society. By closing down the ES she was effectively silencing the doctrinal heart of the Theosophical Society, the inner core, whose secret machinations had been so lovingly cultured by Madame Blavatsky during her lifetime. It was an extraordinary display of Annie's devotion to Krishna; but it was also a responsible move from a leader who realised that her organisation was on the verge of losing its chief asset.

After an all-night conference with Besant, George Arundale grudgingly agreed to continue acknowledging Krishna, but only on the condition that there could be two paths open to Theosophists – Krishna's and his own, which would involve the LCC, ceremony and other occult disciplines of the Leadbeater tradition; 'I also have something to teach,' he indignantly informed Krishna when they met at the end of the year. Leadbeater himself characteristically took the middle line, ingratiating himself with Krishna by accepting the position of Australian National Organiser for the Order of the Star, while holding out for others' points of view: 'so long as each will do his own work along his own line, and not abuse others whose lines are different, they will all reach the same level.'[34] In public he put paid to any question of a schism by writing: 'I doubt whether there is anyone who knows Krishnaji better and loves him more reverently than I do ... So I ask you not to believe stories about quarrels, about separation, or any of the nonsense people talk. Krishnaji and I are bound together by a tie that nothing can break.'[35]

Despite the show of unity, members of the Order and the Society were listening for the most part to Krishna, not to their other leaders, and Krishna was denouncing Orders and Societies. Having peaked early in 1928, membership figures began to diminish in the wake of the charismatic teacher's remarks. Audiences at Krishna's talks, on the other hand, continued to swell.

He had come a great distance since his stirring calls to arms in the early 1920s, which had been influenced by Annie Besant's missionary zeal. There was not even a shadow of Victorian rhetoric in Krishna's prose, no hint of the 'Onward Christian Soldiers' spirit that had formed the backbone of his education. Gone were the political ambitions, the focussed goal of Universal Brotherhood, a Theosophical League of Nations, and the image of himself as a global keystone. Krishna had scaled his approach down to the individual. The world problem at large would only be solved, he maintained, at the level of the individual, and his or her personal realisation of Truth. Furthermore, his extravagant references to metaphysical entities and controlling powers operating on an occult plane had now all but vanished. His listeners still assumed that some evangelistic purpose underscored his appearances, and they questioned him about the nature of his mission, to which he replied, 'Why do you make it my mission and teaching? Isn't it what you people want? Don't you want to be free and happy? It isn't my mission. It is your mission. It is what you are seeking, and not what I am seeking ... So, as it is yours, my purpose is only to awaken that knowledge, that desire to discover for yourself.'[36] He had reduced his own role to that of a lamp, enlightening what was already there but could not be seen. In another favourite metaphor, which he continued to use until the 1980s, he likened himself to a flower – he had no more motive than the flower that opens to the sun and gives off its scent in accordance with its nature, perfect in itself, but not deserving of applause or reward.

How much more Annie Besant and Leadbeater would have preferred him to process in triumph through city avenues, to invite peoples' worship and devotion, to draw up a set of commandments, a philosophical stronghold complete with concrete goals and esoteric rules, to assume a crown, a throne. Leadbeater tried, even in 1929, to tempt Krishna over to Sydney for some appearances at the Pythagorean amphitheatre above the harbour. But the ritualistic pomp for which the structure had been designed was now alien to Krishna's vision, at best an absurd mistake, at worst a wicked delusion.

Early in June 1929, on the eve of his departure for Europe, Krishna was involved in a serious car crash and narrowly escaped fatal injury. It would have been ironic had he died at this juncture, immediately before his most celebrated appearance, the defining moment of his life and the final curtain of his epic Theosophical drama. He would doubtless have been apotheosised, like so many others who lived in the public eye and died young, but even more so because of the extraordinary claims associated with him.

However, Krishna did not die in a fast car on a Californian highway, but travelled to Europe with Rosalind and Rajagopal, proceeding straight to the Alps for a rest before the start of what promised to be a momentous gathering at Ommen. He arrived at Eerde refreshed and ready to face the biggest challenge of his life; and this time he would have to accomplish his task in the presence of Annie Besant. Members of his inner circle were given a foretaste of what was to come during the customary gathering at Eerde Castle: 'I feel very strongly that a time has come when each one of us must change drastically; that is, entirely disassociate ourselves from everything of the past . . . It is absolutely necessary that there should be disruption and revolt . . . You must be free.'[37]

The teachings of the previous two years were reaching their inevitable consummation. He could no longer contain his impatience with the Theosophical Society, with its prejudices and preconceptions, its blinkered reliance on leaders and voluntary submission to dogma, its mediocrity, false morality and spiritual snobbery. He had, of course, by acquiescing to the system of his seniors, contributed personally over the years to the development of Theosophy along precisely those lines he now abhorred, and his own contradictory behaviour in recent times made him vulnerable to accusations of hypocrisy, to which the only solution was a decisive and public *volte face*. If his message were ever to ring true and free, and if he ever hoped for credibility in the world beyond Theosophy, he would have to take his surgeon's knife to his own organisation and cut out the cancer he had so long despised.

So it was, that on the morning of 3 August 1929, in front of a massive gathering of followers, together with Annie Besant and an array of Theosophical leaders, all assembled in the forest at Ommen, that the thirty-four-year-old Krishnamurti took the stand and proceeded to dissolve the Order of the Star. The speech he gave, though much of it drawn from material he had used earlier, was seminal, and marked the start of his mature teaching. Indeed, towards the end of his life, when asked to summarise the core of his philosophy for future generations, he began by quoting the dissolution speech. It was a remarkable statement for its courage and conviction, and it demonstrates dazzlingly how far the speaker had journeyed since that far-off day when he was spotted, gormless, illiterate and under-nourished, on the beach at Adyar.

I maintain that Truth is a pathless land, and you cannot approach it by any path whatsoever, by any religion, by any sect . . . Truth, being limitless, unconditioned, unapproachable by any path whatsoever, cannot be organised; nor should any organisation be formed to lead or to coerce people along any particular path. If you first understand that, then you will see how impossible it is to organise a belief . . . If you do, it becomes dead, crystallised; it becomes a creed, a sect, a religion, to be imposed on others. This is what everyone throughout the world is attempting to do. Truth is narrowed down and made a plaything for those who are weak, for those who are only momentarily discontented. Truth cannot be brought down, rather the individual must make the effort to ascend to it. You cannot bring the mountain-top to the valley. If you would attain the mountain-top you must pass through the valley, climb the steeps, unafraid of the dangerous precipices. You must climb towards the Truth, it cannot be 'stepped down' or organised for you . . . The organisation becomes a framework into which its members can conveniently fit. They no longer strive after Truth or the mountain-top, but rather carve for themselves a convenient niche in which they put themselves, or let the organisation place them, and consider that the organisation will thereby lead them to Truth . . . If an organisation be created for this purpose, it becomes a crutch, a weakness, a bondage, and must cripple the individual, and prevent him from growing, from establishing his uniqueness, which lies in the discovery for himself of that absolute, unconditioned Truth. So that is another reason why I have decided, as I happen to be Head of the Order, to dissolve it . . . This is no magnificent deed, because I do not want followers, and I mean this. The moment you follow someone you cease to follow Truth. I am not concerned whether you pay attention to what I say, or not. I want to do a certain thing in the world and I am going to do it with unwavering concentration. I am concerning myself with only one essential thing: to set man free. I desire to free him from all cages, from all fears, and not to found religions, new sects, nor to establish new theories and new philosophies . . . Because I am free, unconditioned, whole – not the part, not the relative but the whole Truth that is eternal – I desire those who seek to understand me to be free; not to follow me, not to make out of me a cage which will become a religion, a sect. Rather should they be free from all fears – from the fear of religion, from the fear of salvation, from the fear of spirituality, from the fear of love, from the fear of death, from the fear of life itself . . . For eighteen years you have been preparing for this event, for the Coming of the World-Teacher. For eighteen years you have organised, you have looked for someone who would give a new delight to your hearts and minds, who would transform your whole life, who would give you a new understanding; for someone who would raise you to a new plane of life, who would give you a new encouragement, who would set you free – and now look what is happening! Consider, reason with yourselves, and discover in what way that belief has made you different – not with the superficial difference of the wearing of a badge, which is trivial, absurd. In what manner has such a belief swept away all the unessential things of life? That is the only way to judge: in what way are you freer, greater, more dangerous to every Society which is based on the false and unessential? In what way have members of this organisation of the Star become different? . . . 'How many followers are there in it?' That is the first question I am asked by all newspaper reporters. 'How many followers have you? By their number we shall judge whether what you say is true or false.' I am not concerned with that. As I said, if there were even one man who had been set free, that were enough ... You can form other organisations and expect someone else. With that I am not concerned, nor with creating new cages, new decorations for those cages. My only concern is to set men absolutely, unconditionally free.[38]

Krishnamurti has been widely praised for what has been seen as a monumental act of renunciation on moral grounds, displaying qualities of foresight and wisdom. As Rom Landau put it, 'There existed an organisation with many thousands of members; there were platforms from which to speak in four of the most important corners of the globe; there was an independent commercial organisation with its magazines, its books and various publications in a dozen different languages; there were helpers among all classes of society, willing to make practically any mental or material sacrifice; there was, in short, a working machine for the transmission of a spiritual message, as powerful as any institution had ever been ... To throw it overboard as though it meant nothing required personal courage, moral purity and spiritual conviction.'[39] In some senses this judgement is apt. Krishna had renounced what many others would have been tempted to retain. But there is another perspective, that reveals how minimal the actual changes in his life and status were to be after the momentous act.

The dissolution would not have been undertaken without a good deal of forward planning, if for no other reason than to sort out the practicalities. Krishna and Rajagopal had had plenty of time to discuss the consequences of cutting themselves adrift. The months of rest at Ojai and then in the Alps would have seen the two men working out what to do with the Order's property, how to fund themselves in future, what direction to take, and how to cope with the inevitable Theosophical backlash. Administration was not Krishna's strong point, and most of these considerations would have been worked out meticulously by Rajagopal.

Castle Eerde was returned to Philip van Pallandt, who now had a wife and heir, but a patch of forest was retained for future camps – now no longer restricted to members, but open to the public at large. The Star Publishing Trust, established by Rajagopal three years before the dissolution, would continue to provide a medium for the distribution of Krishna's teachings and a means of generating funds for future work. Other assets held in trust for Krishna by the Order, were readministered by mutual agreement between Rajagopal and the trustees or returned to the original donors. A base was retained at Ojai, where Rosalind and Rajagopal continued to live, and which was to become Krishna's principal home for the immediate future. The gatherings continued in Europe, California and India, the publications flourished, and the teachings, if anything, began to reach an even wider audience than they had in the days when they were restricted to the Order's members.

In terms of financial security, Krishna's life did not change dramatically, either. He had become accustomed to a certain style of living, and doubtless appreciated that arrangements were in place to ensure that he could continue in the same manner – though the accumulation of luxuries was never attractive to him. We shall never know how he would have fared if compelled to survive with little or no money, but there is no evidence to suggest that he was in any way dependent on material comfort. He was fortunate in that his needs were looked after entirely by others, and this had been the case ever since his adoption as a boy. Annie Besant recognised that he had never matured in terms of worldly matters, was concerned that he might not cope without the Theosophical Society to support him. It is unlikely that such considerations even crossed Krishna's mind at the time of the dissolution. Just as he had always had his material needs provided for, he had also been surrounded by groups of devotees ready to care for him. He saw no reason why this should ever stop, and, indeed, it did not. Friends and associates continued to mother him, just as others had done in his Theosophical days, up to the end of his life, and, like their nineteenth-century-born predecessors, they saw it as a privilege to do so. Krishnamurti's subsequent history therefore shows us that the dissolution, though well-intended, did not represent the great sacrifice for which he has been admired so handsomely ever since. In reality, he was compelled to renounce his status as leader of the Order of the Star; to have done otherwise would have been pure hypocrisy, in the light of his teachings of the previous two years. The writing had been on the wall for some time.

He did, however, show considerable courage in rising to the occasion. He had to overcome his fear of injuring Annie Besant to the extent that he could openly and publicly, in her presence, deride badges and spiritual hierarchies as childish absurdities. He displayed a steel-edged side to his personality, a refusal to be compromised. The portrayal of Krishnamurti as an eternal child in practical matters may be inconsistent with the stereotypical image of a messiah figure – titanic and self-reliant – but his bold statement that morning at Ommen showed he possessed the metal of a formidable teacher. It also proved once and for all that he was no one's pet monkey.

Krishna emerged cheerfully from the rubble of Theosophy's crumbling edifice, carefree and without a look back at the murky shambles he was leaving in his wake. However, thousands felt betrayed and insulted. He had abandoned his post, they thought, and in doing so had capitalised on their misfortune by exposing them as spiritual snobs and pious hypo-crites in order to enhance his own pure image. Many of them had abandoned the religion of their home culture to take up the creed of Theosophy, and now felt sickened that their risky spiritual investment had proved so hollow. He had fed them a bitter pill, as many of his closest Theosophical associates, such as Lady Emily, now discovered. For Krishna, however, the dissolution was not a moral issue – there was no right or wrong in freedom. It was as plain as air.

He could easily have sailed the tide and tried to become the world-sweeping messiah they all wanted. The world's press was ready and waiting for the word, an administrative structure was in place, and there was even a bona fide Church organisation at his disposal. He might also have succumbed to be a leading Theosophist like Jinarajadasa or Arund-ale, or a grotesquely glorified version of them, venerated within his own circle but the laughing-stock of the world outside. Or he could have quietly retired from the whole turgid mess, with its squabbles, its sexual scandals, hyperbole and prophet-mongering, in which case he might well have disappeared without trace to emerge decades later as the author of bitter memoirs, forgotten by all except a few die-hard veterans.

But he chose a different path. Whilst shedding his messianic label and denying spiritual authority, he retained the stance and stature of a divine representative. He did not wish to be regarded as a religious leader, for all the reasons we have seen, and yet he was aware to the end that he was special, and had been born to fulfil a unique role. It is unlikely that Krishna had any idea in 1929 who or what had ordained his birth, and it is of course possible that the whole idea was just the product of his having been fed such notions consistently from an early age, though he continually denied having any trace of conditioning in his psyche. But there can be no doubt that he kept a place in his heart for the World Teacher concept – the state of man made perfect through union with divinity. Even in 1929, pausing between denunciations of Theosophy, and while setting up a secular platform for his own future work, he was capable of pronouncements about himself that were heavy with messianic portent: 'When it becomes necessary for humanity to receive in a new form the ancient wisdom, someone whose duty it is to repeat these truths is incarnated.'[40]

His abandonment of the Order of the Star was a definite move in the direction of spontaneity and away from formality. There was no progress to be made in systems, belief structures and logical matrices, nor was there any point in delving ever deeper in search of answers for sacred mysteries that would forever remain beyond the reach of language. He was making a blow for life and simplicity. E. A. Wodehouse concluded that his greatest spiritual gift to the world was the fresh cleanliness he imparted, free of pontification and unnecessary complications. When one has been with Krishna, he wrote, one 'has found a new meaning for the word "holy" . . . One discovers for the first time, that the true essence of holiness is far more of the blue sky than of the thundercloud, and that the authentic odour of sanctity is less that of incense than it is the scent of wild flowers in the hedge-row and the breath of early spring. A bluebell or a daffodil, rejoicing in its life, is the typically holy thing. The fawn playing in the forest, the mountain torrent leaping in glee from crag to crag, are apt emblems of things spiritual. The voice of spiritual life is not a sermon but a song.'[41]

10

Farewell to Things Past

———— ❋ ————

Krishnamurti's dissolution of the Order of the Star was the climax of an extraordinary tale; yet the main bulk of his life's work, the oeuvre for which he is revered today, was yet to be commenced. In 1991 the Krishnamurti Foundation Trust produced a CD ROM containing the teacher's complete published works, the equivalent of around 200 books, covering the years 1933–86. Those currently responsible for the dissemination of his teachings do not consider the voluminous talks and writings prior to 1933 to have been fully mature, though at the time thousands marvelled at their insight and originality. From a doctrinal perspective, then, we are presented with a double career: the first occupying the period up until Krishnamurti's rejection of Theosophy – a romantic adventure, but ultimately irrelevant (as Krishnamurti himself tacitly endorsed by losing his memory); and the second represented by more than half a century of consistent, fully developed teachings. But this simple 'before and after' equation seriously underestimates the influence that Theosophy had on Krishnamurti's mature thought and the role he ultimately fulfilled in the history of western spiritual philosophy. The World Teacher project was far from dead, and although use of the term was tactfully withdrawn by those loyal to his wishes, much messianic speculation continued to be centred on the figure of Krishnamurti well beyond the 1930s, and continues to this day.

The desolate economic crisis of the years following the Great

Depression, together with its dark political consequences, did more to stimulate the the public's hunger for a spiritual Saviour than any number of Besantian diatribes. Krishnamurti, transcending all religious frontiers, yet melting them down to a common source, offered hope equilaterally to a world taut with diplomatic tension. He was an intriguingly indefinite figure; he belonged to no particular nationality, was beautiful and chaste enough to appear almost without gender, had been compared to a delicate flower as well as an Old Testament prophet and, most mysteriously, appeared to denounce all accepted religions while retaining a profound religiosity of his own. In the cultural climate of the 1930s, with the rise of Abstract and Expressionist art, when previously revered laws of form and harmony were tossed aside in the name of experimentalism, Krishnamurti's nihilistic stance and denials of authority were fashionably modern.

The Theosophical Society was in disarray. It had been on the decline since the scandals in Sydney and the subsequent defections of splinter groups around the world. What had started life as a forum for the open debate of universal spiritual truths was now nothing more than an exclusive cult, with set rules, goals and rituals. The conservative rigidity of its structure was an anachronism in the 1920s, yet the popularity of Krishnamurti and his Order of the Star had kept the Society's membership deceptively high. Like Squealer's list of ever-increasing productivity at Animal Farm, the official Theosophical publications of the time proudly announce the Society's growth, its new enterprises and glories. But they fail to reveal the degree to which the movement's leaders, especially Leadbeater, had begun to be liabilities in the eyes of the membership at large. Even Annie Besant, revered though she may have been, was not immune from criticism. Her adoption of new fads, such as the World Mother and World Religion movements, together with her floundering antics in the Indian political arena, had cost the Society the loyalty of some of its most stalwart devotees. The membership fall-off actually began in 1928, as a result of Krishnamurti's denunciation of organisations. Most new members had joined to listen to the World Teacher, not because they were attracted to the baroque Theosophical system. They felt perfectly comfortable, therefore, to resign their membership when Krishnamurti finally dissolved the Order of the Star.

The same Theosophical publications that boasted new achievements for the Society in the late 1920s also pointedly refused to give much column space to the dramatic dissolution of 1929. They stood aloof from it, in true Leadbeaterian style, stubbornly maintaining that the Order of the Star was only one of several offshoots of the parent Society, and that its termination did not warrant the dignity of a prolonged debate. The truth, of course, was that the Theosophical Society had been pole-axed. As an esoteric movement it required a symbolic figurehead, a priestly person to mediate between earth and heaven, an inheritor of the secret doctrine. Blavatsky, and, to a lesser extent, Besant and Lead-beater had fulfilled this function, but everyone's hopes for the previous two decades had been focussed on Krishnamurti – Alcyone, the World Teacher, the body made perfect for occupation by Christ, the Lord Maitreya. Not only had Theosophy's former keystone now removed himself from the structure, he had combatively challenged the central tenet of its beliefs, maintaining that the occult hierarchy of Masters was a complete irrelevance.

Theosophy had also been a movement with definite political objectives, which were to have entailed diplomatic activity on an international scale – to bring about universal brotherhood within a federation of religiously sympathetic states. Krishnamurti had been groomed as chief standard-bearer, an ambassador of divinity to the many cultures of the world, a king of kings. This role he now unconditionally rejected. But he never went as far as to deny being the World Teacher, just that it made no difference who or what he was. The subtlety of the distinction he made was lost on many devotees, who continued to invest their hopes in the concept of a new age and a World Teacher, except that now they did so outside the auspices of the Theosophical Society. Annie Besant, through years of toil, had carved the springboard that was to launch her protégé on his stellar career, but she and her movement had been drowned in the tide.

The inevitable backlash from certain quarters of the Theosophical Society against Krishnamurti was initially restrained by the leaders' need to limit the damage as much as possible. Krishna was incensed by their public shows of friendliness towards him at the Adyar Convention of December 1929, when he knew full well the extent of their resentment, and had heard reports of vituperative remarks about him behind his back. Although he now realised that he 'must get out of all this rot',[1] once and for all, he appears to have somewhat relished the chaos he was causing. 'They are out for my scalp,' he wrote to Lady Emily, referring to the Leadbeater camp, '& it will be fun.'[2] After he had formally resigned from the Theosophical Society, in 1930, he was more outspoken in public, though he always prefaced his remarks with polite apologies for the offence that they might cause. 'You go on living a life of utter hypocrisy,' he declared to a Theosophical audience, 'from morning till night, a deceitful life, a counterfeit life ... and because you are afraid, you will seek exploiters who will exploit you, who will invent cages that hold you, that bind your mind and heart, and create sorrow.'[3] And on another occasion, 'societies based on religious hopes and beliefs are pernicious.'[4] The intimation that the Society's leaders were exploiters was particularly difficult for his Adyar audiences to swallow. Yet still he was invited back regularly to address his former following, at least while Besant and her deputy, Jinarajadasa, held the reins.

Leadbeater could not be seen publicly to denounce his protégé, despite the jibes, and the deliberate belittling of his life's work, because that would be to admit a monstrous error in his own clairvoyancy. The old bishop was cornered, and took refuge in superciliousness – a situation viewed with delight by his old opponents, such as Steiner's Anthroposophists, and the back-to-Blavatsky campaigners. The immediate practical solution as to what should be the objective of the Liberal Catholic Church, now that the World Teacher project had floundered, was for the General Episcopal Synod to issue the following statement: '[The Synod] has withdrawn from the *Summary of Doctrine* any mention of the World-Teacher, and has modified those Collects in the Liturgy which speak of the physical return of our Lord, so that they now refer to the awakening and progressive unfoldment of the Christ in the human heart.'[5] This was a typically evasive modulation which neither strayed too far from the Church's original intent nor contradicted too strongly what Krishnamurti appeared to be teaching.

Krishnamurti's prescription stripped all religious officers and Churches of their authority, an emasculation Leadbeater was unwilling to accept, but he was compelled to hide his contempt in order to achieve at least a theoretical reconciliation with the dissident. His tone in the debate, according to E. A. Wodehouse, was one of 'sweet reasonableness; and his attitude towards those who had been worried about the general situation is almost that of a soothing nurse. "There, there!" he seems to say.'[6] Jinarajadasa wrote to Krishnamurti that Leadbeater considered his own work different but complementary to that of his former pupil. 'Isn't it like the two halves of scissors, angry & opposing each other, & yet there is no cutting possible if they weren't opposed!'[7] This was the general line of argument Leadbeater adopted in his definitive statement about the situation, an article entitled, 'Art thou He that should come?' printed in various Theosophical magazines in 1930. 'I have on several occasions heard the World-Teacher speak through Krishnaji,' he concedes before adding, 'but there are occasions when He does *not*.' The same was true for Jesus, Leadbeater maintains, and one need only acknowledge the many religions left on the planet after the death of Christ to understand that a multiplicity of creeds exists because God wishes it so.

Arundale, younger and more combative by nature, attempted a similarly reasonable tone in his published responses, but could not resist an occasional return punch at Krishnamurti. The previous status quo in the Theosophical Society, he argues, is 'being replaced by another tyranny, by another orthodoxy . . . by what I am constrained to call a Krishnamurti orthodoxy'.[8] Indignant though he was, Arundale was also keen to secure votes for what now appeared to be an imminent presidential election, and so wooed World Teacher sympathisers with a transparently sycophantic article entitled 'The Wonderfulness of Krishnaji', published in August 1930. Wedgwood, always a more outspoken opponent of Krishnamurti, pronounced that the former Vehicle refused to see the good in others' opinions and was most 'untheosophical'. Wedgwood's own occult talent for measuring invisible vibrations, he claimed, had revealed without doubt that Krishnamurti was not the real World Teacher. This typically unanswerable assertion was worthy of Leadbeater himself.

One rising star of Theosophy, Geoffrey Hodson, penned a critical pamphlet about the situation. Though a great admirer of Krishnamurti (to the extent that he still considered him a potential saviour of the world), Hodson could not help but be outraged by what he described as the former Vehicle's intellectual arrogance. 'He alone is right. Everyone else from the Lord Buddha down to the latest teacher of the Law, is wrong, criminally wrong.' It was morally unacceptable, Hodson argued, for Krishnamurti to condemn all religious teachers from the dawn of time – great churchmen, saints, holy men, 'all who have given their lives for the helping of humanity' – as exploiters, 'and to class them and the whole body of the priesthood with all the most evil people in the world. Yet this is what Krishnaji continually does.'[9]

It was to Annie Besant, however, as President and long-time advocate of Krishnamurti's divinity, that most members looked for direction in the chaos. The old matriarch, now ailing and clearly tired of her responsibilities, never faltered in her devotion to her 'son', and would gladly have resigned to follow him had it not been for her intractable sense of duty and her addiction to self-martyrdom. She frequently begged members to lay aside their expectations and accept his teachings for what they were. She comforted herself by finding much common ground with him, and maintained, like Leadbeater, that she and he represented 'two sides of one work'.[10] She thoroughly sympathised with Krishnamurti's fundamentally Hindu notion that God, or Truth, was absolute, immeasurable, without name or form, and beyond the scope of human thought; that it represented the ground of all creation, the unity in all material diversity, and that it was therefore the common property of each individual. This property, whether called 'Christ', 'the perfectibility of man', or 'the Beloved', was, for her, the divine common denominator that alone could bring about a state of universal brotherhood.

Besant also admired Krishnamurti's sense of mission, his urge to dedicate himself to a life of service, as she herself had done. His stated aim of setting men 'unconditionally free', of wanting to bring about enlightenment for the individual that would lead to a radical transformation of the world at large, was seen by Besant as nothing short of messianic. She still believed that he would be the Saviour, and in this conviction she saw the fulfilment of her life's work. Krishna might well deny his own authority, she argued, because he operated on a level far above the workings of organised religion. 'I do not say that *he* will make [a new religion],' she said. 'But I think that his disciples will form a new religion out of his teachings. I am sure they will. He will not do it. No World Teacher makes a religion. His disciples do it.'[11]

Face to face with their emancipated World Teacher, ordinary members of the Society were not always as accommodating as their President. Krishnamurti was bombarded relentlessly with questions relating to his status, the existence of the Masters, and his treachery. He quickly learned how to deflect these, often turning the question back on the questioner, like a mirror, thereby illuminating to some extent the hollow inconsequentiality of this line of inquiry. After years of answering the same inevitable questions, even though he begged audiences to concentrate on more constructive issues, he was sometimes prone to lose patience. When asked, as occasionally happened, if he was the tool of dark powers on a mission to destroy the work of the Great White Brotherhood, he was reminded of all that was most petty, narrow and puerile in his upbringing, and his responses could be brutal. 'A few years ago,' he said, 'many of you had my picture hung up on your walls, and you offered flowers and candles to "the Expected One" . . . As long as the picture is silent it is divine, you can worship it . . . Let the image in the picture come to life, as I have stepped out of your picture, and you will see how quickly you will destroy it; how quickly with your subtle and deceitful minds, you will invent words: "black" and "white" . . . How utterly false, hypocritical.'[12]

But to those who, without prejudice, were seriously confused by his apparent iconoclasm (as Alan Watts was to write, his 'calling into question our holiest treasures and leaving us without a single hope or comfort'[13]), Krishnamurti tried to express his perspective in a less fiery style. When asked in 1930 why he had previously asserted a faith in the Masters, he replied gently: 'I will explain. In the search for truth, you have in the background of your being a realisation that you are seeking something fundamental, lasting real . . . and you attribute that reality to types – to highly evolved types [ie Masters]. But the moment you approach that type and have adjusted yourself to it, reality is not in that type any longer, and you go further on . . . You are all the time seeking this thing and attributing it to persons whom you may happen to come across. But gradually you will eliminate these imagined types until at last you arrive at your goal. Because I have found reality, I say to everybody who is willing to listen: Do not attribute the totality of truth to individual types. Seek the ultimate, which is of no person, of no sect, of no path . . . You must be empty as a desert to understand . . . All these questions of types arise when there is still this clinging to the illusion of personal aid from the outside.'[14]

By 1933 it was clear that Krishnamurti's presence on the Theosophical compound at Adyar, in any capacity except that of guest speaker, would serve nobody's ends. He made his Indian headquarters at an ample newly-built house on the opposite side of the Adyar River, called Vasanta Vihara. Some, including Lady Emily, considered his occupying a property so near that of his former sponsors was a bad-mannered attempt to outmanoeuvre the Society. But the real reasons were practical rather than competitive. The Adyar area of south Madras had been his home since boyhood, and it was still the principal flash-point of interest in his teachings as far as India was concerned. Besides, many Theosophists still pinned their hopes on him and were glad to think that he would be lodged a mere bridge-length away from them.

Annie Besant's physical and mental health began to deteriorate rapidly in the the year following Krishnamurti's dissolution of the Order of the Star. One body of opinion attributes this decline almost solely to the disappointment she is supposed to have felt as a result of her 'son's' defection, but there is little evidence to support this. Both she and Krishnamurti frequently reiterated publicly and privately that there had never been a rift between them, and Besant was still optimistic that her protégé would fulfil her expectations. What was more likely to have sapped her energy was Krishnamurti's eloquent exposé of the Society's very real decay; he had, with a single gesture, unlocked the door and brought daylight into the stagnant, cobwebbed cellar of Theosophy. She may suddenly have realised the devastating truth about Leadbeater's distorted spiritual matrix, and perhaps even begun to suspect that his opponents over the years had been correct all along. She was also injured by the apparent ineffectiveness of her many years' work for Indian Home Rule. That campaign was now dominated by Gandhi and his inner circle, from which Besant was excluded because, despite her philanthropy and good intentions, she was suspected of being a British imperialist at heart. She must have felt bitter at the apparent pointlessness of her efforts.

Faced with a dead-end of disillusionment, old age and decrepitude, she let go of her mental faculties and retired quietly to her quarters at Adyar. Neither she nor Leadbeater had the energy or resources to pull the Society back onto its feet or unite its various factions.

Reports of her final months describe a pathetic but endearing figure, seated on a sofa on the roof of her rooms, feeding the squirrels, attempting to read, but finding it difficult to concentrate. A leg injury had made her almost immobile, and her conversation wandered from the occasional affirmation of her Theosophical mission, to comments about dancing fairies or the welfare of 'pretty little animals'.[15] Krishnamurti continued to write to her but, as ever, his letters were vacuous, so much so that Jinarajadasa (who probably read them to Annie) was moved to reprimand him for their superficiality.

Krishna came at last to visit his Amma in December 1932, their first encounter in over two years, and he was saddened to see how far her legendary strength had ebbed. Her memory was shaky, but she did recognise him, and was clearly glad to have him near. Their final meeting the following May was poignant, as Krishna realised on the eve of his departure for Europe that they would probably never see each other again. She rallied somewhat and offered him snippets of advice on his health and affairs, but the physical deterioration of this magnificent woman seemed to epitomise for Krishna the tragic failure of the Society as a whole, its flawed enterprises, stale theories, and disoriented membership. He was tired of the whole edifice, too tired now even to find it amusing. He doubtless knew, when he left Annie's side on 2 May 1933, that the compound held nothing more for him and that he might not ever return.

Annie Besant died in the afternoon of 20 September 1933, after having lain barely conscious for five days. The inevitable crowds assembled to file past the body, while newspapers around the world filled their columns with glowing tributes, and various institutions within India closed for the day as a mark of respect. Leadbeater had been alerted and had travelled from Sydney to be at his old partner's side when she finally slipped into that abyss they had both for so long attempted to define. He officiated at her funeral ceremony, dressed in a white cassock adorned with much regalia, masonic and otherwise. He cut a splendidly patriarchal, though frail, figure as he put the torch to her funeral pyre.

Krishnamurti claimed, fifty years on and despite his loss of memory, that he was never officially informed about his adoptive mother's death, but read about it in the New York press. This oversight, deliberate or otherwise, illustrates the distance that was now to be put between the Theosophical leadership and its former chief mascot. An election was held after Besant's death and, as expected, Arundale was elevated to the presidency, defeating – by allegedly dubious means – his only contender, Ernest Wood. It was Arundale who was forced to pick up the pieces of Theosophy in the wake of Krishnamurti's defection and to attempt a reconsolidation on the basis of Besant's tenets. But he had neither her oratorical skills, nor the mysterious charisma of Leadbeater, her maverick associate. Most important of all, he had lost Besant's chief premise for the existence of the Society – the promise of a golden new age and the return, in a physical body, of Christ. After decades of Besant's stirring prophecies and claims, anything uttered by Arundale was bound to be anticlimactic. He sought some consolation in vituperating against Krishnamurti, but the tide was against him, as the former World Teacher's prestige quickly outgrew that of the Society that had moulded him. Arundale, in seeking to repair the damage, led the body of thought that cast Krishnamurti as an appropriate, but failed, candidate for the Lord Maitreya, one who had crumbled under the strain of his responsibility or had been led astray by less than wholesome agents (the term 'black powers' was dropped).

Leadbeater left Madras on 31 January 1934 in an extremely fragile state, bound for Australia. It is unclear why he did not choose to remain at Adyar, considering the state of his health. He perhaps knew that he was dying, and wanted to return as soon as possible to the community of which he was undisputed chieftain in Sydney. For many years he had appeared to defy age, remaining fit and athletic well into his supposed eighties. It is now known, of course, that he was seven years younger than he had always claimed, so that by the time he marked his birthday, en route to Sydney, in February 1934, he was, in fact, only eighty years of age. He was never to complete the journey, but died in Perth on 29 February. His body was taken on to Sydney, where a Liberal Catholic funeral was held before the cremation. Krishnamurti was lecturing in Australia at the time, and by chance arrived in Sydney in the time for the funeral. He had the grace to attend, though preferred to wait outside the crematorium during the ceremony.

Leadbeater, like Besant, had begun to realise at the end of his life that his labours were not bearing the expected fruit. Generation after generation of young people had come into his orbit only to depart after a few years, having rejected his teachings, or reacted violently against them. Few, if any, remained in the Theosophical circle, or carried on his work after his death. But he did not die in complete disappointment. Humiliated as he was by Krishnamurti's defection, he continued privately to express admiration for his former pupil, and cannot but have felt proud to witness the younger man maturing into one of the foremost religious philosophers of the time. Leadbeater's notoriety was to continue long after his death, not just because of his association with Krishnamurti but through his written work, which, even today, is sometimes described as ahead of its time. Ironically, it was Annie Besant's publications (over 400 in all) that were soon to be forgotten and relegated to dusty library shelves, taking their place in the vast acreage of rarely visited Victorian prose.

Other former associates of Krishnamurti settled into new lives or floundered for lack of personal initiative. James Ingall Wedgwood began to lose control of his mind in the early 1930s, a condition ascribed to syphilis. He continued to work in his more sane moments, and helped to establish a Liberal Catholic community at Tekels Park, in Camberley, England, where he lived and was cared for until his death in 1951. Lady Emily and the gopis struggled hard to understand Krishnamurti's post-Theosophical teaching. They had to accept that he would not be drawn into possessive personal relationships, and that, though they may have enjoyed years of intimacy with him in past times, that was no qualification for continued closeness. They must expect nothing from him, but could choose to continue loving and listening to him if they could manage so unilateral a relationship. Those who could not appreciate this level of detachment fell away from his orbit. Some, including Lady Emily, remained, though she found it hard to grasp even the basics of his message. Her love for Krishna was still titanic, and had he not utterly denounced the notion of discipleship, she would gladly have given up everything to follow him. As it was, she wrote that he had cut the ground from under her feet, 'and I felt I was dropping into nothingness.'[16] She also felt stung by guilt that she had for so long neglected her husband and family in order to indulge her own spiritual caprice. Her adventure was over, and although she continued to correspond with Krishna for the remainder of her long life (she died in 1964), she began to drift away from him. Of the gopis, only Mary Lutyens and Mar de Manziarly remained close to him until the end. The former became his authorised biographer, and could justifiably claim to have been his oldest friend.

As Krishnamurti walked away from Sydney's Ryde Crematorium on the day Charles Webster Leadbeater's body was consigned to the flames, he knew that the last of the great moulding influences on his life had now passed. Many of his tutor's more beneficial lessons had taken root, and were to stay with Krishnamurti for life, such as a meticulous attitude towards cleanliness, physical appearance, clothes and exercise. It could also be argued that the uncompromising sincerity with which he approached his teaching work – verging on the tyrannical at times – was ultimately derivative of the example set by his formidable mentor. Yet in all practical senses the frayed strings that had tied him to his past were now finally cut; so, too, was the Theosophical Society's last living link to its notorious founder, Madame Blavatsky. The shadow of nine-teenth-century millenarianism was lifted, and he was finally, in every sense, free to pursue his teaching mission.

Krishnamurti in the 1930s could barely contain his enthusiasm for teaching, although his speaking style was still far from polished. As one observer noted during a lecture in 1930: 'he appeared nervous and ill at ease, his body swaying like a reed in the wind, his gestures stereotyped to a single pattern, his voice falling at times almost to inaudibility, depending too much . . . upon his paper memorandum. The total effect, however, was not one of weakness, but of power imperfectly con-trolled.'[17] He was fuelled by a burning desire to share the realisation he had himself attained. Yet he discovered early on the inherent paradox in his life's mission: that the inexpressible could never be communicated through language; he could teach to the end of his days, he could theorise, intellectualise, convince, cajole or bully his audiences, but, ultimately, the fire he aimed to ignite could not be contained in words or concepts, no matter how inspired the speaker. As an old man he complained that not a single person, despite his sixty years of work, had actually lived the teachings and attained the liberation of which he spoke.

The camps continued at Ommen and Ojai, and lecture tours in previously unvisited countries around the world were embarked upon. He particularly enjoyed visiting Greece, where he first spoke in December 1930, causing a sensation in Athens. A visit to New Zealand, shortly after Leadbeater's funeral, caused widespread interest because the government, fearful of his radical approach, banned him from broadcasting on the radio. The result was a huge increase in his live audiences, all fascinated to hear first-hand the apparently subversive message of this exotic visitor. Bernard Shaw, who happened to be visiting New Zealand at the time, added his voice to those outraged by the ban. 'The authorities are evidently ignorant of Krishnamurti's standing, and his admirably catholic doctrine,' he said to a reporter, 'and class him as just an Indian heathen . . . They will be sorry for it.'[18]

Krishnamurti's travels and personal expenses were now financed by income derived from the Star Publishing Trust (or SPT) publications. These were predominantly 'Verbatim Reports' of his talks, edited by Rajagopal and Lady Emily, and translated into eighteen languages. The tool for the dissemination of his message thus also became the principal source of his, and his retinue's, funding, though he did continue to receive Miss Dodge's annuity and donations from other benefactors. A shrewd marketing operation had been conceived – shrewd enough to include in its list of saleable texts *At the Feet of the Master* (whose authorship had been so hotly disputed nearly twenty years previously), in no less than three different bindings, cloth, paper and 'deluxe'. Krishnamurti certainly lacked for nothing, and his lifestyle remained as affluent as before. He was frequently the guest of wealthy and aristocratic grandees, and was always accommodated in comfort.

The business administration of the SPT, and the organisation of Krishnamurti's affairs as a whole, was left to Rajagopal, as it had been in the days of the OSE. He was also responsible for liaising with and marshalling, the various international representatives, of which the Trust boasted forty-four by May 1930. He would see to the finest details personally, working long hours to the point where his own health began to suffer, so as to ensure that every administrative aspect of the work was water-tight. He was frustrated by Krishnamurti's complete lack of economic sense, and preferred to undertake his own work independently, with as little interference from the teacher as possible. He deeply resented being described as Krishnamurti's secretary, and confrontations between the two men were not infrequent. When a quarrel arose, Krishnamurti more often than not returned to his cowering childhood persona and allowed himself to be bullied, rather than prolong an argument. He was innocent and malleable to an extraordinary degree at times like this; quite different from the stern teacher in front of whom thousands sat spellbound. The relationship teetered from this time onwards between strong affection and mutual antipathy. Part of the problem (but probably only a small part) is said to have been Rajagopal's continued sympathy with the Theosophical Society, which he thought Krishnamurti had treated with callous disdain. He remained nominally loyal to the Society and retained his membership until his death in 1993. Krishnamurti, by contrast, said of his own alleged betrayal of the Society, 'I am not talking about loyalty, I am talking about truth ... you cannot be politic with regard to spiritual things.'

A more complex issue was now to drive a wedge between the two men, though the extent to which it was openly acknowledged by them at the time, rather than tacitly accepted for a period of more than twenty years, remains something of a mystery. Full details of the situation have come to light only recently, causing shockwaves of dismay to reverberate through Krishnamurti's following. From the impartial perspective one cannot but think that the disproportionate scandal resulting from the revelations derives more from the flawed secrecy of the affair, than its actual circumstances.

Krishnamurti was spending more time at Ojai than in previous years, as it had now become his principal home, and from October 1931 to July 1932 was resident there continuously, with the object of meditating and distancing himself from material distractions. Rajagopal, in a diametrically opposite frame of mind, was always working, travelling regularly to and from the official Star office in Hollywood. He also suffered from recurrent ill-health, particularly rheumatism and sinus problems, and was frequently consigned to hospitals. His relationship with Rosalind, which had never been satisfactory, was now under serious strain. The birth of their only child, Radha, in July 1931, did little to improve matters. Indeed, on first seeing the baby, Rajagopal announced to his wife that, having now completed the business of producing a child, they might justifiably cease to have sexual relations. He appears to have grown less enamoured of Rosalind and was perhaps also haunted by Theosophical puritanism with regard to physical indulgence; but he refused to consider a formal separation, out of respect for Annie Besant, who had given her blessing to the union. He needed independence within the marriage in order to devote himself to his work and, by the same token, Rosalind was now granted her freedom. It was an arrangement that was to suit them both, and it also meant that baby Radha would never completely lose either parent.

However, it was Krishnamurti, rather than Rajagopal, who became the child's acting father, playing with her more than any other adult, and showering her with affection. She later wrote, 'He took me on with a fierce protectiveness, hovering like a lion over my crib and never allowing any stranger to touch me. It was he and not Raja[gopal] who did all the things that most fathers of that era left to their wives or nurses.'[19] The small amount of leisure time Rajagopal allowed himself rarely overlapped with that of his family, and Krishnamurti found himself not only adopting the role of father, but that of husband to the lonely and doting Rosalind. He must have been fully aware of the state of her marriage, and been assured by her that an affair between them would not be morally reprehensible – although, of course, it would have to be kept absolutely secret for everyone's sake, including baby Radha's. Thus concealed, their intimate and physical relationship began in the spring of 1932 and continued for over twenty-five years. It was only with the publication of Radha's book in 1991 that knowledge of the affair was made public, although close friends such as Mary Lutyens, had known of it for some long while. Radha claims that Rajagopal himself knew nothing until twenty years had passed, which, if it is to be believed, reveals his lack of interest in domestic life.

This was the first time that Krishnamurti – now thirty-seven years of age – had allowed himself to enter into full sexual relations. He now felt that the restrictions imposed by the Theosophical Society with regard to sex were artificial and unnecessary. He had experienced strong sexual attractions in the past, and had more than once endured the agonies of romantic passion, always denying himself the ultimate physical fulfilment. He had found a solution in mentally twisting his attraction to the opposite sex into a longing for maternal succour; and at one time he had considered celibacy a necessary criterion for the achievement of enlightenment; but in the hot passion of his new discovery, together with his freedom outside the limits of Theosophy, he abandoned this particular philosophy.

The relative seclusion of Ojai ensured that the couple would be safe in their secret, and Krishnamurti's frequent visits to Rosalind's bedroom, most commonly taking her a tray of breakfast or a bunch of flowers in the morning, were not especially noticed. In Europe he was less careful, and even arranged for Rosalind to join him in his forest hut during the Ommen camps. She accompanied him elsewhere on lecturing tours, but this appeared, to observers, like a simple continuation of his previous travelling arrangements. Krishnamurti had always toured with an entourage, often with Rosalind, both before and after her marriage, and there had been others in attendance of both genders. In his Theosophical days it would have been unthinkable that he might have been sexually involved with one of his companions, although the atmosphere was often thick with romance, and this unquestioning attitude continued thereafter. When the affair was finally made public, the injury was in the degree to which people's rigid assumptions about Krishnamurti had been shattered, rather than the facts of the relationship itself. His followers elevated him into a status of their own making, as the Theosophists had done, and sought to keep him there. When they found that the clothes they had made did not fit the real person, many were outraged.

Their resentment would have had just cause, of course, had Krishnamurti spent his life preaching the benefits of celibacy, and advocating the sanctity of the institution of marriage. In fact, he did neither. Quite the opposite; he frequently derided religious traditions of asceticism, eastern and western, as being life-denying; he abhorred the artificial suppression of natural drives, poured scorn on monastic vows of chastity (which he saw as indulgence of the ego), and said that to deny oneself sex on religious grounds was like denying the beauty of creation for the sake of a man-made ethic; it blocked emotions, dehydrated life, and turned the mind into a battleground.[20] On the question of sex, marriage and legitimacy, he pronounced, as early as 1933; 'In most cases marriage is but the sanctification of possessiveness, by religion and by law. Suppose that you love a woman; you want to live with her, to possess her. Now society has innumerable laws to help you to possess, and various ceremonies which sanctify this possessiveness. An act that you would have considered sinful before marriage, you consider lawful after that ceremony. That is, before the law legalizes and religion sanctifies your possessiveness, you consider the act of intercourse illegal, sinful. Where there is love, true love, there is no question of sin, of legality or illegality.'[21]

Marriage meant little to Krishnamurti, but he was awake to the notion of commitment within a relationship. In 1933, he told Rosalind that he would like to take responsibility for her and Radha, which would have meant bringing their relationship into the open and braving a public scandal. They both shrank from the idea, and the clandestine affair continued. A crisis point was reached in 1935 when Rosalind found she was pregnant. An abortion was performed, illegally, by a friend – an osteopath, rather than a doctor. Rosalind had two further pregnancies by Krishnamurti, the first around 1937, which ended in an early miscarriage, and the second in 1939 – again terminated by a covert abortion. They had made their decision to keep the relationship hidden, and the possibility of having a child together was therefore out of the question.

Although Krishnamurti's relationship with Rosalind cannot be described as dishonest, in that it does not contradict his teachings, there is no escaping that he was henceforth leading a double life. Whether he was protecting his own image as a holy figure and fostering the illusions of his followers, as Radha Rajagopal Sloss maintains, or whether he was merely shielding Rosalind and her daughter from scandal, cannot be definitively proved, although the former would imply a flagrant contravention of his own teaching, which would be uncharacteristic, to say the least. A more plausible reason for his secrecy was his natural aversion of vulgarity, of bringing (as he occasionally referred to it) one's dirty linen out into public view. History will not view Krishnamurti in quite the same light, as a result of the revelations about his private life, but it is doubtful whether significant damage has been done to the reputation of either the man or his teachings.

Ojai now became Krishnamurti's family home, the calm backwater to which he would retire, especially at times of exhaustion, and for fifteen years he enjoyed a kind of married bliss there, in close proximity to Rosalind. With the advent of war his travels ceased, and Ojai became his refuge. Despite the turmoil and devastation in the world at large, Krishnamurti enjoyed the longest period of uninterrupted seclusion he was ever to experience. The pace of his life was more relaxed than at any time in the past, and he was subject to less media attention, as public interest in a former would-be messiah paled beside the more pressing issue of a world at war. He gloried in the landscape, the scent of wild herbs on the hill and orange blossom in the valley. Walking became a form of meditation, when he would observe nature silently, with rapt attention, vividly aware of his surroundings, but without judgment or analysis. His energy and aptitude were applied to refining this razor-sharp quality of awareness, which was to become a fundamental element in his teachings after the war and beyond.

With the threat of war in Europe, California became a popular destination for refugee pacifists, writers and artists. They were attracted by the pleasant climate and the intellectual culture of Los Angeles. There was also the allure of Hollywood glamour, and the money-earning opportunities presented by the growing film industry. Ironically, and in contrast to the blatant materialism of Hollywood, one of the focal-points of intellectual pacifism at the time was the Los Angeles Vedanta Center, a Ramakrishna ashram presided over by a Bengali guru called Swami Prabhavananda. He taught the principles of Vedantic philosophy – the ancient cornerstone of Hinduism, that had earlier bewitched both Besant and Blavatsky. Ramakrishna's mission had been established in America at the end of the nineteenth century, by Swami Vivekananda who, along with Annie Besant, had attended the 1893 World Parliament of Religions in Chicago. At the close of the 1930s, with war erupting in Europe, Prabhavananda's disciples included three distinguished British writers and spiritual experimentalists: Gerald Heard, Aldous Huxley and Christopher Isherwood. All three were to enter Krishnamurti's orbit during the war years. Heard was a committed and intellectual spiritual seeker, with an almost medieval penchant for asceticism and self-denial. Isherwood, more attached to the charismatic Swami than either Heard or Huxley, was at this stage something of a religious tourist, floundering about in search of a spiritual path that would suit his own personal and moral inclinations. He entered into the spirit of Prabhavananda's Hindu routines, traditions and ceremonies, and clearly preferred this highly devotional path to the nihilistic teachings of Krishnamurti.

Aldous Huxley was to become a close friend and valued companion during Krishnamurti's Californian sojourn. Already a veteran anti-war activist, and famous not just as a writer but as the latest offshoot of a prodigiously gifted family, Huxley had come to America accompanied by his Belgian wife Maria, in 1937. He went to meet Krishnamurti at Ojai, with Gerald Heard, in April 1938. They immediately discovered much common ground. On the issue of the impending armed conflict, both men shared an abhorrence of gung-ho nationalism and the latent, if irrational, tendency in human nature towards conflict. Huxley had also for many years (indeed, since his school days) had a fascination with the underlying tenets of Theosophy. He acknowledged the presence of divinity, and the necessity for man to realise it, but was convinced that it lay outside the parameters of religious dogma. He discovered in Krishnamurti an approach to living that was in every sense spiritual, but lay quite beyond the scope of conventional religions or his own stockpile of philosophical knowledge, and he soon realised how much more appropriate this was to his own needs than the repetitive devotionalism encouraged by Prabhavananda.

Krishnamurti also encountered many of the other luminaries living in and around Los Angeles at the time. Stravinsky, Brecht, Thomas Mann and Bertrand Russell came to visit, as did Frieda, widow of D. H. Lawrence. Huxley and Isherwood were both employed as script-writers for the Hollywood studios and would mix socially with the celebrity set, some of whom, like Charlie Chaplin and Paulette Goddard, were playfully curious to meet the man who had turned down the opportunity to be a god. There were others, such as Greta Garbo, who considered themselves serious spiritual students. In the 1940s, just as today, there was a religious underpull in the lives of many film stars, and they sought, through men like Krishnamurti and Prabhavananda, to escape the superficiality of their public profiles. As Isherwood noted: 'Garbo was anxious to meet Krishnamurti ... She was very unhappy, restless and frightened. She wanted to be told the secret of eternal youth, the meaning of life, but quickly, in one lesson, before her butterfly attention wandered away again.'[22] In the autumn of 1939, she was invited to join Krishnamurti and Rosalind on a picnic, along with the Huxleys, the Russells, Isherwood, the script-writer Anita Loos, and various other friends. While walking in the woods, the group deliberately ignored a sign which forbade trespassers and burrowed clumsily under a wire fence to find an idyllic spot for their lunch. The forest ranger who furiously evicted them shortly afterwards was deaf to their claims of celebrity status. The dishevelled woman in men's trousers and a tatty straw hat, with a plaster between her eyebrows (to prevent herself from developing creases), bore no resemblance to the screen goddess who had recently impersonated Queen Christina and Anna Karenina.

Maria Huxley formed a close friendship with Rosalind, and her letters often refer to the latter and Krishnamurti as a couple, describing their visits and lamenting the periods in between, when their company was clearly missed. They were invited, with Radha, to spend the summer of 1945 at the Huxleys' home in Wrightwood, a mountainous retreat, surrounded by pine forests, high above the Mojave Desert. They instantly fell in love with Wrightwood and were shortly after to buy their own log cabin retreat there. It was a walker's paradise where both Krishnamurti and Huxley benefitted tremendously from the bracing outdoor life. They always enjoyed walking together, sometimes lapsing into long, natural periods of silence, but more often delving into details of a philosophy they both shared, but approached from different angles. Huxley, the polymath, could theorise, classify and define with great eloquence, whereas the poorly-educated Krishnamurti, although impressed by so powerful an intellect, considered such preoccupations an impediment. He was to develop instead the notion of 'choiceless awareness', which implied direct relationship between the observer and the observed, untainted by thought or the analytical process. The two men frequently entered into discussions on the relative worth of knowledge and whether it had a role in solving the problems of the human psyche. Anyone who has heard Krishnamurti's much later dialogues with the physicist David

Bohm can easily picture this scene with Huxley, as witnessed by Sidney Field: 'Krishnaji would often make a general, sweeping statement, as he was wont to do, minimising the significance of the intellect in resolving the enormous problems of life. Huxley would then launch a rebuttal, very quietly, with always the right word at his command, spoken in the most correct British manner. He would summon all kinds of scientific and historical evidence to indicate the great role intellect had always played in dissipating some of the darkest clouds of ignorance and superstition.'[23]

Their minds did meet on a certain territory, and it was Huxley who persuaded Krishnamurti that he should write definitive texts, rather than merely print transcriptions of his talks. Krishnamurti followed this advice and began to collect notes of his personal encounters, rather like a psychologist's case studies, interspersed with his own observations and some picturesque word-painting. These were later to be published as the first volume of *Commentaries on Living*. However, before that, in 1954, Victor Gollancz published Krishnamurti's first major book of philosophical observations, entitled, *The First and Last Freedom*. Huxley added a lucid introduction to this work, which no doubt contributed to its credibility and sales potential. His statement not only reveals a sympathy with Krishnamurti's thinking, but that he was willing to lend his own literary reputation in support of a message that he believed would greatly benefit mankind. Indeed, he appears now to endorse Krishnamurti's views on the limited value of intellect: 'Choiceless self-awareness will bring us to the creative Reality which underlies all our destructive make-believes, to the tranquil wisdom which is always there, in spite of ignorance, in spite of the knowledge which is merely ignorance in another form. Knowledge is an affair of symbols and is, all too often, a hindrance to wisdom.' For Krishnamurti to have thus engaged and intoxicated a mind such as Huxley's is no mean testament to the persuasive brilliance of his philosophy.

In August 1938 Krishnamurti attended what was to be the last Star Camp at Ommen. The threat of a German advance the following year rendered another gathering at the van Pallandt estate impossible. As expected, Nazi forces did sweep across Holland, and the Star premises was used by the invaders as an internment camp. During the course of the war this rural site, that had for fifteen years hosted a generation of egalitarian idealists in pursuit of a better world, became a concentration camp where Jews were assembled before being transported to unimaginable horrors in Poland, and a munitions factory. When the conflict finally came to an end, the castle was used as a prison for Dutch nationals who had collaborated with the Nazis. The fires in the forest had been extinguished forever.

Krishnamurti had talked a great deal, since the early 1930s, about the violent consequences of nationalism and the false sense of security it fostered. In 1939 his worst fears became reality, and the era of hope that he himself had so picturesquely symbolised in the 1920s now crashed in ruins. Throughout the ensuing conflict, he remained as unaffected by patriotic Allied hyperbole as by anti-German propaganda, just as he had as a young man during the First World War. He maintained that there was no moral high ground to be held in this conflict by either side, and that it was pure hypocrisy for one plainly imperialist nation to condemn as evil the military ambitions of another. He remained impartial throughout the war, and deeply critical of both sides. The root of the crisis, he maintained, lay within the minds and attitudes of individual people: entrenched opinion and self-determination leads inevitably to fear and hatred, and as long as there exists any form of prejudice, be it a matter of race, gender, class or creed, the result will be conflict. This theory drew Krishnamurti to the assertion that 'you are the world'; cure the problem within yourself and you cure the problem of the world. The war was merely a surface symptom. He took the opposite view to Annie Besant, who aimed to solve the evils of the world through global alliances and the hegemony of a new culture, populated by beings whose enlightenment derived from their race and religion. Krishnamurti had reduced such grandiose schemes down to the level of an individual's struggle to liberate him or herself from inner turmoil.

This approach did not prove popular with audiences at the outset of the war, who felt such philosophical niceties were not just irrelevant at this period of crisis, but almost callous. They would have preferred the teacher to have tackled the immediate problems head on: the tragedy of young men slain on the battlefield, the atrocity of children bombed in their homes, the devastation of entire cities, the wholesale extermination of a religious culture. They begged for moral truisms or prayers for peace, but Krishnamurti would acidly reply: 'You are the cause of war . . . Do not think by merely wishing for peace, you will have peace, when in your daily life of relationship you are aggressive, acquisitive, seeking psychological security here or in the hereafter. You have to understand the central cause of conflict and sorrow and then dissolve it and not merely look to the outside for peace.'[24] Some audiences were infuriated by this, and what they saw as Krishnamurti's unpatriotic stance, so much so, that a scuffle nearly broke out at one of his 1940 lectures. The teacher now came under FBI scrutiny as a potentially subversive influence, and at one time the authorities even suspected that he might be involved in a plot to assassinate Roosevelt. It was therefore decided, in everyone's best interests, that he should refrain from further lectures until the political climate had changed. He gave his last talk on 14 July 1940, and was not heard again in public until 14 May 1944.[25]

Krishnamurti scornfully rejected the role of mighty saviour at this time of global crisis, and retreated into lonely obscurity. A rumour was even spread across the east coast of America that he had died, and telegrams of condolence were received at Arya Vihara. Though hibernating, he was in fact in good health and spirits, undertaking long, meditative walks on his own, and sometimes going for weeks without looking at a newspaper. He had decided what he thought about the war, and believed the best way he could serve the world, true to his own philosophy, was to put himself to rights, or, in the terminology he was to adopt, 'set his own house in order'. In this reclusive state, cut off from the horror in Europe and elsewhere, he attracted some criticism, not least from old friends like Lady Emily, who openly accused him of escaping from reality. His whole philosophy, she felt, was ethereal – incomprehensible, almost – and she complained bitterly that his constant retreats and journeys into himself offered no practical help to mankind. Krishnamurti did not view this period of his life in such negative terms; far from it, he saw it as a time of intense encounter with the world, with the essence of life itself, pure and undistracted. It was also a period of consolidation, as he braced himself for the teaching mission that was to occupy the remainder of his life.

A certain amount of readjustment would have to be done, in the wake of the changing world. The Theosophical Society's myth about the returning messiah and the glorious new age would be dashed by the war, as would be the spirit of idealism that had etched itself into 1920s and '30s western culture. The post-Second World War generation would be haunted by the fear of yet more conflicts, and the new fear of total annihilation. If the 1920s was a time when youth culture was characterised by earnest spiritual experimentation and the hope of enlightenment, the 1950s and '60s were to see the rise of political pragmatism, giving birth to a generation of activists, cynics and extremists. Krishnamurti's teaching would have to change in style and language to accommodate the needs of this new generation. The war was a sobering reminder that human nature cannot attain permanent goals. There would never be a war to end all wars, nor a state of universal brotherhood, as envisaged by Besant. Enlightenment was not a vaccine to be sold wholesale to the world; nor was it a prize, which, once attained, could be put up on a shelf to gather dust. The golden era had not arrived; just more killing, misery and poverty.

Life at Ojai during the war was not all meditation and philosophical discussion. Because of rationing and shortages, Arya Vihara was trans-formed into a small-holding farmstead, and Krishnamurti entered will-ingly into his share of the hard labour. There was a vegetable plot, fruit trees, bees, chickens and cows, most of which required daily attention. Any surplus produce was tinned or dried for aid boxes that were then sent on to Europe. Krishnamurti, far from being frustrated at having his wings clipped, was happy working hard in this secluded paradise alongside the woman he adored. Rajagopal, as ever, was always too much occupied with other business to interfere, and it was generally accepted by visitors that Krishnamurti and Rosalind were host and hostess of the establishment. Radha remembers his devotion to family life at Arya Vihara – he would always walk her to the school bus in the morning and be there when she returned; and he preferred not to go out in the evenings, but to stay and talk with the company at home. The occasional horrifying piece of war news darkened their idyll, and they constantly feared for their friends in Europe, but the atrocities seemed distant and were rarely discussed openly.

Krishna on holiday at Pergine, north Italy, August 1924.

August 1924, at Pergine, north Italy. *Front row, l to r:* Krishna, Lady Emily, Betty Lutyens, Mary Lutyens, two Indian friends (Sivakamu and Malati), and Ruth Roberts; *back row, l to r:* Helen Knothe, Rama Rao (a long-term friend and worker for Krishna), Rajagopal and John Cordes (national representative of the OSE in Austria).

Krishna dressed in Indian clothes during his impressive fortnight of talks at Castle Eerde, summer 1926.

The camp fire at Ommen in 1926, a magical and memorable time for followers of the Star.

Krishna addresses the Ommen Star camp in 1926.

Krishna and Annie Besant mingle with camp participants. Ommen, 1926.

Switzerland, August 1927. Krishna with (*l to r*) Rajagopal and Jadunandam
Prasad, two friends who helped to fill the void left by the death of Nitya.
Jadunandam was to die prematurely in 1931.

Krishna sitting with Annie Besant at the momentous Ommen gathering of 1929.

Rosalind and Krishna in Holland, c1930.

Krishnamurti with Radha Rajagopal, California, 1939.

Krishnamurti in 1948, shortly after his return to India,
every inch the dynamic spiritual master.

Krishnamurti meets students at Brockwood Park, 1975.

Krishnamurti with David Bohm, in 1983.

Krishnamurti in 1985.

The small community at Ojai, with the inclusion of Huxley, conceived the idea of fulfilling Annie Besant's plan to found a school in the valley, one of the reasons for which she had raised money and formed the Happy Valley Association. Krishnamurti was less concerned with furthering the ambitions of his bête noir, the Theosophical Society, than with putting into practice his own educational theory, and, more pressingly, finding a solution to the problem of where Radha and her classmates could go to high school. The Happy Valley School opened, in defiance of multiple financial difficulties, in September 1946, with twelve children and eight staff. Rosalind shouldered the bulk of the school's administrative work, and this responsibility meant that she had less time to devote to Krishnamurti's needs, a circumstance that may have brought a note of mutual resentment into their relationship.

By the end of the war, this eternal boy-man, who had always enchanted the world with his youth and beauty, and seemed immune to the ravages of time, had suddenly arrived at the age of fifty. Christopher Isherwood describes a middle-aged man starkly different from the princely and dapper messiah of the 1920s: 'Krishnamurti was a slight, sallow little man with a scrubby chin and rather bloodshot eyes, whose face bore only faint traces of the extraordinary beauty he must have had as a boy. He was very quiet and modest, and never talked in ordinary company about philosophy or religion. He seemed fondest of animals and most at ease with children . . . he had a kind of simple dignity which was very touching.'[26] He had shed the pious aura that had accompanied him in earlier times, partly because of his change in status and partly because he was now surrounded by practical, working human beings, rather than priests, disciples and clairvoyants. The Savile Row suits and silk shirts were packed away for a while, making way for comfortable ranch-wear and a broad-brimmed sun-hat. Sidney Field remembered him as 'a prince in faded Levi's and worn cotton shirt'.[27] There was no more mention of throbbing engines in the air at Arya Vihara, or of visitations from astral entities; the pepper tree outside Pine Cottage, once declared a sacred site where mile-stone events in the new scripture had been enacted, was no longer endowed with particular significance, and Krishnamurti forbade any mention of the events that had taken place there in 1922. There were fewer devotees on hand to hang on his every utterance or reach out for a touch of his sleeve, and the remaining companions who did share his life grew less tolerant of his idiosyncracies. As with so many adults who are catapulted to fame in childhood, there were sides to his character that had never matured; these now grew disproportionately irritating to those around him (especially to Rajagopal and, increasingly, Rosalind) and led to his becoming the victim of increasing abuse. His passive nature let the criticisms and intimidations pass unchecked.

The situation was exacerbated when Krishnamurti fell seriously ill with nephritis, to the point where Huxley and others feared for his life. His refusal to be nursed by anyone other than Rosalind, over-burdened as she was, was to cause her much exasperation, especially as he took more than six months fully to recover. His plan to embark on a tour of India, Australia and New Zealand in 1946 had to be cancelled, as he would not be fit to travel until September 1947, by which time he had begun to feel that his life had become suffocatingly circumscribed. He also felt restless to address new audiences and redefine his message now that his Theosophical connection had been severed by a space of more than fifteen years. He longed to break out of the claustrophobic atmosphere at Ojai and return to his vocation which, no matter how awkward he felt on the platform, was to teach the world.

11

Teaching the World

———— ✳ ————

The single most striking difference in the public teaching style that Krishnamurti was to adopt after his long sojourn in California was his abandonment of mystery. He played down any connection between himself and Besant's predicted messiah and was at pains to draw a veil over some of the enigmas of his own person, such as his much-attested gift for healing through the laying-on of hands. He jettisoned traditionally devotional terminology, such as references to the Beloved, and messianic expressions which had adorned his lectures in former times. Aware of his audiences' tendency to invest him with sanctity, he now adopted the habit of referring to himself in the third person, as 'K', 'the body', or 'the teacher'. He sought to break the spell that he had cast over his listeners in the days of his poetic outpourings and to extinguish, once and for all, their almost erotic desire to deify him. For the remainder of his life he would implore audiences to listen and question rather than stare in meditative wonder at 'the speaker.'

Besantesque orations were ditched as he began to find his strength in the more intimate medium of the question-and-answer session. His style underwent a mutation, from that of Saviour pronouncing cosmic truths, to that of personal counsellor, responding to the crisis within each individual's psyche. The goal of transforming the world was no different, but the means of achieving it had shifted. The language he employed became less florid and more practical, though the simplicity of his prose belied the sophistication of the concepts he attempted to impart. Henry Miller was to write that his 'language is naked, revelatory and inspiring. It pierces the clouds of philosophy which confound our thought and restores the springs of action. It levels the tottering super-structures of the verbal gymnasts and clears the ground of rubbish.'[1] Yet he was never secular in approach, and the very premise of his teaching mission was the immanence of the sacred in creation. His audiences could never forget that their speaker was a profoundly religious man, who had been in the presence of spiritual infallibility. The purpose of his message for humanity was the solution of psychological suffering, but with every word that he uttered he affirmed his conviction that the answer to this problem was to be found in a truly spiritual way of life. This alone would transform the world.

His public profile was now defined not by sensation, exoticism, or an apotheosising pedestal, nor even by system and method, but by the example of his own living. He was clear that enlightenment could not be taught in one or one thousand lessons, and that theorising would never bring about transformation. Krishnamurti, with his intensity, powers of observation and sheer wakefulness was for his followers the living embodiment of his own teachings. He claimed that his life was spent in meditation, not in the traditional sense of withdrawing from the world, or focussing the mind on a given theme, but participating fully in life, at the moment, with all senses alert, attentive, undistracted by the activi-ties of thought. Central to this way of life, which his followers increasingly attempted to emulate, was a respect for order. He maintained there was no chaos in nature, only in the muddled thoughts of man, and that through an orderly life mankind could approach the inviolable purity of creation. In his own life this extended to the most banal every day activities, the way he dressed, ate, drank, worked and used language. He purposefully regulated the mechanics of his brain so as to deny the infiltration of disorder, which would lead to conflict. Order, he main-tained, was a property of intelligence.

It is important to understand that nothing Krishnamurti taught was new. This does not mean that he was unoriginal (especially in the com-municative style he developed, which was fresh and appropriate for a twentieth-century audience), but that the essence of his personal vision, his Truth, was not to be contained in what is implied by terms like old, new, original or derivative. Whether or not he was conditioned by his own background remains a subject of hot debate, but his output certainly contains elements that are in sympathy with both Hindu and Theosophical philosophy. The conviction that an unnameable and transcendent divine energy is immanent in all creation, and that man's liberation from bondage is achieved through a state of union with this energy, is fundamental to ancient Vedantic philosophy of the type that inspired both Blavatsky and Besant. Furthermore, Krishnamurti's emphasis that this liberation is dependent on a disciplined awareness of mental distractions such as desire, personal achievement, pleasure and thought, has resonances in mainstream Buddhist and Hindu traditions. He reveals a more western slant in his rejection of creeds, superstitions and codes of religious morality. This is reminiscent of the type of Enlightenment rationalism that characterised theosophical speculators of the eighteenth century, Blavatsky's forerunners.

It was neither originality nor a logical system that Krishnamurti sought. His talks, instead, were intended to light a fuse, to set his audience questioning, so that they might discover uncharted illuminations within themselves, ultimately leading to a revolution of the psyche. As such, his teachings were emotive and rhetorical rather than structured or argued. There is no such thing as a Krishnamurti spiritual technique, although he gave innumerable recommendations on ways to tidy one's 'house' in preparation for insight. He never allowed an audience to look to him for systematical solutions or formulas for salvation. That would be to set himself up as an authority, a crutch. It was only in pointing out spiritual obstacles to be avoided that he began to develop certain pet themes over the years. These were refined, massaged and moulded as he grew older, according to the circumstances of the audience he happened to be addressing, culturally, politically and socially. The advent of the nuclear menace, the cold war, the savagery of interracial strife, the technological revolution, the prospect of an environmental crisis, and the dawn of a new youth movement in the 1960s, all served to draw fresh perspectives and language from Krishnamurti, though the underlying pillars of his message remained consistent from the 1930s until his death.

These fundamentals are best summarised in a statement Krishnamurti himself composed in 1980, entitled, *The Revolutionary Core of Krishnamurti's Teaching*:

The core of Krishnamurti's teaching is contained in the statement he made in 1929 when he said 'Truth is a pathless land.' Man cannot come to it through any organisation, through any creed, through any dogma, priest or ritual, not through any philosophical knowledge or psychological technique. He has to find it through the mirror of relationship, through the understanding of the contents of his own mind, through observation and not through intellectual analysis or introspective dissection. Man has built in himself images as a fence of security – religious, political, personal. These manifest as symbols, ideas, beliefs. The burden of these dominate man's thinking, relationships and daily life. These are the causes of our problems for they divide man from man in every relationship. His perception of life is shaped by the concepts already established in his mind. The content of his consciousness *is* this consciousness. This content is common to all humanity. The individuality is the name, the form and superficial culture he acquires from his environment. The uniqueness of the individual does not lie in the superficial but in the total freedom from the content of consciousness.

Freedom is not a reaction; freedom is not choice. It is man's pretence that because he has choice he is free. Freedom is pure observation without direction, without fear of punishment and reward. Freedom is without motive; freedom is not at the end of the evolution of man but lies in the first step of his existence. In observation one begins to discover the lack of freedom. Freedom is found in the choiceless awareness of our daily existence.

Thought is time. Thought is born of experience, of knowledge, which are inseparable from time. Time is the psychological enemy of man. Our action is based on knowledge and therefore time, so man is always a slave to the past.

When man becomes aware of the movement of his own consciousness he will see the division between the thinker and the thought, the observer and the observed, the experiencer and the experience. He will discover that this division is an illusion. Then only is there pure observation which is insight without any shadow of the past. This timeless insight brings about a deep radical change in the mind.

Total negation is the essence of the positive. When there is negation of all those things which are not love – desire, pleasure – then love is, with all its compassion and intelligence.[2]

The essence of the radical change Krishnamurti advocated (which in other theologies and philosophies is variously described as enlightenment, realisation, awakening or rebirth), is contained in the title of one of his shortest but most effective books, *Freedom from the Known*. All security, pleasure and happiness, together with their opposites, fear, sorrow and suffering, derive from our confinement within and addiction to the known, our constant dependence upon the particular field of reference which defines our individuality. A typical illustration is our fear of death. It is not death itself we fear, but the idea of death, based on mental impressions we have formed during our years of thinking on the subject. Death is in fact the one certain and most natural consequence of life, observable all around us, all the time, at the close of each day, the turn of each season. Yet within our limited field of reference, personal death has taken on a shape and entity of its own, an illusory monster. Living, as we do, within the parameters of thought, we cannot face the unknown; the unknown can never be understood because the very process of 'understanding' implies that it is already within our field of reference, which personal death clearly is not. The one defining element within this field, its regulator and structure, is psychological time. It is the notion of ending time, losing the hand-rail of our continuity, that renders death unthinkable. We therefore try not to think about it, because the only alternative offered by knowledge is to form a thought-image of death as an ultimate, insuperable foe – a terrifying ogre, perhaps, pacing ever nearer, ready at any moment to pounce.

Krishnamurti sought to point out the limitations of existing within a field of reference by demonstrating that it is created by the past – experiences, memories and conditioning – and is therefore a barrier to our full participation in life. It gives rise to monolithic and illusory constructs (illusory in that they are the product only of conditioned thought), such as ideologies, prejudice, the division of man from man, which are responsible for the fragmentation of creation. He taught that there is no fragmentation, no division or conflict in nature; quite the opposite, there is nothing but oneness. Fragmentation is the product of thought, of self-determination, all of which derives from an individual's storehouse of knowledge, which then translates into judgments, likes and dislikes. Our very notion of ourselves as individuals, the 'me', is nothing but a bottled preserve of memories, labelled with a name and characterised by a set of opinions that derive from the personally known. Freedom from the known, he maintained, is the key to a truly religious life, a life spent in union with creation and the divine energy inherent within it.

Controversially, and in opposition to almost every established religious outlook, Krishnamurti maintained that the psychological revolution he demanded was available to anyone, at any time, regardless of personal history, moral outlook, devotional background, spiritual faith or learning. Indeed, these might all block a person's perception of the truly sacred because they are divisive. Here is just one of the many paradoxes about Krishnamurti: that he dedicated his life to the proliferation of religious awareness, while at the same time undermining the fortress of what has been conventionally termed religion.

When Krishnamurti finally left Ojai in the autumn of 1947, bound for India, he was entering a new and exciting period of his life. He wrote amorous daily letters to Rosalind, but continued his life without apparently mourning the separation and, as was the case with Lady Emily in the 1920s, found it unnecessary to justify or share his new interests with those who had appeared to be so close to him in the recent past. Deliberate or not, he was always prone to withold details of one side of his life from those who were prominent in another. Significantly, Rajagopal did not accompany him to India, and Krishnamurti was now to be apart from his Californian 'family' for nineteen months. He was returning to India an independent middle-aged man, not without an extraordinary reputation, but unaffiliated and free of any organisational restraint. Many of the old Theosophical brigade came to hear him as soon as he arrived, but they did so on his terms, and if they felt nostalgia for the old days they kept it quiet. George Arundale had recently died, and Jinarajadasa, the last of the old guard (and certainly the most sympathetic to Krishnamurti's new stance) had been elected President of the Society. Although the term World Teacher was not one many dared utter in Krishnamurti's company, some faithful old Theosophists silently believed that this mature and free-standing phenomenon who returned to their midst in 1947 was at last fulfilling his mission in the world. He certainly rose to the occasion, stirred from the pleasant inertia of Ojai by the clarion call of a new and vibrant audience.

It was a remarkable time for India. Weeks prior to Krishnamurti's arrival the Republican flag had been raised above the dome of the palace built by Edwin Lutyens in New Delhi, now the official home not of a British Viceroy but the Indian President. A nation had been born; but the euphoria of independence was soon dampened by the carnage of Hindu–Moslem conflict. Thousands were butchered on both sides as the religious prejudices of centuries struggled to assert themselves in defiance of Nehru's secular democracy.

Krishnamurti cut an impressive figure on his return, dignified, perhaps even majestic in his Indian kurta and dhoti, still handsome with a full head of hair, and a physical presence that was variously described as explosive, monumental, celestial. He immediately attracted a following of young intellectuals, forward-looking men and women, many of them former freedom campaigners. They were enthusiastic, questioning people, ready to take up the challenge of a nation in crisis, and sincere in their desire to construct a brave new world in India. They looked to Krishnamurti for a practical way forward, a twentieth-century way, free from the misty opacity of traditional religion, and open to the inevitable advent of modern technology. He was a new type of guru, emancipated and free of superstition, yet still, to their minds, steeped in the Vedantic philosophy of their fathers. This recipe, perhaps in some way reminiscent of the Gandhi–Nehru blend that had given rise to the free republic, was a crucial factor in securing Krishnamurti's place as a spiritual influence in the new India.

Despite his lifelong aversion of being labelled a guru, Krishnamurti was tactful enough not to breach cultural etiquette in India or cause offence. He understood that, whereas he might be a novelty in Europe or the States, in India he was one of a long line of spiritual teachers who had dedicated their lives to imparting realised Truth. He was literally a 'guru' (one who brings light to the darkness) and, as such, it was his cultural role to receive gifts, such as fruit and flowers, and to accept the devotion of his audience. Many of them merely wanted to taste his presence – the Hindu concept *darshan* – and touch his feet as a mark of respect. The holy and wise came from far to view and hear the teacher. Monks, swamis, sannyasis, learned pandits, and religious devotees of different persuasions littered the ranks of his listeners, each claiming a place for him within the spiritual lineage of their preference. They were deaf to his denials of tradition but alert to the perspicacity of his vision.

Amongst the bright young people who became close to Krishnamurti on this first return visit to India were two sisters, Pupul Jayakar and Nandini Mehta, daughters of an eminent civil servant with a Theosophical background, and members of Bombay high society. Krishnamurti adopted them as trusted friends from the start, with Pupul often acting as his intellectual amanuensis. The beautiful and vulnerable Nandini touched his heart in a special way. They were to become intimate and devoted friends, a teacher–pupil alliance that inevitably gave rise to whispers in certain quarters. In May 1948 the two sisters sealed their friendship with the teacher by helping him through the first major recurrence of his mysterious 'process' since 1925. They had retired for a few weeks to the anglicised hill-station of Ootacamund, and in this verdant retreat, peppered with quaint cottages and rose gardens, Krishnamurti began to feel the familiar symptoms – agonising neck and skull pain, together with intense heat, and a feeling that his body was being cleansed by the band of 'spotless' entities to whom his life's work was entrusted. The sisters, unaware of the events at Ojai and elsewhere in the 1920s, were alarmed and dazzled by the transformation that was taking place before their eyes. Once again, he appeared to drift away, leaving a childlike shell to provide an outsider's commentary on the events, but in moments of coherence bade them remain calm and just stay with him, protecting his body and seeing to its needs. By the time the process came to an end, in mid-June, the women were convinced they had been privy to sacred events. Krishnamurti declared that he had been fuelled up, like a car in preparation for a long journey.

He certainly had need of fuel. His speaking schedule from this time on, together with the time he reserved for private interviews (up to thirty a day), was physically demanding. His reputation as a leading seer of modern India soon brought Jawaharlal Nehru to his door, seeking spiritual advice. The assassination of Gandhi, on 30 January 1948, had been a tremendous blow to the besieged prime minister, both personally and politically. The nation he had envisaged, with his ideals of social democracy and egalitarianism, was floundering on a wave of civil strife. Nehru had come into contact with the Theosophical Society in his youth, and had met Krishnamurti in the 1930s. Now he had to sit and listen as Annie Besant's former protégé told him how social transformation would never save India while the minds of men remained unchanged. Transformation must first occur within. It was a difficult lesson for the pandit to hear, as leader of an impoverished, deprived, and blood-stained nation. Krishnamurti was later to play a pivotal role in the political life of Nehru's daughter, prime minister Indhira Gandhi, and could justifiably be described as her spiritual guru.

Krishnamurti's first extended visit to the Republic of India, served to ensure that it would remain an important centre for the dissemination of his ideas, as Annie Besant had always envisaged. His relationship with the country would be volatile over the years, and he would frequently express in private his frustration at the cultural idiosyncrasies of its people, but he never lost the conviction (perhaps a remnant of his Theosophical background) that the fabric of India, its philosophies and its very soil, were sacred. The annual pattern of speaking engagements he was now to adopt centred on three principal territories: California, Europe and India, and he was to divide his time between the three, visiting the States in the spring, continental Europe in the summer, England towards the close of summer, and India during the winter.

On his return to Ojai, Krishnamurti's private life with Rosalind began to show signs of strain again. She suspected that he was witholding secrets from her about his activities in India, even to the extent of concealing the identity of a new lover. Rosalind's worst nightmares appeared to be taking shape in January 1950 when *Time* magazine published an article about Krishnamurti's role in the break-up of a prominent Bombay family. The piece was headed 'Revolt of the Doormat', and outlined the case of his friend, Nandini Mehta, who was suing her husband for legal separation on grounds of domestic violence and cruelty. The husband, a 'textile millionaire', publicly blamed Krishnamurti for inciting her rebellion, through his iconoclastic teachings on the institution of marriage and the traditional role of women in Indian families. Nandini subsequently lost the case, her position in society, and custody of her three young children. Much emphasis had been put on her refusal to continue sexual relations with her husband, which was interpreted by some as a sign that she had transferred her affections to another man – Krishnamurti.

The rumours were probably unfounded, and the publicity surrounding the case vastly disproportionate because of the high profile of the family involved. In fact, Krishnamurti's advice to women at the time (not just Nandini) was mild by contemporary western standards. It was also wholly consistent with what he had been saying for years, and would continue to say, about marriage, and the economic and social subjugation of women in India. In this regard he was a worthy successor to Annie Besant, who campaigned tirelessly for the same cause. Nandini had indeed been swept off her feet by the charismatic teacher who took her to his heart, but her husband was an overbearing and violent man, and she was by no means the only woman at that time to be stirred into revolt by Krishnamurti's words. Several others were simultaneously going to court against their husbands, but did not have the money or social standing of the Mehta family.

In September 1950 Krishnamurti announced that he would be going into retreat for a year, ostensibly to rest after three years of almost continuous work, but he was privately keen to heal relations with the Rajagopals. Rosalind and her husband both resented the degree to which they had been excluded from his activities in India, and were concerned that the future direction of his work might take him beyond their control. Krishnamurti was not to return to India for nearly a year-and-a-half, but remained in California, pursuing a peaceful life, not unlike the one he had enjoyed during the war – walking, contemplating, gardening, and observing a rule of silence for much of the time. These periods of retreat, which he undertook at various points in his life, helped focus and revitalise him in a way that was later to find expression in the rhapsodic prose of his published *Notebooks*. When he did return to India, in December 1951, it was in the company of a suspicious and watchful Rajagopal. Before leaving Ojai, Krishnamurti had been asked to assure Rosalind that he would distance himself from Nandini. He kept this promise, even to the point of not responding to an urgent telegram from Pupul, in July 1952, telling him that Nandini was seriously ill with cervical cancer. She was fortunately to recover, and relations between them would later be restored to normal.

The seeds were now being sown for what was to become the ugliest chapter in Krishnamurti's life, one that was to shadow his public career to the very end. It has given rise to accusations of hypocrisy on the part of the teacher who famously and repeatedly claimed that his life was entirely without conflict. The problem stemmed from the gradual disintegration of his relations with Rosalind and Rajagopal.

His gradual refusal to be answerable to Rajagopal, in an administrative context, and Rosalind in a romantic one, and his preference for remaining silent rather than admit truths that would lead to arguments, they regarded as disloyal, even deceitful. But that he would not willingly submit to their possessiveness was entirely in keeping with what he had always taught and observed. He certainly did not apply double standards; jealousy and possession had no place in his vocabulary of life, nor did constancy, which he considered a false virtue because it implied stagnancy. Despite his dependence on certain people, and his need for physical care and succour, he remained throughout an isolated person. He lived alone in his extraordinary world, unencumbered by the complexities that beleaguer ordinary human relationships. He was not unlike a lighthouse, perched out on a lonely rock, sending beams of light indiscriminately and unexclusively into the night; occasionally the light would find its mark, and illuminate some stray vessel, before moving on to fresh horizons. Too often the vessels would come like moths towards the light, to live in its beam, instead of steering the wise course, and too often they were wrecked. Krishnamurti would say that it was not love that bound them to him, but the brain seeking to catch love and trap it. Underneath the child in his nature was the steely teacher who consistently refused to be anyone's toy, and that periodically meant discarding those who had clung to him.

A turning point in Krishnamurti's relationship with the Rajagopals came about in 1955, when it was decided that Rosalind would accompany him to India to see for herself the scene of his new influence and meet some of the people involved. She was no longer perturbed so much by the threat of Nandini as by the adulation that surrounded Krishnamurti everywhere he went. She found the devotion of his entourage overly obsequious, and had difficulty reconciling his acceptance of it with the attitudes he had embodied during their life together in Ojai. She was irritated at having to stand aside and witness the sanctification of a man she knew to possess human flaws and weaknesses. She finally decided that she could no longer have any part in his life and, as they paused in Stockholm for Krishnamurti to fulfil some speaking engagements, declared that he would not be welcome to return to Ojai. As ever, Krishnamurti acquiesced without complaint, thus relinquishing his home like an errant husband. The ban was to stay in place for four years, after which Rosalind took it upon herself to heal the breach. But by this time she felt isolated and embittered in the wake of a romance that had sprung up between her husband, Rajagopal, and a pretty young Swiss-Italian woman whom he was later to marry. She was also concerned that deteriorating relations between her husband and Krishnamurti had left Rajagopal in a state of deep depression. She therefore wrote and invited her former lover back to Ojai, in the hope that their differences could be sorted out. There was a reconciliation of sorts on Krishnamurti's return in 1960; however, by this time an added complication had arisen, which was ultimately to lead to a complete rupture.

Rajagopal had for years had sole control of Krishnamurti's talking and travel schedule and, more importantly, the increasingly wealthy organisation that was responsible for the publication and dissemination of his teachings, known now as Krishnamurti Writings Incorporated, or KWINC. It had become his own little empire, over which he had complete autonomy, and Rajagopal was notoriously fond of managing matters personally, down to the smallest detail. It was an arrangement that suited both men, as it allowed Krishnamurti to detach himself from administrative matters, while Rajagopal retained his dignity, independent of his employer rather than subservient to him. The person of Krishnamurti, his teaching and reputation, had given rise to what was now a multimillion dollar concern, but the commercial success of the operation was the fruit of Rajagopal's hard work, editorial skills and fussy directorship. It is little wonder he was prepared to defend his achievement with the tenacity of a successful businessman, and that he was increasingly irritated at Krishnamurti's nonchalant attitude towards money. The deterioration of the two men's friendship after the war led Rajagopal to demand legal definition of his position with regard to control of copyright and publications. What had before been an informal understanding was legally sealed in the presence of a public notary in Madras, on 13 November 1958. Krishnamurti later claimed, ingenuously but characteristically, that he had not really understood what had been handed to him for signature.

Rajagopal had succeeded in stabilising his position, on paper, at least; but for the remainder of their lives the two were to regard each other with a kind of hatred, fed, perhaps, by an undercurrent of love, discernible to no one else and perhaps not even to themselves, like husband and wife in a poisoned marriage. Rajagopal, always destined to remain in the shadow of his fellow Brahmin, developed a dependence on alcohol, and grew more depressed and reclusive with age.

Faced with these developments, Krishnamurti was now advised to reassert his control over the affairs of KWINC, for which he had in the past happily relinquished responsibility, as he began to suspect that Rajagopal's secrecy in the management of his affairs might conceal a mishandling of KWINC funds. He was also persuaded of his duty towards those who had donated large sums for the proliferation of his teachings, and who were concerned that their funds were being intercepted. Matters came to a head when Rajagopal began to restrict the amount of money available to Krishnamurti on his speaking tours, occasionally leaving him with barely enough to cover his travel and hotel bills. Communication between them soon degenerated to the point where they both became childishly spiteful when referring to the other; accusations of insanity, hypocrisy and fraudulence were made on both sides, much to the distress of mutual friends. Their attempt at a reconciliation, when Krishnamurti returned to Ojai in 1960 after his prolonged absence, was foiled when Rajagopal refused adamantly to allow him back onto the board of KWINC, the body that bore his name and was responsible for the distribution of his work. Krishnamurti pressed him to hand back manuscripts and other archive material from a collection that Rajagopal had put together in a specially constructed vault underneath his house, and which he seemed vehemently determined to retain. These became the issues that were now to drive them apart and although Krishnamurti persisted for eight years in reiterating his requests, Rajagopal refused to change his mind. There were renewed attempts to achieve a truce for the continued smooth running of KWINC, but neither man was prepared to compromise his position; and Rajagopal never let Krishnamurti forget that his entire reputation might be at stake if word of his clandestine affair with Rosalind were ever to escape.

The result was a stalemate, with Krishnamurti staying away from Ojai for a further five years and a state of open discord between the two camps representing the same man's work. A return to Ojai in 1966 convinced both sides that the position was untenable. Krishnamurti had become hopelessly alienated from Rajagopal and Rosalind, and even convinced himself that Pine Cottage, the scene of spiritual wonders and happy days in the past, had been electronically bugged by his enemies. By the summer of 1968 Krishnamurti decided that he could have nothing more to do with KWINC so long as Rajagopal remained. He issued a statement to the effect that he was detaching himself from KWINC and announced the birth of the Krishnamurti Foundation Trust, to be based in London, which would thenceforth be responsible for his speaking engagements in Europe, his recordings, receipts of charitable donations, and publications. This KFT, as it would be known, was to be allied with a Krishnamurti Foundation of India and a Krishnamurti Foundation of America, to complete the world picture.

A series of legal battles were now commenced, first to revoke the Madras agreement of 1958, which had assigned copyright control to Rajagopal, and then to recover KWINC funds and property, together with Krishnamurti's archives. Millions of dollars were at stake, as were the houses at Ojai and Madras, and the future control of Krishnamurti's books. After both sides failed to reach a settlement out of court legal proceedings were initiated against Rajagopal in 1971. The matter was settled in December 1974 in Krishnamurti's favour, except for some minor provisions for the duration of Rajagopal's life, and KWINC was dissolved. The eighty-year-old teacher was now able to return without complication, to his beloved Pine Cottage. However, a dispute continued over the possession of certain archives, and a new lawsuit was initiated against Rajagopal in December 1980. At this point Rosalind intervened and warned Krishnamurti that their former love-affair would be made public if this case were to proceed. It is unclear whether she was attempting to blackmail him or make him understand that the archive material soon to come under the lawyers' scrutiny was of a highly sensitive nature, and perhaps included their private letters. At a deposition hearing in March 1983 Krishnamurti was questioned about his relationship with Rosalind, but on the advice of his lawyers refused to answer and the matter remained concealed. The case continued until June 1986, when a further million dollars, together with some archives, were handed over to the Krishnamurti Foundation of America. Rajagopal was permitted to retain certain documents deemed to be his own property, and in addition was officially declared to 'have done nothing wrong, and have not committed any acts which might be the basis for civil or criminal charges or complaints'.[3] Seventeen years of legal action had finally been settled.

It is very easy when examining this record of events to label Rajagopal the intransigent aggressor and Krishnamurti the innocent victim. It would be wrong to picture him in this way, as there is evidence to suggest that, like any human being, he was capable of contradicting himself and manipulating events to his own ends, some of which were darker than his followers might like to admit. This became apparent in the 1950s when the consolidation of his mature teachings led to his adopting a defensive and not entirely straightforward position with regard to his own past. In defiance of his own principles he developed a fixed notion of how he wanted to be perceived by the contemporary audience. It was as if an edifice was under construction that must be protected and kept free from taint. Above all, he was keen to withold from the public as much as possible about his Theosophical connection, the messianic ambitions of Besant, and the mysterious 'process'. When Lady Emily attempted to include a detailed account of all these in her autobiographical *Candles in the Sun* in 1954, Krishnamurti vehemently forbade her to publish the book. It was eventually published, in a truncated form, in accordance with his wishes, three years later. He clearly believed, with good reason, that the sensationalism of his early story would cloud the public's perception of his current work. And Lady Emily's experience of him in the 1920s revealed him as an insecure, overly-romantic, at times embittered youth, who was ultimately capable of jettisoning those who had spent their money and lives promoting him. This would be bad publicity, pure and simple. The extreme assertiveness with which he was later to attempt to regain possession of his early papers and manuscripts from Rajagopal's archive implied that he wanted to select what material from his past was to be available for future historians. This kind of censorship reveals a man aware of a potential crisis in his public image – an issue that he repeatedly claimed was an irrelevance. By 1975 he lifted his objection to having the record set straight, when he allowed Mary Lutyens to publish a biography including much of the material that he had previously banned, but by this stage half a century had passed, and everybody's sensitivity to those events had been dampened.

Many of those who knew him personally, friends, disciples and dis-senters, support the theory that there were two people in Krishnamurti. They are united in admiration for the teacher, the strength, sincerity, charisma, consistency and inspiration that marked his performance in public. The other, human personality, evokes different responses. Detrac-tors maintain that he had a cold, deceitful side, that he would use any means available to have his way, even if it meant hurting and abusing his friends. They draw attention to his excessive vanity, his fussing over trivial details, his impatience with certain individuals whom he quite obviously disliked, and his apparent tactlessness in criticising those who worked hardest for him. This would appear to paint an overly negative picture of the man. A more balanced view, and one entirely consistent with the boy Krishna, reveals a human being largely devoid of strong personality, one who, when not teaching, was vulnerable and helpless to the point of torpidity. As such he was easily intimidated and manipu-lated by other, more determined characters. Many of the inconsistencies of his private life can be traced to this very quality. He cherished this vacuousness as central to his life as a teacher (as, indeed, had Leadbeater), and once declared to the staff at one of his schools that the most important thing in his life was 'To be nothing, to be absolutely nothing.'[4]

Yet this, again, does not complete the picture, as he was periodically capable of great strength of character, stunning his associates with his forthrightness. In many ways he was less than human; in some, more; but it would be a mistake to deny him humanity altogether, and to expect more from his sixty years of teaching than any human operating in the real world, not cloistered in a remote monastery, would be capable of providing.

While the confrontation with Rajagopal was brewing, Krishnamurti's Ojai appearances were suspended indefinitely, and new avenues for the dissemination of his teachings were being explored. Relations between Ojai and Krishnamurti's workers in Europe were strained, and in 1961 the latter formed a committee, in practice independent of KWINC, to arrange an annual group of talks at a European location, along the lines of the former Ommen and Ojai gatherings. This would centralise Krishnamurti's summer schedule, bringing audiences to him rather than subjecting him to a punishing round of international tours. This committee also recommended, with the agreement of Rajagopal (who still maintained complete control of all publications), that Krishnamurti's talks and formal conversations should henceforth be recorded, both for posterity and to make them available, through a more vivid medium than the printed book, all around the world. Rajagopal insisted on immediate possession of any recordings made in Europe, but suspected that his own influence was being undermined by the new committee.

Krishnamurti was also growing close to a more recent friend, Mary Zimbalist, the widow of an eminent film producer, whom he would call Maria in order to differentiate her from the several other Marys of his acquaintanceship. She had first heard Krishnamurti speak in 1944, but became particularly interested in his teachings after the death of her husband in 1958. By the mid-1960s she had become part of the close inner circle, volunteering herself to drive Krishnamurti to engagements around Europe, travel the world as his personal assistant, and look after him when ill. Unlike Rosalind, she asked for nothing in return for her devotion, except the privilege of being close to a man she saw as the light of the world. They were to share homes in California and at

Brockwood, and Krishnamurti became dependent on her in a physical sense. He had always selected certain individuals to look after 'the body', and Mary, with her gentle humility, but firm motherly control, rose willingly to the task.

The village of Saanen, near Gstaad in Switzerland, was selected in 1961 as the new European centre, and a portion of land acquired for the purpose. The neutral diplomatic status of Switzerland was significant, as was the proximity of mountains, lush valleys and forests, which had always held an attraction for Krishnamurti. A huge marquee was erected on the site, with capacity for one thousand visitors, and for the next twenty-five years the word Saanen became synonymous, in the minds of spiritual seekers, with the annual Krishnamurti summer event. In 1969 another centre was founded at Brockwood Park, a Georgian house in southern England, which would serve not only as a venue for further gatherings, but also as a school, and a home for Krishnamurti himself.

The audiences he attracted at these talks belonged to no particular type, age, class, income bracket or esoteric persuasion. They all shared an interest in alternative spirituality and were perhaps of a more than average intellectual ability but, unlike members of the various cults that prospered in the 1960s and '70s, did not subscribe to a common agenda of salvation, and drug culture was strictly prohibited. Professionals, academics, vagrants, young, old, rich and poor rubbed shoulders as they silently listened to the now aging and diminutive figure on the platform, who spoke without notes, his hands tucked under his thighs, to still a slight shake in his wrists. The pleasant and harmonious quality of the audiences, together with their spirit of optimistic enquiry, was reminiscent of the early Ommen camps. Indeed, many veterans of that era were still attending Krishnamurti's gatherings in the 1960s.

Aside from giving talks, Krishnamurti developed a fondness for the medium of dialogue in the post-war period, and this was to prove an important new tool in the dissemination of his ideas. His dialogues, with one or several interlocutors, were intended to be an egalitarian journey of discovery through the exchange of ideas. Unlike his question-and-answer sessions, dialogue proposed that questions should give rise to further questions, rather than assertions, and that this process of enquiry would release a participant from the constraints of opinion, leading to fresh insights. Contrary to the western religious tradition of faith and dogma, dialogue encouraged a dissolution of belief in favour of perpetual questioning. Krishnamurti was to have hundreds of formal dialogues, many of them published in book form as seminal expositions of his thought, whether they were with scientists, religious leaders or school children.

The resolute strength of Krishnamurti's teaching style acted like a magnet to the weak, and many of the same people would return again and again to his talks, often travelling the globe to sit at his feet. This sort of blank, inactive acceptance of his words infuriated him and led him to deride audiences for their spineless devotion. By the early 1960s it became clear that he was looking for new ways of transmitting his message, and that reiterating the same themes to predictable audiences year after year was leaving him frustrated. He sought a more challenging arena, and his change of style around this period reflected a new sense of urgency that was to characterise the later teachings. He had lived through two major world crises and felt that another, more devastating still, was looming, if fundamental change were not soon to be brought about. He now chose, therefore, to engage leading specialists in various fields, through formal dialogues, tackling them face to face at the heart of their subjects in an attempt to throw up revolutionary insights. He approached this task with the ease and confidence of one who had spent a lifetime receiving society's most eminent grandees, and once through the barrier of his own personal shyness, no individual, regardless of rank or qualification, constituted a threat to his way of thinking. He only ever shrank from an encounter when there was a possibility that he might cause offence to a genuinely kind and sincere person, such as the Dalai Lama, whom he dreaded having to inform about the absurdity of institutionalised religion and spiritual authority.

One specialist field of enquiry he tackled regularly was that of psychotherapy. Many of his own books and case study observations centred on the issue of psychological bondage and the need for transformation, and it was therefore apposite that he should challenge contemporary attitudes towards mental health, which he believed were fundamentally misdirected. He met with groups of therapists and psychologists to thrash out his own conviction – in opposition to current theories – that psychological suffering could only be resolved through a dissolution of the separate self and a complete detachment from past and experience. Delving into the past, he maintained, would confine the patient to an already troubled field of reference that would not permit a breakthrough. The encouragement of a sense of 'self', he further argued, promoted that which is at the heart of all divisiveness in human society (self-determination), and would only serve to integrate a sick person into a sick community. Psychological injury should instead be tackled at source, beyond the limits of an individual's personal history, in realms common to all humanity, such as fear, desire and insecurity.

Krishnamurti also became intrigued by what he saw as breakthroughs in modern science, pioneered by certain maverick biologists and physicists who sought to reconcile the empirical results of their studies with philosophical truths. Although he dismissed mainstream science as something of an irrelevance, limited by its dependence on reasoned logic, he felt that the twentieth century offered an opportunity to invent a new grammar of scientific enquiry, one that might bring it into dialogue with spirituality. It was by no means an original idea. Newton, Faraday, Planck, Einstein, Pauli and Bohr, to name but a few, had all been tantalised by the lure of metaphysical revelations hovering across the frontiers of their research. Krishnamurti believed the scientist shared common ground with the mystic (although he avoided that term) in the former's flash of inspiration – the moment when accumulated knowledge is suspended, and insight emerges from the unknown. Where their paths diverge is in the scientist's requirement for controlled verification of his findings. He was eager to explore the indeterminacy of post-relativity science, where it had been demonstrated, in accordance with his own tenets, that an object of observation is tied in relationship to the subject who observes. This assertion implies an indivisibility of matter at a sub-atomic level, a unified cosmos in which thought, time and matter are contingent and by no means self-determined.

The most important bridge Krishnamurti was to build with science centred on the person of Professor David Bohm, the theoretical physicist, pioneer of quantum mechanics, and one-time collaborator with both Einstein and Oppenheimer. Bohm, one of the most eminent and fascinating scientists of the century, was as excited as Krishnamurti by the prospect of physics pointing a gateway to the transcendental; he believed passionately that a convergence of his own work with philosophy might bring about a transformative understanding of the condition of man. He first met Krishnamurti in 1961, having stumbled across one of his books in a public library, and determined to meet the teacher at the first available opportunity. During the course of the 1960s he attended the annual Saanen gatherings and entered into a series of recorded dialogues with the teacher, many of them later published in book form, that reached fruition in the 1970s. Krishnamurti was thrilled by Bohm's sympathetic response to his thinking, and for a decade the two men's relationship was intense. They were on a common wavelength, and Krishnamurti greatly benefitted from Bohm's coherency when his own powers of articulation faltered. There was no equivalent individual, in all his years of teaching, who possessed the linguistic command and knowledge of semantics that Krishnamurti felt would do justice his own ideas. He would enthusistically corroborate Bohm's neat intermittent summaries of ground they had covered with 'That's it, that's right,' and was so moved on occasions that he would get up in the middle of dialogues and embrace Bohm, or leave the room, overwhelmed by the profundity of their joint adventure. The result was twofold: a new clarity for Krishnamurti's teaching, especially for western audiences, that has been both praised and criticised for its more intellectual quality; and, secondly, an endorsement of his ideas by a leading member of the scientific community.

Bohm became a Trustee of the Krishnamurti Foundation Trust, and was to be deeply involved in the schools in England and California. But his association with Krishnamurti was not ultimately to provide him with the fabulous breakthrough in his own work that he dreamed of achieving. He had to suffer the derision of his colleagues in mainstream physics, and was eventually confused by the contradictions he perceived in Krishnamurti's own personality. This, and Bohm's own deteriorating mental health, led to a breakdown of relations between the two men, which should not (though it inevitably will) taint the reputation of the illuminating body of work they earlier achieved together.

The stimulus of his new gatherings at Saanen, coupled with the challenge of engaging academics and scientists, contributed to drawing Krishnamurti's focus westwards in the early 1960s. He had grown impatient with India, and frustrated by a people who had absorbed the teachings of Vedantic masters for centuries without having achieved the necessary transformation; whereas in the west he now began to scent an opportunity for real change. The influence of the Beat movement in the 1950s had shown a younger generation the attractions of non-conformism particularly with regard to religious alternatives; it was suddenly fashionable to deny authority, to doubt received opinion and to question orthodoxy of any kind. Patriotism was undermined, war was stripped of its glamour, and issues like racial equality and the brotherhood of man were added to the moral agenda of the time. The extremes of the youth movement were symptomatic of a general shift in western cultural values, which was heading towards wide-scale secularisation, social emancipation, and post-modernism. Krishnamurti responded positively to the shift, just as he had in the 1920s when a generation of practical idealists had come to him in reaction against the blood-stained orthodoxy responsible for the First World War. Now the opportunities were even greater than before: the stakes were higher, in terms of potential world disasters, the exclusivity of cultures and philosophies appeared to be crumbling, and the far corners of the earth were suddenly accessible to anyone who could buy a plane ticket. The stage was set, it seemed for a final and definitive statement of his message.

Krishnamurti was the man of the moment, a key player in the 1960s spiritual upheaval. Nothing had changed in what he said, but it suddenly took on a special significance, addressing, as it did, the dilemmas of an entire generation. His *The First and Last Freedom*, with its introduction by Huxley, had anticipated the preoccupations of an up-and-coming youth culture, and had perhaps helped to form it, as had Huxley's own controversial book, *The Doors of Perception*, describing his experiments with hallucinogenic drugs. Students who came to hear Krishnamurti at this time, knowing nothing of his messianic history, saw him, perhaps rightly, as the standard-bearer of anti-establishmentarianism, but wrongly as a guru of liberal radicalism and political revolution. Krishnamurti was to remain a central figure in the opening of the western spiritual psyche to new philosophies, but he did not become a hippie icon, like several other representatives of Hinduism to Europe and America, who rose on the tide of youth demand, and subsequently fell in ruins, finally corrupted and destroyed by the west they had come to transform. Unlike many of these (and in open disagreement with Huxley), Krishnamurti consistently denounced the use of drugs as a pathetic attempt to short-circuit the spiritual process; he had no time for the culture of indulgence, whether it involved wearing tinted clothes, worshipping images of the guru, cultivating sexual libido, or practising ritualised forms of meditation. These were all symptomatic of egos that desired massage rather than dissolution. The so-called revolution of the 1960s represented for Krishn-amurti not a bid for transformation, but the replacement of one set of social conditions for another. New Age culture was ultimately no different from Brahmin, Christian or Muslim culture. They were all exploitative, they all defined and imposed a system of values in the name of spirituality.

Aware that his adult audiences continually seemed to be missing the point, Krishnamurti gave new impetus to his school enterprises from the 1960s onwards, convinced that freedom from conditioning would be most easily achieved by those young enough not yet to have suc-cumbed to psychological crystallisation. He turned his attention to founding schools along the same principles as those that already existed at Rishi Valley and Rajghat, with the added plan of providing centres for adult study. Education, which had always held an interest for him, was now to become a passionate preoccupation. He himself had, of course, been a poor pupil and had absorbed very little by way of school-ing; but he had been nurtured by some of the most progressive education-alists of the western world, many of whose ideas he unwittingly incorporated into his own educational scheme.

The Theosophical Society under Annie Besant was in the vanguard of educational reform in the early twentieth century, pioneering the theory that the perfection of man could only be achieved if children were free to develop in accordance with their particular strengths and intuitive natures, and not subjected to the tyranny of competitive examin-ations. These principles had been laid down eloquently by Blavatsky herself in *The Key to Theosophy*. The Society had supported thirty-seven schools in India, on the premise that learning was a sacred enterprise, not merely a process of absorbing information. Theosophy was influential in defining the radical New Education Movement that took shape in the wave of idealism following the First World War, and it helped shape the educational philosophies of Tagore, Steiner and Montessori, all of whom had a connection to the Society. Krishnamurti had been present at the dawn of this movement and had matured under its auspices, working hard to establish his own schools before his break with the Theosophical Society. His later scholastic foundations, while not imitative of New Education, were certainly related in spirit to the movement, and thereby to Theosophy's endeavours in the same field. He, too, reacted against the rigidity of conventonal education, with its emphasis on discipline, conformity and punishment, and maintained that education should prepare children for the many different aspects of life, not merely fill them with knowledge; different areas of intelligence, other than intellect, should be cultivated, as must a child's emotional and social vocabulary. Central to this vision was the relationship between child and teacher, which in former times had been based on hierarchical respect and fear. Despite the acrimonious split with the Society in 1929, one senses that in the field of education, as in certain other areas, Krishnamurti was carrying the torch of Besant's Theosophy towards the closing years of the millenium.

He was to found seven schools, five in India, one in California, and one in Hampshire, England. Aside from Rishi Valley and Rajghat, the Indian schools were located in Madras, Bangalore, and Bombay. He took a close interest in all of them, sending open letters (later published in two volumes as *Letters to the Schools*), visiting as often as his schedule would allow, and participating in numerous dialogues with staff and students. On arrival at the schools he was treated with a mixture of reverent awe, as would befit a cardinal at a convent, and warm affection, like a beloved father returning to his family, both of which roles he appeared to appreciate. Small children were drawn to his charismatic presence as much as adults, and he would adapt his message to suit the limits of their vocabulary and perceptual abilities with masterly ease. Two further Krishnamurti Foundation schools have been started in India since his death (in addition to the five that still exist), one in the Uttarakhand district of the Himalayas, and the other at Pune. Brockwood Park, in England, continues to operate along the principles laid down by its founder, and remains the most radical of all the Krishnamurti schools. The Happy Valley School, that had been set up at Ojai in 1946, diverged from his educational ideals and Krishnamurti grew detached from it, in the main because of his deteriorating relations with Rosalind, who had been the main power behind the school since its foundation. He was finally to side-step his involvement with it altogether when he founded the Oak Grove School, located further along the Ojai Valley, in 1975.

Krishnamurti frequently made the point that the sacred aspect of learning would be enhanced by the beauty and atmosphere of the schools' environments. The buildings were to be located within landscapes that would reflect the reverence and awe expected of staff and students as they approached the business of education. Similarly, the ambience indoors should be orderly, calm and harmonious, not unlike a temple, he would say. The relationships of the inmates should be in tune with the sincerity of their undertaking; relaxed intimacy would go hand-in-hand with seriousness; opinions should be exchanged in a spirit of openness and without prejudice. This approach continues today to lend the schools a tangibly intense and religious feel that gives them an atmosphere unusual in equivalent boarding institutions – warm and homely, while at the same time subdued and monastic.

Krishnamurti's six books on education, the first published in 1953, are not concerned with practical or curriculum matters, but deal with the wider issues of the subject, all of which tie in with his general philosophy, such as an awareness of the living world, learning through enquiry, a journey of discovery, freeing the mind of fear, observing the process of thought, and seeing both the uses and limitations of knowledge. His principal objection to conventional education was in its emphasis on competition, of striving towards high examination grades, thereby instilling the notion that success, social or professional, should be the goal of life. He acknowledged the importance of vocational qualifications, but felt that they should not determine the entire premise of education. He strove in his own schools to apply his agenda for living and learning as an end in itself, within a closed community structure, and with respect to the routines and formalities that any educative project would demand. If approached in the right spirit, and with a sense of order, academic study would flower of its own accord, motivated by the student's natural drive to learn and relate, without the need of authority, threats or coercion. There would be no fear of the social consequences of failure or non-achievement, nor would the schools be factories geared merely towards cultivating children's memories. Instead, there would be excitement in the air, an alertness to fresh wonders.

It was and is an admirable project, and has succeeded in many respects; yet there are certain contradictions in the approach. Krishnamurti was a teacher who tirelessly denounced ideals as belonging to the same stable as beliefs, faiths, and thought; they are all limited and subject to an individual's experience or opinions. He was also opposed to methods or systems, be they political, physical or religious; again, they are by nature circumscribed and vulnerable to the imposition of authority. Yet in his books and talks on the subject of education we hear the voice of an idealist of the most passionate and radical kind, and we read a method eloquently and plainly defined. His followers nowadays are cornered in the terminology open to them because of the apparent contradiction, and rather weak euphemisms are adopted by way of a solution, so that, for example, one must describe his marvellous body of work in this field as Krishnamurti's 'suggestions' for education.

Inevitably, the schools were to encounter problems, chief amongst which derived from the limitations of staff members who, with the best intentions, were attempting to live and teach in accordance with Krishnamurti's 'Truth' while not having found it for themselves. There was tension between individuals, resentment of head-teachers' policies, and even conflict with the students, who were understandably confused as to the precise parameters of their so-called freedom. Krishnamurti was distressed by the various disputes but tended to stay aloof from them, as ever, preferring to avoid conflict, even if it involved leaving others to fight out issues in his own name.

It was perhaps the distance he kept from the unpleasant aspects of life and his refusal to succumb to stress that accounted for his remarkable state of preservation up until the age of ninety. Despite the rigours of his schedule, he retained outstanding physical and mental energy, and his body showed few outward signs of decline – aside from the loss of his hair, suddenly, around 1960, an event that clearly injured his vanity, as he would spend the remainder of his life carefully covering up the deficiency with combed sweep-overs from either side.

His resilience to old age and decrepitude belied a lifetime of frail physical health, dating back to the deprivations of his youth, prior to Leadbeater's intervention. His medical record reads like a catalogue of illnesses, all of which afflicted him in addition to the recurrent 'process' symptoms, although the latter eased somewhat in later years. One of his more disturbing conditions, in the light of Nitya's fate, was a predisposition to bronchial complaints, exacerbated by the chronic hay-fever he suffered. He regularly went down with kidney diseases and urinary tract infections, some of which put him out of action for months at a time; he also had to endure mumps as an adult, prostate gland trouble, a hernia, hearing problems and much discomfort in his teeth. Small and slight of build, he never had much resilience, and would both tire and faint easily. The talks left him particularly drained, as he would imbue them with a high voltage of energy that appeared almost alien in an old man of such a delicate physique. Several of his associates have reported their alarm when he would occasionally go to bed the night before a talk, exhausted, sick at heart and in no way capable of addressing an audience. Yet the following day, having taken no remedy or treatment, he would appear transformed, poised and replete, and would climb the speaker's podium radiantly composed. It was an eerie experience for those close to him, and theories arose, as they had since his childhood, that some outside agency or energy had intervened to galvanise him.

His stamina was bolstered by the daily exercise routine he maintained with characteristic discipline throughout his life. He was meticulous in his choice of healthy vegetarian food, and frugal in the amount he consumed; he never drank alcohol or smoked, rarely tasted coffee, and resisted others' attempts to make him take remedial drugs. When compelled by ill-health to swallow a child's dose, he would feel dizzy; and on the first occasion that he took antibiotics (for a kidney infection, in 1960) suffered temporary paralysis in his legs. His exercise pattern included regular yoga, which he stressed was purely physical, and had no religious or ritualistic significance; and he never lost his love for long country walks, on which he would embark at a brisk pace, and usually in silence, no matter how distinguished the company. His physical resistance to decay was spurred on by a mental capacity that he believed was increasing with age. This was a subject that fascinated him, and he would maintain to Bohm and others that his brain was actually expanding, its cells replenishing, in defiance of biological feasibility.

At other times, however, it appeared as if his attachment to life was tenuous, and he remarked on the ever-proximity of death, sometimes even personalising it as an entity that came to lay claim to his body. This was most evident, of course, during the 'processes', when some part of him would apparently leave his physical body to participate in an encounter on another plane. He would also refer to metaphysical dialogues he had experienced under anaesthetic or in the delirium of ill-health, that would suggest he was frequently faced with the option to 'slip' into a pleasant of death. He claimed to have resisted this temptation in order to return and continue his work; but he would also claim, in accordance with others who have been through what is known as the near death experience, that the encounter left him psychologically purged. The thin gauze between life and the immeasurable state beyond clearly offered Krishnamurti regular glimpses of his enlightenment, and he would return from the experience, even within a matter of hours, to give some of his most inspired talks.

As he grew older, members of his inner circle began to question him as to how he intended 'the work' to be continued after his death, and when that event might come about. He claimed at times to have a good idea about when he would die, but gave vague and contradictory indications to different people. What he resolutely maintained was that he was here to do a job, and that job was to talk. As soon as 'the body' was no longer able to continue with the work, for whatever reason, the source of his life and motivation would recede, and death would follow soon after. But as he reached the mid-1980s there did not appear to be any such recession on the horizon and he continued his work with ever greater vigour, more and more convinced of his unique role in history. Despite his resilience, however, during the course of 1985 he at last began to show signs of exhaustion.

Krishnamurti began what was to be his final year in India, where he made many public appearances before proceeding to America for a glittering round of talks, including one at the United Nations, four in

Ojai, and two in Washington, together with several dialogues and public question sessions. He then travelled to Europe for the summer, making eight appearances at Saanen, giving four talks at Brockwood Park, and holding a series of dialogues with staff and students there. He finally left for India again in October, where his schedule included talks at Varanasi (Benares), Rishi Valley and was to be concluded at Madras. It was here that his career as a public speaker came to an end, close to where it had begun, with a series of three talks, finishing on 4 January 1986.

Before embarking on the final trip to India, it was clear that his health was declining, and that he probably would not be able to fulfil all the scheduled engagements. This fear was reinforced by his dramatic loss of weight and strength during the course of November and December, together with his constant need of warm clothing and blankets, even in the heat of southern India. His voice began to weaken, he felt nauseous and suffered a recurrent fever. Everyone around him began to suspect the worst. He expressed a wish to return home to Ojai as soon as possible and began to give away his Indian clothes to friends in Madras. His last talks were followed by some uncomfortable meetings with Trustees of the Krishnamurti Foundation of India, at which thorny adminis-trative matters were sorted out, before he finally flew out of the country of his birth in the very early morning of 11 January. Some hours prior to leaving for the airport, he took a final walk along the beach at Adyar, close to the spot where he had encountered Leadbeater. Before leaving, he paused and stared out to sea, observed by a group of friends from a distance, the strong wind blowing his hair wildly around his emaciated face.

He arrived at Ojai on the morning of 12 January and rested a day before visiting his trusted doctor, Gary M. Deutsch, at his Santa Paula surgery. A firm diagnosis could not be made until Krishnamurti was admitted to hospital on 22 January, where he received intravenous feeding and was subjected to various scans and tests. He stayed in hospital for a week, attended loyally by Mary Zimbalist and Scott Forbes, a member of staff from Brockwood Park. Krishnamurti was evidently unhappy with the ambience and discomfort of hospital and longed to return to Pine Cottage, a wish that was granted as soon as it became clear that nothing more could be done for him other than relieving the pain. The condition was diagnosed as cancer of the pancreas that had spread to a secondary tumor in the liver.

Krishnamurti, now wasted and shrunken, was delivered back to Ojai, in the sheeting rain on 30 January, and lodged in the same room where he had experienced the extraordinary spiritual awakening more than six decades earlier, in the company of his brother. Dr Deutsch came regularly to his bedside to check on him, give him food supplements, morphine and sleeping pills. When it became clear that the last weeks might be slow and agonising, Deutsch 'specifically asked him about taking his own life and he stated that he [did] not want to die "artificially" but qualified this by stating that he [did] not want to suffer'.[5] Doctor and patient struck up a close friendship in these last days, and Deutsch claims to have been Krishnamurti's last student.

Inevitably, many friends and associates came from around the world when news of the great man's imminent death began to spread. They were torn between wanting to pay their last respects at the same time as not yet giving up hope of a miraculous recovery. Nothing was impossible in such a man, they believed, and when Deutsch intimated on 4 February that there were signs of a possible remission, hopes began to soar. Meanwhile, Krishnamurti prepared himself for the end. He sent enquiries to Brahmin pandits in India to find out the appropriate funeral arrangements for a holy man, only to reject them later out of hand as ridiculous and full of superstition. He went on to make some final recordings and cleared up a few administrative and publishing loose ends. Close to his heart were plans for a new adult study centre at Brockwood, the foundation stone for which, funds permitting, would be laid the following summer. He was also particularly keen to see the younger people involved in his work, those who had long lives ahead but little experience of him personally, in order to ensure that their commitment was grounded in his principles and would not be corrupted. His mind remained lucid during these discussions, despite the drugs he was intermittently receiving, and he felt the need to reiterate that he was still in control of his affairs. Visitors, choking back their tears, were struck by his continued inner authority, and what appeared to be a radiance shining from him. He was holding on to life by a thread, in the shadow of a drip feed, dependent on undignified tubes attached to his body, and barely able to move, they report, but his fabulous energy still filled the room as much as ever in the past. And as he lay in this pathetic state he astonished one and all by stating firmly that while he was alive he was still 'the World Teacher'.[6]

It was felt by some, unfairly, that it was inappropriate for one such as Krishnamurti to succumb to a disease like cancer. He himself expressed this sentiment on one occasion, intimating that the condition may have been caused by something he had done wrong, some constitutional or psychological impurity. However, the suggestion that an alternative diagnosis be publicly announced was wisely rejected, and his disciples were left with the perhaps unpalatable truth that even saints can develop fatal tumors.

On 3 February, Krishnamurti was lifted down from the verandah of Pine Cottage, in his wheelchair, and placed under the pepper tree, no longer the sapling of 1922, but which now provided an ample and spreading shade. It was to be his final excursion out of doors, and he sat in quiet thought at this scene of past adventures. Behind him, attentive and alert, stood a group of devoted acolytes, just as in former days, their predecessors, equally enamoured and self-sacrificing, having departed decades earlier. Two members of that generation had survived, of course, and both had been major players in those remarkable formative experiences. Rosalind and Rajagopal remained resident not far away, but by this time were so completely estranged from Krishnamurti, they may not even have known the seriousness of his condition. No effort was made on either side to reach a reconciliation or bid farewell. Rajagopal was to live on until April 1993, still a member of the Theosophical Society and as old as the century. Rosalind survived until January 1996, also nearly ninety-three, her secret at last revealed to the world through her daughter's book.

When it became clear that the precise day of Krishnamurti's final parting would be hard to predict, and that it would be in no one's interests for a large group of mourners to wait at Ojai for the dreaded event, Krishnamurti tactfully asked most of them to leave, and they reluctantly respected his wishes. As he drifted into the second half of February, he remained conscious but became increasingly dependent on medication to relieve the pain. On his last evening, having taken a sleeping dose, he gently bid Scott Forbes and Mary Zimbalist goodnight. They held a hand each, convinced that they had heard his final words. His heart stopped beating at 12.10 a.m. local time on Monday 17 February.

His body was washed and wrapped in unused silk. A few hours later he was taken in a cardboard coffin to the crematorium at Ventura, accompanied in the hearse by Mary Zimbalist, who was fulfilling an earlier promise that she would attend him right to the very end. In order to ensure that his ashes were kept pure, Krishnamurti had personally given instructions in advance that the furnace should be thoroughly cleaned out and then inspected by a member of his own staff. Once this had been accomplished, with a minimum of ceremony and in the presence of a few local friends, Krishnamurti's body was committed to the fire. In accordance with his wishes, the ashes were split into three, one part to remain at Ojai, one to be scattered at Brockwood, and the other in the River Ganges. He had specifically instructed that no particular ritual was to accompany these tasks, and that no memorial was to be set up in his honour, then or thereafter.

12

The Empty Throne

————— ✳ —————

Krishnamurti was dead. The star had set, its mission at an end. A comprehensive body of teachings remained for future generations – scores of books, recordings and video tapes; but the Brahmin magus who had engendered them, who had probed the spiritual mind of man in all parts of the world for the best part of a century, had at last been silenced. His style had always been to pose a question rather than present the answer, and it is appropriate that his own life should pose the biggest question of them all, an enigma central to the spiritual aspirations of mankind: who or what was the immensity to which he appeared to have access? What was the source of his inspiration, the mystery that he preferred not to clarify for fear that it might be leapt on in judgment or cheapened by the spiritually ambitious?

Ten days before he died, and with a failing voice, Krishnamurti recorded a remarkable statement. He chose this sombre moment to give greater definition to the enigma of his life than he had ever dared to in the past: 'For seventy years that super energy – no – that immense energy, immense intelligence, has been using this body. I don't think people realise what tremendous energy and intelligence went through this body . . . You won't find another body like this, or that supreme intelligence operating in a body for many hundred years. You won't see it again. When he [Krishnamurti] goes, it goes.'[1] So who, or what was Krishnamurti, and how far can we allow ourselves to indulge the dizzy hypothesis, as Annie Besant would have us believe, that he might indeed have been the representative on earth of a divine power?

A sceptic would observe that a good deal of the mystique surrounding Krishnamurti derived from his exotic origins and the veneration afforded him as an Indian holy man. He certainly cut the image of a superhuman sage when residing in India, where it was accepted that he was the latest in a line of 'realised' men, whose talents would naturally include clairvoyance, miracle-working and a benedictory presence. All three were claimed on Krishnamurti's behalf, and not without considerable support- ing evidence. He was frequently asked to lay his hands on the sick, to beneficial effect, although he would insist that this gift was of no great significance and certainly should not be used to endorse his credibility as a teacher. The content and style of his talks given in India reveal that he was aware how much he was venerated there, and have an air of sanctity about them that he might have scorned in the west. He was known in India to chant Sanskrit texts, refer to Hindu mythologies, and speak rhapsodically about certain sacred sites in the subcontinent. This inspired what Rosalind condemned as idolatory in his Indian audiences; but it could also be explained as his communicating in a language that was acceptable to the indigenous culture, the very threshold of which was religious. The demi-god profile was jettisoned as soon as he embarked for the west, where tweed suits were donned instead of cotton kurta pyjamas, and polished handmade brogues replaced the simple wooden sandals. After his break with the Theosophical Society (and unlike several of his guru contemporaries) he refused to wear Indian clothes out of context or for emotive effect. But the nobility of his performance on the dais, with its reverential intensity, remained unchanged in the west, even if the language he chose was of a more secular inclination.

Away from the teaching platform, and in the company of friends, his behaviour was decidedly more human than Christ-like. He never lost his enjoyment of telling irreverent jokes around the dining table – usually about God, St Peter at the gates of heaven, the Pope, or political leaders. The childlike side of his nature was attracted to novelties, mechanical inventions and movies, and he continued into old age to admire the design and performance of expensive cars, finally settling on a Mercedes for himself. He was impetuous, especially when handing out responsibilities and gifts, a loose cannon of diplomacy, leaving others to make good the trail of impracticalities he would frequently leave in his wake. He could be fussy, especially about punctuality, and insisted that his prized watch was kept accurate to the second; running late for a train could leave him 'violently upset',[2] as Isherwood noted. His insistence on certain standards of hygiene (perhaps a throwback to his Brahmin background) struck some as amusingly petty, for example, his insistence that covers of second-hand books be wiped clean before he could read them. He was a stickler for etiquette and thoroughly disapproved of bad table manners, noticing minor deviations when others did not, and in many respects upheld the old-world standards that had formed a part of his training as a boy. In later years his western audiences would be charmed by his linguistic anachronisms, his 'old boys' and 'by Joves', reminiscent more of Bertie Wooster than a latter day prophet or messiah.

The revelation of his long affair with Rosalind has promoted the image of a very human Krishnamurti at the expense of the priestly mould many would have him fit. He was not an asexual being, but greatly enjoyed the company of women and became intimate friends with several of them. This was movingly demonstrated by his close relationship with Mary Zimbalist for the last two decades of his life. He was clearly a man like any other in his physical needs, temperamental swings, daily habits, likes, dislikes and personal foibles. Yet this does not tell the whole story, and there remains a nagging mystery about him, or about one side of him, that needs to be addressed if one is to assess his place in the evolution of spirituality. The sceptical onlooker, again, would maintain that this is an oft-repeated example of human gullibility, and that Krishnamurti's so-called mystery was either a personal delusion or a deliberate hoax. It would be all too easy to relegate Krishnamurti to the growing battalion of fashionable gurus, past and present, confidence tricksters and exploiters, as he shares many of the attributes common to the formula: oriental roots, a history of esoteric wisdom, a rarified, somewhat isolated childhood, a spiritual crisis that occurred around the age of thirty, charisma that lends credibility to his convictions, articulacy, good looks, and a forthrightness that is irresistible to lost souls. However, condemnation of those who fit this pattern, including Krishnamurti, is dependent on a single basic argument: that the person under scrutiny is

a liar, that his teaching is without substance because it has been manufactured for the greater glory and profit of the teacher. If Krishnamurti
falls into this category he can be dismissed with all the other tin-pot
gurus.

But he differs in too many respects. Krishnamurti never cultivated
power for its own sake, and actively set out to tear down the institutionalisation of communities that began to form in his name; he never
demanded a particular way of life, did not prescribe rules of behaviour
or dress, did not amass personal wealth (though he was always comfortable), did not encourage a personality cult, did not use his position to
take sexual advantage of followers, nor did he subject those around him
to irrational cruelties or regimes. On the contrary; he was always perceived as the respectable face of spiritual adventurism, his approach
noted for its wholesome and undogmatic quality. It was this that attracted
statesmen, intellectuals and establishment grandees from a variety of
fields into his orbit. He was alone amongst alternative religious speculators of his time not to be branded the leader of a cult. Nor was he
definitively descended from either oriental or occidental traditions of
philosophy. As such, he was unique, and cannot be compared to figures
such as the Bhagwan Rajneesh of ninety-three Rolls-Royces and free
love fame; or the Beatles' guru, Maharishi-Mahesh; or the boy-wonder
Guru Maharaj Ji; or the charismatic tyrant, Gurdjieff; or more sinister
characters, like Jim Jones and Dave Koresh, both of whom led their
followers to death; nor even the pious and ambiguously pious, such as
Ramana Maharshi and Swami Muktananda.

Unlike these men, Krishnamurti refused to be regarded as an authority,
and continually denied that he, personally, possessed any significance
other than as a mouthpiece for the teachings. However, there was, and
is, amongst his following, a tacit understanding that the phenomenon
of Krishnamurti was a unique, or at least very rare, event in the history
of mankind. Towards the end of his life he could not disguise that he
shared this sentiment, as his death-bed statement quoted above makes
clear. He grew intrigued with the mystery of his own existence, delving
into the subject in the company of friends, particularly in relation to the
circumstances of his upbringing. He lent considerable significance to the
spotlessness of his childhood, both as the inheritor of a pure Brahmin

body, and as the untouchable icon of a messianic project. The blueprint of his physical heritage, together with the spiritual role that he appeared predestined to fulfil, led him to conclude that his life may have been ordained.

The thesis that gradually emerges from his musings proposes that something, some metaphysical 'other', had apparently selected him as its tool, perhaps because of the immaculate condition of his body and vacant personality, and had endowed him with a predisposition for what might be termed transcendental sensitivity, or enlightenment; from this sprang his compulsion to teach, and hence his role as a kind of saviour for humanity. For a man who had spent a lifetime denouncing the tenets of Theosophy, this now sounds like an approximate acceptance of the Society's theory that he had been chosen as the Lord Maitreya's Vehicle, the World Teacher. Perhaps Krishnamurti had never fully rejected the idea; or perhaps he had now come to realise that it may have had some substance after all.

This mysterious 'other', that returns to the Krishnamurti equation later in his life, does not now have a label; it cannot be personified or defined, and has nothing to do with Masters, Brotherhoods, hierarchies or Arhats. And yet it has a more tangible presence than the nameless no-thing of Vedantic philosophy. He refers to 'it' in his published notebooks as if he can physically detect it, like a perfume; it is an immense sacredness inherent within creation, a presence that imbues everything it touches with benediction. It is not separate from the world, nor does it exist on a different level of reality. It is simply there, a 'wordless ecstasy', usually neglected by man because of the preoccupations of the brain, but the property of life itself. Increasingly with age, Krishnamurti felt he was existing in the company of this 'other', that it was in a continuous state of revelation to him, the source of his perspicacity.

Occasionally (and, again, in the company of close friends) his language when discussing this mystery was reminiscent of Theosophy. As he floundered for words to describe the indescribable he fell back on terminology derived from his own religious past. This is not uncommon in those who claim to have had a mystical experience, be they Christian, Hindu, Muslim or atheist; they pick upon 'whatever symbols of ultimacy are available in the attic of the mind'[3] – which does not at all imply that

Krishnamurti in late life was returning to the beliefs of his sponsors. Yet he would refer to the presence of 'eminent holy beings' attending him, invisible to others; and also to a 'face' that appeared plainly, merging with his own in moments of spiritual rapture. There were times when he was clairvoyantly aware of etheric entities, some of them benificent, like angels, and others less so. On one occasion, when he was visiting a temple near Rishi Valley, he felt a mischievous presence following close behind, and turned to cast it off with firm words. He would frequently mention to friends the fine balance he perceived between good and evil operators in the environment, and would demonstrably 'cleanse' rooms of unwholesome presences when entering them. If he was ill or incapacitated by the process, he claimed to need the 'protection' of two intimate friends, a notion that Annie Besant had upheld years before, when she had insisted that he always be attended by two Initiates, whose responsibility it was to ensure that no harm came to his body. During his final illness he spoke often of the hazardous proximity of evil, an indeterminate threat, and how he must be never be left alone or vulnerable to its machinations.

All this would appear inconsistent with the main body of his teachings, which confidently dismissed the concept of supernatural entities as pure superstition. He berated man's pathological need to create anthropo-morphic images of the divine. God was a human invention, he claimed, *the* super-mage, the biggest single enslaver of the mind. This was the flawed path of religion, the trap of man's own making. His abhorrence of Leadbeater's densely populated spirit-world was absolute. The mind had to be its own light, he stressed, and to dwell on personifications of God or any other spiritual agency, good or evil, as the Theosophists had done, was a load of 'rot'.

There emerges a paradox in what Krishnamurti was saying. On the one hand he would pour scorn on people's attempts to spin mystery around him; yet he could equally baffle his friends with esoteric pro-nouncements. Similarly, his audiences basked in the practical secularity of his teachings, enjoying the freedom they granted from religious tra-ditions; yet the same people would swear to the presence of a holy grace when he spoke, or even when he entered the room, some claiming to feel it like a rushing wind.

Krishnamurti was fully aware of the paradox – that he was caught between an acceptance and denial of mystery – and was as keen as any to explore it. An unsatisfactory resolution might throw his entire body of teachings into question. At the core of the issue was the implication that he was a 'biological freak' (his term), a one-off, a human being made perfect by a singular set of evolutionary circumstances, and therefore uniquely capable of metaphysical insights. Annie Besant would have us accept this, and it would be difficult for Krishnamurti to have felt any different, in the deepest recesses of his psyche, having been worshipped and deified since childhood. But this theory entails the possibility that his teachings might remain ultimately inapplicable to ordinary humans. As he grew older, and the transformation of man appeared not to be happening, this became a serious consideration. He therefore put forward the idea that the teachings were relevant despite his own uniqueness: he was a pioneer, blazing a trail that others could follow, even though they would not and could not possess his particular gifts. He used the appropriate metaphor of a light-bulb. We need not all be Edisons, he would say, to turn on an electric light. In other words, there was a mysterious dimension to his life, which it was neither his nor our business to understand, simply because it lay beyond mental comprehension; this mystery had endowed him with unique gifts that would enable him to point the way for ordinary people, who, through his example might perceive, and even merge with, the 'source', though they could never hope to attain the particular capacities that his life had demonstrated.

This assertion is a short step away from a monumental claim: that Krishnamurti was a messenger of divine revelation whose mission was nothing less than the redemption of mankind. Are we then to believe that he was equivalent to the originators of the world's great religions? It is perhaps wiser not to ask what the similarities are between Krishnamurti and men like the Buddha and Jesus, but, instead, whether the example of Krishnamurti's well-chronicled life and work might give us a better idea of what Jesus and the Buddha represented to their contemporaries, before the institutionalisation of their 'joyous song' began to blur the picture. Krishnamurti frequently claimed that the great religious teachers had come not actually to found religions but to destroy them, and there is certainly evidence of this revolutionary tendency in what little we know about the lives of both Jesus and the Buddha. A comparison with the latter is particularly appropriate in that both he and Krishnamurti redefined principles rooted in ancient Hindu tradition by breaking away from established religious practice, employing a philosophy of negation. Krishnamurti always felt a strong affinity with his venerable forbear, and shared a common language with many Buddhist scholars, particularly those who fled from Tibet to India in the 1950s.

It is not within the scope of this book to analyse the respective philosophies of Krishnamurti, Jesus, Mohammed, Confucius, Lao-Tzu and the Buddha, although scholars have done so with interesting results. It is largely the social and political context of a religious figure's life, in addition to his philosophy, that results in whether he is regarded by history as potentially messianic. Judgment cannot yet be cast on Krishnamurti because his historical niche is still in the early days of construction; but it is doubtful that he will ever rise to the cultural pre-eminence of the great religious leaders, most obviously because it is so clearly on record that he forbade the establishment of a doctrinal system in his name. There was also not the political context that propelled Jesus into the role of saviour, and the question of physical martyrdom fortunately never entered the equation of Krishnamurti's or his followers' lives. Had the British in India persecuted Theosophists and crucified their mascot in 1928, in the full flower of his beauty and wisdom, it may well have been a different story!

Setting aside these speculative parallels, it is perhaps more appropriate, from an anthropological point of view, to place Krishnamurti in the ranks of the Indian god-men, or Avatars – included amongst whom is the person of Jesus – and to view his role not so much as that of a messiah, but as a culturally-approved incarnation of the divine. The Hindu Avatar (literally 'one who comes down') is a rare but not unique pheneomenon: a person who bestrides the divine and temporal, thus demonstrating, through the example of his life and insight, the possibility of human union with the supreme godhead. Avatars are related to the Christian tradition of saints, but are theologically closer to Christ, in that they physically embody God and therefore display the attributes of man perfected – the very 'Christ principle' that Krishnamurti described so poetically in his references to the Beloved.⁴ Modern Avatars are said to have included Ramakrishna (who famously declared his spiritual relationship to Jesus in 1874), Sri Aurobindo, Meher Baba and, more recently, the renowned miracle-worker, Satya Sai Baba.

An Avatar is also traditionally seen as the herald of a new age, and arrives amongst ordinary men at a moment of particular need. Their followers promote that blend of woe and optimism that characterises those who look starry-eyed to an imminent apocalypse. The promise is of a golden dawn, defined by the divine inspiration of the god-man who has been sent to prepare for it. This was the stuff of Besant's millenarian forecast, and the Theosophical profile of Krishnamurti as World Teacher fits squarely into this Avatar tradition. In this light he can be described, in the sight of a cultural tradition that has spread rapidly this century from east to west, as a 'son of God'. He never denied the role, and was capable of blatantly messianic remarks, such as on one occasion in later life declaring, 'The tears of all the world have produced the World Teacher.'⁵

A less sensational placement for Krishnamurti would be alongside the many enlightened mystics, whose number include representatives of all the major religions; and although reports of their unitive states are couched in the jargon of their particular culture, it is clear the ground of their experiences was not dissimilar to that of Krishnamurti. And yet if the insight of all mystics is fundamentally the same, if they are tapping the one and only source, albeit at different stages of history and in different sociological contexts, what is the essential difference, in terms of divine revelation, between an enlightened monk in his obscure monastery and the founder of a great world religion? The answer is perhaps to be found in their corporeal rather than spiritual circumstances: the socio-political world in which they live, their personal charisma, zealousness, originality, drive, fitness, and daring. The difference is in the extent to which they employ their insight with a sense of novelty and mission to galvanise others and turn the tables on an established order. As *the* World Teacher Krishnamurti approaches the status of the religious colossi and shares many of their attributes; but as *a* world teacher he is perhaps best compared to dozens of other similarly inspired individuals who did not have the fortune of his particular opportunities.

There is a body of opinion, by way of contrast, that doubts the assumption of Krishnamurti's uniqueness, even to the point of questioning the veracity of his inspiration. Whilst some dissenters deserve serious consideration, one must beware the venom of those whose personal feelings have been injured because their ambitions of achieving intimacy with the teacher were thwarted. Many of his critics belong to this category. Ever since his early Theosophical days, Krishnamurti lived surrounded by sycophants jostling for his favour, which, once achieved, was guarded jealously and used like a prefect's badge to establish the seniority of a chosen few within a community. A comment he made to Lady Emily as early as 1926 would have been equally appropriate sixty years later: 'Everybody is the same – they all think they have some special claim – some special road to me.'[6] Some abandoned him because they felt their devotion was never sufficiently recognised; others did succeed in carving themselves a place within his inner circle, often to be sidelined at a later stage, which, again, usually resulted in them turning against him. There were also objections to a guru preaching inner strength and self-sufficiency who at the same time depended on an infrastructure of supporters to compensate for his own deficiencies. When a new favourite was welcomed into the troop and swept to a position of high influence, often impetuously and at the expense of faithful old devotees, Krishnamurti was branded disloyal. It was an understandable and only too human reaction, in the face of which his repeated denunciations of attachment and possessive love rang hollow.

Mary Lutyens and other stalwarts shielded their hero even when their feelings had been hurt, nobly taking the blame on their own shoulders: 'Indeed, the closer we were to the sun the more likely we were to get burnt.'[7] Michael Krohnen, the cook at Ojai during Krishnamurti's last years, eloquently confesses what others felt but could not admit, about life in close proximity to the teacher: 'It could be demanding, even distressing, to be so close to the flame. Since the nature of the flame was to be without a center, it tended to show up starkly the solidity of the selves within its range. More than ever, I came into contact with the ways in which I compared myself to others, with my desire to be appreciated, and with the resulting divisiveness, envy and jealousy.'[8] Krishnamurti would not flatter or bolster an injured ego; instead, if he felt that friends had become blasé or had lost the desire to learn, he would let them drop away like dead flies, apparently without a care. Many of the disillusioned casualties saw this as callous, and claim to this day that he preferred to surround himself with blind devotees rather than accept contradiction or work out a difficult relationship.

A number of the criticisms levelled at Krishnamurti should in fact be borne by this tight-knit band of inner helpers – whether in India, Europe or California – whose behaviour at times resembled that traditionally associated with sectarian communities, especially in their exclusivity. They were defensive of criticism, even before it had been stated, wary of outsiders, and fiercely protective of their guru. There are numerous reports of Krishnamurti's friends who, happening to find themselves in his vicinity, but out of the usual context in which they had come to know him, would attempt to make an impromptu visit. His local guardians would invariably treat them with suspicion bordering on hostility and ask innumerable questions. It proved very difficult indeed to make an appointment, although on the occasions when word of their visits filtered through to Krishnamurti himself, they would be welcomed into his presence with open arms. This behaviour on the part of the inner helpers showed their tendency, like their Theosophical predecessors, to over-sanctify the teacher – in contradiction of the teachings. It also gave rise to the unfair myth that Krishnamurti only had time for the rich and influential who appeared to have greater ease in gaining access to him. In truth, he was of an entirely egalitarian disposition, treating pauper, prime minister, sceptic, holy man, child, stranger or friend with the same degree of respect – much to the chagrin of those who felt they deserved more.

Krishnamurti must share at least a part of the blame for the behaviour of his close circle, as they showed symptoms of a consistent discipular condition that coexisted alongside his teaching life all the way from adolescence to the grave. Although he periodically took steps to annihilate what he would jokingly (and rather disgustedly) refer to as 'the circus' around him, he none the less allowed it to reconstitute itself, at least in order to look after his administrative needs.

More serious to the long-term credibility of Krishnamurti was the deterioration of his relationship with David Bohm, his closest dialogue partner and colleague in the hope for human transformation. Bohm was confused by the paradox of Krishnamurti's acceptance and rejection of mystery, which was, in a sense, a manifestation of his own psychological dilemma, torn as he was between the empiricism of physics and the speculations of spirituality. He wanted to believe that Krishnamurti was a unique human being, but simply could not accept that the World Teacher project had not left a lasting impression on him. How else could he allow his entourage to deify him, even though such behaviour went against his own teachings? Bohm also objected to Krishnamurti's claims of complete infallibility, his use of linguistic absolutes that would not tolerate contradiction, and his abrupt dismissal of scientific endeavour. Furthermore, he grew disillusioned with the way the Foundations and schools were being run, with their unwholesome rivalries, disputes and administrative deadlocks. He suspected he was being edged out of Krishnamurti's orbit because some felt his influence was overly intellectual or, worse still, that he was beginning to steal the limelight from the teacher. Krishnamurti himself began to neglect him, consistently refusing to resolve Bohm's confusion, asserting instead that his eminent interlocutor had clearly failed to understand anything. This was deeply distressing for Bohm who had at one time staked his career, social life and marriage on the viability of Krishnamurti's philosophy. His friends in mainstream physics – predominantly materialist Marxists – had poured scorn on his flirtation with spirituality, and his wife, Saral, had been forced to take second place to her husband's mystical adventure. Increasingly prone to depression, Bohm now sank into despair, haunted by the possibility that his life and work had got him nowhere. There were times when he contemplated suicide and in 1980 he suffered a severe heart attack. He was to recover and live for another twelve years.

Krishnamurti doubtless lacked tact in his handling of the affair, but his behaviour is understandable. He had grown aware of Bohm's deteriorating mental health and bouts of depression, which he would have viewed not as a clinical condition but as the scientist's failure to make the psychological breakthrough they had long discussed. This was equally disappointing for Krishnamurti, who felt that, of all people, Bohm seemed close to achieving transformation, and might even carry on the teaching work after his own death. The story after 1980 was not all gloom. Although the two men were never again to achieve the electric intimacy they had enjoyed in the early 1970s, they remained on cordial terms and continued to have some illuminating dialogues. Bohm rediscovered a passion for his own work, but his biographer maintains that, as far as his inner reflections on Krishnamurti were concerned, he remained 'deeply troubled until he died'.[9]

Another critic of Krishnamurti deserves mention because his life in many respects represents a close parallel to that of his bête noir, even to the point of sharing his name. U. G. Krishnamurti (henceforth, to avoid confusion, U. G.) is a South Indian Brahmin, born in 1918, who showed remarkable spiritual insight as a child, and was subsequently educated by the Theosophical Society at Adyar. As he rose through the ranks of the Society he came into contact with both Beasant and Leadbeater, and for seven years lectured as a Theosophist, before rejecting the movement. He had grown up surrounded by images of the wondrous World Teacher, and in later life came to know him well. Like Krishnamurti, U. G. divided his time between India, California and Europe, the similarity of pattern even extending to his spending an annual summer holiday at Saanen. It was after hearing one of Krishnamurti's talks at Saanen, in 1967, that U. G. underwent a physical and spiritual crisis very similar to the former's 1922 process. Since that time U. G. has become an eminent teacher in his own right, adopting a drastically nihilistic philosophy, beside which Krishnamurti's appears almost conventional. Shortly after the death of Krishnamurti, in May 1986, the *Illustrated Weekly of India* summed up the difference: 'Those who are evaluating the contribution of the two Krishnamurtis to mankind maintain that U. G. Krishnamurti begins where J. Krishnamurti ends. Does this mean that one era has faded out and the new one is fading in?'[10]

U. G. reserves a mixture of vitriol and laconic contempt for his namesake, whom he considers to have been flawed by obvious contradictions. How could he denounce systems and conditioning, U. G. asks, while at the same time founding institutions that prescribe a method and foster more conditioning? The 'kind of organisation he has now, with worldwide real estate holdings, boards of trustees, vaults of insured tape recordings, millions of dollars, all runs counter to his basic teaching, which is that you can't organise truth. He shouldn't be building an empire in the name of spirituality.'[11] U. G. goes on to question the validity of Krishnamurti's realisation, claiming that he had seen but never tasted 'the sugar cube', that he was 'the greatest fraud of the twentieth century', and 'a purveyor of archaic, outmoded, outdated, Victorian hogwash'. All of these remarks, he said, were returning to Krishnamurti 'a dose of his own medicine'. U. G. enjoys his role of 'spiritual terrorist' and relishes the opportunity to annihilate venerability when he sees it institutionalised. He was delighted to hear news of Radha Rajagopal Sloss's critical book about Krishnamurti, in 1992. 'She has dumped a keg of dynamite!' he responded, 'The story of the sex, lies and flippancy of Krishnamurti is more absorbing than his teachings.'[12] Much of what U. G. says is clearly intended to shatter people's psychological quietude, and must be taken in that context. On other occasions he has been known to state that Krishnamurti was the most remarkable man he had ever encountered.

Another reproving opinion comes from the pen of Helen Knothe Nearing, Krishnamurti's one time sweetheart, whose memoirs, written late in life, paint a common sense picture of the young World Teacher by one who had shared his most intimate company. Their relationship was to have a disappointing epilogue when Helen happened to be in Madras decades after their last meeting and attempted to contact him for old time's sake. She managed to obtain an appointment for a short interview, during which Krishnamurti behaved with formal detachment, barely recognising her and appearing totally oblivious of their former friendship. 'He had no more care for me or interest than he had for the fly on the wall,' Helen recalled, concluding that, although possessed of inner greatness, Krishnamurti lacked ordinary human compassion and kindness; he was intolerant, even contemptuous, of those who could not rise to his own high plane. As for the claim that he was unconditioned and lived a life free of attachments, Helen wrote that it was hardly consistent with the man she and many of her friends had known, 'the Krishnamurti who slept in comfortable beds in costly houses, who got up in the morning, gargled, abluted, combed his hair, and dressed in fine clothes bought in elegant shops . . . He was conditioned and affected every second of his life, just as everyone else was and is.'[13]

Krishnamurti's impatience with audiences and individuals who seemed to be missing his point or questioning his assertions earned him a reputation as something of a martinet. After so many years surrounded by an inner circle, like a monarch attended by his courtiers who adored him and believed he could do no wrong, he had grown unused to being contradicted. He could at times be overly authoritarian which, again, was inconsistent in one who denounced authority and upheld the virtues of open discussion. His recorded dialogues, though purportedly a melting pot for the ideas of all participants, invariably became a showcase for Krishnamurti's point of view, to which other interlocutors would happily defer; or object, at their peril. The usual pattern was to begin with generalisations, the whole group contributing, before the discussion became more specifically centred on one of Krishnamurti's favourite themes. Then one can witness a gradual increase in tension as the teacher's conviction mounts. It is compelling to watch such unshakeable assurance. He becomes forceful and, although still inviting the opinions of others, is prone to passionate interruptions, at times hardly listening to what another has said. An eventual pause is achieved, either through the force of his argument or the intimidation of other participants, and Krishnamurti backs off calmly, half closes his eyes, and pronounces his conclusions in an oracular style. This technique, and the rather bullying way in which he was occasionally seen to treat his audiences, leads sceptics to believe that this so-called exponent of spiritual freedom was in reality an arch dogmatist. He had learnt from Annie Besant, they would say, that incontrovertibility was the most effective form of dissemination.

These criticisms made little difference to those who claimed to benefit from his teachings. The water tasted good, the words seemed to make sense; and when they did not, there was always the extraordinary presence of the teacher, which, even if no words were spoken, would have been sufficient for many to have departed his gatherings with a sense of benediction. This explains why many of the same group returned again and again, or followed him around the world. It was not that his message or themes were any different from talk to talk; indeed, there was an inevitable degree of repetition. The invigoration came through the sharing of space and time with the guru (*darshan*), an experience that appeared to equip his followers to live better lives.

It was a natural consequence of such devotion that these followers should have remained blind to any hint of deficiency in Krishnamurti or his teachings. They were unperturbed by his sweeping denunciations of all teachers, philosophies and methods of education other than his own. They were not disquieted by his derision of books as useful for spiritual growth, while allowing many to be published in his own name. And they ignored the most glaring contradiction of them all, at the core of his message – that a theoretical argument cannot help one attain a state of non-thought, because both the argument and the notion of non-thought are in themselves the product of thought. It is a self-defeating enterprise. Krishnamurti endlessly repeated that 'the word is not the thing,' that his talks and teachings could not be the tool to bring about an individual's realisation of truth; and yet his whole life was dedicated to giving talks, haranguing crowds and spreading 'the word'. U. G. once confronted him on the issue, demanding that he, 'Come clean for once.' Krishnamurti replied, 'You have no way of knowing it,' to which U. G. characteristically retorted, 'If I have no way of knowing it and you have no way of communicating it, what the hell have we been doing! I have wasted seven years listening to you.'[14] Those followers who claim a faultlessness, in terms of both theory and applicability in Krishnamurti's teachings, have succeeded somehow in fitting the square peg in a round hole. They ingenuously excuse the contradictions as being the product of Krishnamurti's enigmatic status. He belonged to a superior order of beings for whom the normal rules of logic, analysis and morality do not apply. It is in the upholding of such unanswerable tenets that a minority of Krishnamurti followers share a devotional language with the disciples of more stereotypical gurus; and the fierce defensiveness with which they close ranks to protect Krishnamurti's reputation merely contributes to the resemblance.

The difficulties, inconsistencies and obstacles in Krishnamurti's teachings do not present a problem for the many thousands, perhaps millions, whose brief encounter with them has had a constructive effect on their thinking. Complications arise when an attempt is made to live the teachings to the letter, or when they are subjected to over-analysis, which reveals flaws, contradictions and paradoxes. That Krishnamurti in one sense demanded this of his followers was perhaps his one weakness as a teacher. He was a person of tremendous conviction. His faith in what he perceived to be Truth was complete, perfect and irrefutable, and as such he was incapable of ceding ground or tolerating criticism. Truth cannot be contradicted. His perspective was direct, his sincerity absolute, and his purpose single-minded. This kind of resoluteness attracted the needy, and the weaker they were, the closer they attached themselves to his teaching, regarding it as their salvation. Yet Krishnamurti was not for the weak, and his words do not submit to a literal reading. If there was a prerequisite for anyone prepared to open themselves to his ideas it was that they equip themselves with inner strength and banish the notion of dependency. He failed to guard himself from being swamped by spiritual flounderers, because, ultimately, he never succeeded in persuading followers that he was not another Jesus, that he had not come to be the good shepherd, a comfort to the needy.

Annie Besant predicted that a religious movement would be set up in Krishnamurti's name after his death. The possibility is upon us, now that he himself is no longer here to prevent it. A large proportion of the staff at the various institutions he founded guard against such a tendency; but, as detractors delight in pointing out, the indulgent streak in human nature will not be suppressed, and devotionalism is one of its favourite indulgences. Groups of enthusiasts, bereft of their hero, have come together to form organisations hosting seminars, camps, retreats and expeditions, so that they can meet others with the same interests and keep their enthusiasm for the teachings alive. It is a disguised and unofficial club for cognoscenti, publishing its own delightfully illustrated international newsletter; and with the three Foundations, of America, India and Britain, still prospering, and around forty Krishnamurti organisations operating in other countries, the 'movement' would appear to be gaining strength. The old books are translated into ever more languages, while new anthologies are published, extracting original texts, out of context, to make up theme books or compilations with a certain slant. Thus the financial turnover is maintained and the mission given a contemporary face, even if Krishnamurti's insistence that there should be no manipulation of the teachings is not entirely respected.

The centenary celebrations of 1995 acted as a catalyst for devotees, with Krishnamurti conferences, lectures and exhibitions organised in commemoration of the great man's birth. A Dutch exhibition, given the title 'Pathless Truth', and doubtless put on in the name of historical interest, strayed dangerously close to promoting Krishnamurti memorabilia as holy relics, with display items that included a pair of his shoes, handwritten letters, and assorted paraphernalia bearing the Star insignia. This is hardly in keeping with the wishes of a man who demanded that there be no memorial or significance associated with his physical person after death. Nor can the various academic papers contributed to Foundation conferences, analysing different aspects of his work, be seen as respecting his decree that there should be no interpretations or paraphrasing of his original texts.

A devotional tendency is also apparent in the reverential ambience that characterises gatherings of Krishnamurti enthusiasts nowadays, especially on the occasions when images of the teacher are brought to life in video presentations, or if his voice is relayed through speakers at hushed group assemblies. At such gatherings the participants bestow upon themselves and others a mantle of pious sobriety, to the point where a critical opinion of the teacher is regarded as unconstructive, if not blasphemous. Freedom of speech is encouraged, as is the notion of open discussion, but only within certain tacitly acknowledged limits. There is also an idiosyncratic attitude towards language that can present a minefield of potential faux pas for the uninitiated. Certain terms recur frequently with an electricity not inherent in their purely dictionary meaning (words like individual, mind, intelligence, dialogue), while others are frowned upon as potentially insolent if employed in relation to Krishnamurtu (guru, disciple, doctrine, method). A regime of sanctimonious goodwill is imposed, in emulation of the teacher and with the best intentions of living in accordance with his ideas, but without, of course, realisation of the inner fire that had inspired them. The result can be tense and artificial, with too heavy an emphasis laid on the image of Krishnamurti as a papier maché saint – something that goes against the spirit of his life's work, surely to its future detriment.

Yet Krishnamurti certainly intended that the work should go on after his death, particularly at the schools, and the last weeks saw him emotionally galvanising his retinue, passing on the fire to kindle their long-term commitment. If only a few people within the schools and Foundations would live the teachings, he would stress, a radical change in human consciousness at large might be precipitated. It is understandably difficult for those left with the responsibility of disseminating his work to steer the subtle path that avoids evangelism but facilitates availability of Krishnamurti to as many people as possible. Are they actively to spread the word, or just make accessible the texts? They have been entrusted to keep alive his zeal, and yet must resist the temptation to preach. Above all they have been forbidden to set themselves up as an authority in his name. There were most definitely to be no successors.

The Krishnamurti schools have succeeded in sustaining their educational project, but not without having to face the same problem. There is a determination to continue in the spirit of their founder but, in the second decade after his death, the schools are having to define their position in the contemporary world, avoiding the obvious dangers of being perceived either as a stale experiment or as representative of an esoteric sect. In order to ensure their own survival they have had to play down too overt an association with Krishnamurti, reducing the prominence of his name from much of the publicity material, and dispel the notion that staff members might be followers of a cult rather than serious educators.

There is also a danger that the schools might become ivory towers, solitary outposts where Krishnamurti's teachings are adopted as a doctrinal system, closed off from, and disapproving of the outside world. Each separate institution has tackled the problem in its own way, and each has therefore developed its own particular character. There are no blanket administrative or ideological guidelines to which all the schools have to comply, although regular communication and exchanges are cultivated.

If a school is to be judged by the rounded, open and positive outlook of its student leavers, together with their genuine affection for the staff and institution, the Krishnamurti schools must be said to have succeeded. Brockwood Park, for example, maintains a spirit of industry voluntarily undertaken, albeit in an atmosphere rather more restrained and serious than at a conventional school; moral issues and philosophical perspectives form much of the currency for discussion, while the preoccupations of ordinary youth culture, such as glamour and fashion, appear less prevalent. The students encountered are usually of an enquiring, unintimidated disposition, and have available to them facilities, class sizes and a physical environment that would make them the envy of even the best private schools. Krishnamurti's work is freely available, but no longer part of the curriculum, and although he is frequently mentioned as the inspiration behind their community, few of the students cultivate a particular enthusiasm for his teachings.

There are downsides to the schools. The rarified atmosphere, isolated position and stunning natural surroundings might be said to induce too much introspection on the part of young people who are easily enough entangled in their own emotions. It can also create false expectations of the outside world, either as a corrupted hell-hole that should be guarded against, or as a morally flawed construct which Krishnamurti school graduates, with their superior philosophical outlook, will be able to rectify. These attitudes can lead to disappointment and integration problems for the students later in life, something that was clearly not an issue for Krishnamurti, who intended that his schools should be hubs of wisdom and light, from which a new culture of spiritual awareness might spread. There is also the danger, as with all schools that cultivate a particular philosophy, that a code of values is imposed on students which does not suit them all. The deliberate discouragement of competition, for example, while admirably egalitarian, removes a zest from school life that a number of children do find natural and stimulating. Sport is viewed as a provider of fresh air and exercise, and those who enjoy the competitive element either have to suppress their interest or choose a different school. Discipline is a thorny issue because rules are difficult to impose in a community that exists and defines its parameters through democratic means. It is usually maintained through mutual agreement between staff and students based on respect for a smooth-running community, but there are grey areas relating to subjects like sexual relations or, as one student wryly told me, 'rules that are optional but compulsory'. Academic excellence, for its own sake, is not considered a laudable goal to be striven towards, and is therefore rarely achieved. This applies more to Brockwood than the Indian schools, which are more tuned to the economic requisites of the country. The Oak Grove School, in California, also places greater emphasis on preparing students for university education.

Worldwide interest in Krishnamurti is also gaining focus through the establishment of adult retreat centres around the world, which allow people to pursue their interest in Krishnamurti and encounter others of the same persuasion. Book sales and translations continue to mount; in addition to the fifty books published during Krishnamurti's life, around twenty-five have been produced since, some of which are currently available in as many as fifty different languages. Academic interest in the teachings is on the increase, with ever more papers published, lectures given, e-mail dialogues initiated and doctorate theses undertaken. The future of the Foundations would appear at present to be secure.

What became of the Theosophical Society, the organisation that prepared the ground for Krishnamurti, launched his career, and to a large extent initiated the shift in spiritual attitudes in the western world that was to make available to him so large an audience of religious seekers?

The Krishnamurti Foundations today do not rewrite the teacher's early history, but take the line that it is largely irrelevant. They acknowledge in passing the events of his youth, the World Teacher project and the role of the Theosophical Society, but emphasise that Krishnamurti's career began in earnest only after his dissolution of the Order of the Star in 1929. They do not publish the talks that were delivered prior to 1933, and in order to find copies of these texts one must either consult antique Theosophical magazines or a seven-volume edition of *Early Writings*, available only in India. The Foundations are thus in accord with Krishnamurti's own claim that the Theosophical Society was not influential in defining his mature teachings and that he had remained totally unconditioned by his past. An introductory book entitled *Unconditionally Free*, published by the joint Foundations to mark the centenary, gives virtually no mention of Krishnamurti's Theosophical past, Leadbeater or Besant. He owed nothing to anyone or any influence, it is claimed, other than the unknowable inspiration with which he was uniquely endowed.

Krishnamurti may well have tapped a divine source, something beyond time or category, although the essence of this claim can never be proved or quantified. What is more apparent to the impartial observer is that his expression of the mystery, and the role he assumed in society to publicise that expression, were very much the children of time, and in this sense he owes his eminence to the circumstances of history.

The emergence of Jesus as an historical figure was linked to the political circumstances of Palestine, the state of the Jewish people and the imperial policy of Rome. Krishnamurti, when examined from a similarly historical perspective, was the inheritor of a seed sown by Blavatsky, who in her own right stood at the confluence of several historical strands. She prepared the way for the acceptance of eastern spirituality in a world that was increasingly dominated by a mind-set rooted in the Greco-Roman tradition – a materialist, occidental mind-set. A number of factors contributed to the evolutionary movement of which she and Krishnarmuti were a part: the Enlightenment, the industrial revolution, denominational sectarianism in the nineteenth century, the rise of socialism, the First World War, the fall of empires, improved global communication, and the ascent of the New World, to name but a few.

The Theosophical Society, under the founding inspiration of Madame Blavatsky, was one of the principal agents facilitating the spread of non-affiliated religious philosophies in the twentieth century – a move-ment which has gathered momentum to form what is now called New Age thinking. The life and work of this controversial woman are directly connected to that of Jiddu Krishnamurti, no matter how unpalatable such an idea might be to some of his followers today. He was one of the first and most widely publicised figures to present eastern spirituality in a context comprehensible to those conditioned by western theological and philosophical traditions. Unlike Ramakrishna, who had preceded him, Krishnamurti was an international statesman of spirituality, con-stantly travelling, with no political or religious ties. He was an ambassador for Blavatsky's objective of Universal Brotherhood; and the means he employed to bring this about was the sharing of his own enlightenment – the abiding, immeasurable Truth that Blavatsky referred to as the 'impersonal divine Principle, the Infinite All, which is no Being or thing'.[15] Krishnamurti's teachings may thus be seen to correlate with Blavatsky's concept of the Ancient Wisdom, the core from which all religious expression derives or, as Huxley termed it, the Perennial Philosophy.

Blavatsky's preoccupations also foreshadow those of Krishnamurti on a practical level. As W. Q. Judge wrote: 'The aim and object of her life were to strike off the shackles forged by priestcraft for the mind of man ... by showing the real unity and essential non-separateness of every being. And her books were written with the declared object of furnishing the material for intellectual and scientific progress on those lines.'[16] A similar assessment could be made of Krishnamurti's career, and one can confidently assume that Blavatsky would have joined in his denunciation of the Liberal Catholic Church, Co-Masonry and other ritualistic enterprises taken up by her successors at Adyar. She also shared Krishnamurti's concerns for right education, his disregard for exams, competition and the cultivation of mechanical memory. Her terminology at times uncannily anticipates that of the man who abandoned her Society and went on to found his own schools.[17]

Satyat nasti paro dharma, announces Blavatsky's motto for Theosophy, emblazoned on the cover of *The Secret Doctrine*: 'There is no Religion higher than Truth.' A century after her death, leaving behind her, as she did, a disjointed organisation and a jumbled mass of texts, she could scarcely have asked for a more effective descendant than Krishnamurti. He evolved in his own right, jostled and shaped by the world in which he lived and the experiences he encountered, but the roots of his mission were planted deep. While he rejected Theosophy, he can be said to have fulfilled its highest expectations.

There were and are other figures descended from the Blavatsky lineage, some of whom continue to have a following quite distinct from the Theosophical Society and, like Krishnamurti, can be said to have contributed in a major way to the development of New Age thinking. These include Rudolf Steiner with Anthroposophy, Alice Bailey and the Arcane School, the Ballard family and the I Am movement, Gurdjieff with his own theories of cosmic order, Elizabeth Clare Prophet and the Summit Lighthouse movement and, more recently, Benjamin Creme, who has written a number of books as mouthpiece of the Lord Maitreya (whose latest vehicle, as yet unnamed, is expected shortly to declare himself to the world). However, there is little common ground between the doctrines of these people and the teachings of Krishnamurti. All of them (with the exception, perhaps, of Steiner) elaborated on the esoteric aspect of Theosophy, which is precisely the area jettisoned by Krishnamurti. He relinquished his ready-made position as the Society's future Prospero, and the role was greedily assumed by others, of various persuasions, whose careers took them off at tangents, and their descendants continue to multiply. Their general judgment of Krishnamurti was that he had not possessed the requisite stamina and divinity for the job. Had they but read the metaphysical speculations of his late years, which resonate with perspicacity and mystery, they may well have reversed both judgments.

It would be inaccurate to claim that Krishnamurti remained a closet Theosophist in all but name. He fundamentally rejected the vast, complex and lugubrious system crafted by Besant and Leadbeater, the basis of which had its roots in Blavatsky's work and her hierarchy of Masters, but which was subjected to distortions. He further dismissed many of the theories Theosophy had borrowed from Hinduism and Buddhism, such as the notion of a permanent ego that is reincarnated over the course of centuries, evolving according to the law of karma, before its final absorption in the godhead. Krishnamurti's understanding of a religious life had nothing to do with an adherence to creeds, patterns of behaviour, cosmogonic theories or ecclesiastical pomp; he urged his listeners to relinquish spiritual clutter and discover Truth through a quiet but vivid acceptance of 'what is'. His approach surely facilitated a more direct route to Besant's objective of trans-cultural empathy than her own rigidly partisan methods. In many ways he appears to have been more Theosophical than the Theosophists themselves, but they had become too entrenched in their system to recognise the fact. However, Krishnamurti remained in tune with his beloved Amma on the two principles closest to her heart: that we should strive towards a transformation in human consciousness on a universal scale, and that it should be the World Teacher's role on earth to instigate such a transformation. He carried the torch of this project with him to his dying breath.

Krishnamurti's relationship with the Theosophical Society underwent a surprising change in the very last years of his life. He had been totally estranged from the Adyar organisation during the presidency of George Arundale and, although he received repeated invitations from the succeeding President, his former tutor and friend Jinarajadasa, to return and speak to the Society as of old, he still resisted. Jinarajadasa'a death in 1953 marked the very end of the Besant–Leadbeater era, but Krishnamurti continued to refuse offers of a reconciliation. By 1980 he appeared to have changed his mind, partly because of the election of a friend as President, Radha Burnier, who also happened to be a niece of Rukmini Arundale. Burnier had already been active in the Krishnamurti Foundation of India and was to become a Trustee. A bridge was thus built between the Foundation and the Theosophical Society, and none too soon for Krishnamurti, who in later life had begun to delve into the mystery of his background in an attempt to come to terms with his own uniqueness. He intimated that the old Theosophical belief in the inherent sanctity of India was relevant to his present work and that, because of this, the Society might again have a role to play. It was not the geography of India he was referring to, but 'the Indian mind that has produced the *Upanishads*, the Buddha. India has been the storehouse of something very very great.'[18] He now feared that it was in danger of obliteration because of the spread of western materialism, a preoccupation that had been paramount to Annie Besant and fuel for her world scheme.

So it was that on 3 November 1980 Krishnamurti returned in triumph to the Adyar compound of the Theosophical Society, after an absence of forty-six years. He went to view his own and Annie Besant's rooms, left unchanged since the 1930s, and was surprised to see a large framed portrait of Bishop Leadbeater which had not previously hung there. For an electric moment the celebrated eighty-five-year-old sage stared into the sharp eyes of his old mentor behind the glass, absorbed in a silent dialogue, before he raised a hand to the long-dead Theosophist and said, 'Pax, pax.'[19] From this time on he became a regular visitor, and though he claimed to remember almost nothing of the place, his return marks something of a completed circle, the resolution of an extraordinary tale that had been left open-ended.

Radha Burnier now promotes the view that the old Theosophical Society had lost sight of its fundamental aims, and had run adrift in its confusion, while the example of Krishnamurti had consistently shone like a beacon of truth. She completes his official rehabilitation with statements like: 'He was a theosophist in the full sense, a *brahma-jnanin*, or knower of Truth ... The Theosophical Society can be justly proud of having sponsored and made known a teacher who has had such a profound impact on contemporary thought, whose influence is likely to grow, and not diminish, with time.'[20] In 1995 the Theosophical Society in India put on a ten-week seminar gathering for the purpose of studying Krishnamurti's work, and his themes are frequently used at conventions as a springboard for discussions.

The Society today bears little resemblance to the thrusting missionary enterprise presided over by Annie Besant, with its ambitions of world influence and millenarian goals. Its Lodges worldwide are diminishing in numbers, its membership aging and depleted, and its finances a perpetual concern. Unlike many sects and plainly esoteric organisations, it has not greatly benefitted from the resurgence of spiritual experimentation that has characterised the New Age which it helped to engender, although this is perhaps to its credit. Since the defection of Krishnamurti and his subsequent reconciliation, the Theosophical Society has learnt the perils of dogma, and is more mindful of its motto and original three objects. The Adyar leadership evades any line of questioning from non-Theosophists relating to its chequered past, and will certainly not offer an official opinion on the World Teacher, the hierarchy of Masters, the 'new civilisation', the Root Races, or Charles Leadbeater. It also shies away from ascribing any set agenda or body of opinion as being part of the Society's character. Freedom of belief is cherished and protected as the prime concern.

The Liberal Catholic Church similarly has no official opinion about Krishnamurti or his role as World Teacher, and casts a blind eye over the millenarian aspirations of its founders. It is now concerned more with its role as a specifically Christian organisation, along the lines of the Old Catholic Church, from which it originally sprang. Many older Liberal Catholics still retain fond memories of Krishnamurti, but the majority of younger lay and clergy members either possess no interest or have not even heard of him. The old alliance with the Theosophical Society has declined, but there are still informal links and a small overlap of membership between the two. Leadbeater is largely forgotten except as the author of *The Science of Sacraments*, still considered an important text for Liberal Catholics.

*   *   *

The death knell of Besant's grand scheme for the salvation of mankind rang long ago. Even her admirers are tempted nowadays to condemn her work in this area as a regrettable deviation, perhaps the result of incipient senility or religious hysteria, both maybe brought on by an exaggerated view of her own importance. And yet the World Teacher project never really died. It changed appearance, adopted a fresh vocabulary and enlisted a new generation of foot-soldiers, but its captain, its centre and inspiration remained untouched, leading from the fore with remarkable consistency of purpose into his ninety-first year. Up until that time those working closely with him still held to the conviction that they were participants in a momentous enterprise. They may no longer have believed, like their predecessors, that they were players in the Gospels of the future, but there was a feeling that the work they were undertaking, in support of their wondrous leader would mark a turning point for mankind. The feeling continues to this day. The Foundations are preparing the ground to disseminate his work for centuries to come, convinced, just as the early Theosophists were, that Krishnamurti's utterances have a critical significance for the spiritual evolution of humanity.

Would it be too far-fetched, in the light of this, to claim that Krishnamurti fulfilled Leadbeater's prophecy, and did in fact become a 'great spiritual master', as the bearded old Theosopher predicted in 1909, one who would 'be able to work for the good of humanity, and to pour out at these levels influence which otherwise could not descend thereto'?[21] There seems little doubt that he achieved the latter; but the messianic profile urged upon him as a youth, rich in Victorian undertones and cloud-breaking Christological imagery, was never to materialise. Instead, he became something of a post-modern saviour, if such a bizarre notion can be permitted. He represents a religious paradigm for the late twentieth century – the product of multiple historical movements and influences, yet answerable to none and, in fact, in perpetual revolt against them. He sews the ancient and golden thread of spirituality into the fabric of modern life, employing a strategy that is staggeringly avant garde. He smashes our understanding of what is real, what has substance and value; he overturns our dependence on the 'authoritative centres of thought,' such as God, hierarchy, love, measured time, the mind. Our perception of the world, its people, and even of ourselves, he argues, are mere images produced by a fragmentary thought process, subject to the limitations of language and interpretation. True to the post-modern idiom, he points out that knowledge can never lead to universal certainties; there are no comfortable markers except those invented by society to contain itself; as far as the brain's capacity is concerned, the 'known' can only ever be partial. In every sense he was a contemporary thinker. The great achievement of his life was not that he rejected the throne that was Christ's (because it is questionable that he ever did), but that he succeeded in stepping out of his robes, adorned as he was with every sacred trapping short of a halo, and sat down instead with ordinary human beings, to thrash out the practicalities of living a religious life in a modern secular society. It was here, face to face with mothers, plumbers, teachers, students, builders, wasters, or ministers, in the banality of a seminar room and on a plastic chair, that he fulfilled the role prescribed for him in Leadbeater's exotic prophecy.

His Theosophical sponsors, steeped in the values of nineteenth-century Britain, cannot be blamed for their miscalculation of the young paragon. Who could have predicted one hundred years ago the world in which we live today, let alone the shape of our spiritual inclinations as we head into the next millennium? Krishnamurti evolved with the century; his teachings were tuned to the contemporary idiom, at the same time shaping it and responding to its needs.

He spoke to a society increasingly enslaved by linear time and obsessed with the individual. The disintegration of communities, the dispersal of people pursuing novelty and opportunity, has ruptured the old support structures – families, villages and churches, and modern people are challenged to make the best of their lives, as individuals, within the time available. Everyone today is responsible for his or herself, home, health, income and spiritual well-being. Krishnamurti addressed this condition, focussing on the state of the personal psyche, the modern obsession. His mission was thus simultaneously personal and global, directly mirroring the needs of the contemporary world, which harbours ever greater individualism, while becoming smaller by the day, the common property of all.

The universalism that Krishnamurti represents is perfectly adjusted to an increasingly liberal and eclectic world culture. Traditional creeds and ideologies no longer possess the authority to demand complete allegiance. Diversity and choice have displaced dogmatism and the security it brought. The present era offers man the right, for better or worse, to select what he wants from the various religions and philosophies of the world, adding some to his shopping basket, while rejecting others, at all times aware that his ultimate loyalty is only to himself and his own salvation. This emancipated, self-absorbed creature, who travels alone across the spiritual landscape of the world, surprisingly finds in Krishnamurti something that resembles the home he has lost. The teachings, though disguised, repeat what has been stated and restated in various religious traditions of the past, and hence its hidden warmth. But what is important for the traveller is that it has now been put in a language suited to his modern outlook. The eternal questions and answers are no different to what they were 2000 or 20,000 years ago.

The late twentieth century, with its communication networks and multi-media, has given us an unprecedentedly clear, though sterile, view of history and the shifting sands of time. Like the gods of Greece we look down with detachment on the follies of our past, convinced, in the hubris of the moment, that we know more and better than ever before. Religion has been one of the greatest casualities of this would-be Olympian perspective. Those who do remain within the established traditions are tending towards a more ecstatic expression of their faith, which involves a shedding of past values, rebirth, and a new highly personal union with the godhead. They are not as far removed as they think from their New Age brethren, for whom a similarly unitive experience has become the ultimate spiritual goal, albeit outside the nomenclature of mainstream faiths. The mistakes of our ancestors have led us to desire a new beginning, and a new understanding of God, free of past or misleading iconology. The motivation for present-day religion, in a predominantly secular western society, is enlightenment, whether it be attained on the psychiatrist's couch, the pew, the rush mat or the plastic chair. Advocates of enlightenment are the modern-day prophets, though they can never teach the experience, but merely share their own realisation of it in a comprehensible manner.

Krishnamurti was one of the first and most prolific of these modern prophets, and his mould is being cast and recast with ever greater frequency. Unlike an enlightened guru in his ashram, receiving western spiritual tourists by the plane-load, Krishnamurti did not retreat from the world, or escape from materialist preoccupations into a beatific trance. He relentlessly confronted the modern condition on its own terms: he fathomed the implications of the technological revolution, he engaged scientists and doctors, he questioned school children, and used the logistics of rational argument as part of his idiom. But it was all undertaken from the perspective of the unitive state – divine, mystical enlightenment. His teachings always retained the quality of scripture, rather than textbook. His words were utterances rather than statements – a subtle difference, the former implying a character of incontestability. It was an authority even he was powerless to deny. The World Teacher's message was applicable to all people, regardless of national, social, religious, racial, age or gender divisions. He touched the contemporary nerve, and left a residue of influence that is incalculable. He was a herald for the new age, a sign-post for the future of man's metaphysical aspirations, a star in the east.

Notes

Chapter One: The Boy on the Beach (pages 1–6)

1. C. W. Leadbeater, *Man Visible and Invisible.*
2. Ibid.

Chapter Two: The Melting Pot (pages 7–22)

1. I am differentiating between 'Theosophy' as expounded by Madame Blavatsky's Society and the generic school of theosophical thought by using the capital 'T' when referring to the former.
2. For a full exposition of the Masters' relation to historical individuals, see K. Paul Johnson's valuable research in *The Masters Revealed: Madame Blavatsky and the Myth of the Great White Lodge.*
3. See *The Elder Brother: a Biography of Charles Webster Leadbeater* by Gregory Tillett.
4. In years to come Leadbeater would deny that he could ever have been anything but a Theosophist. The opening paragraph of his *How Theosophy Came to Me* begins with the sentence: 'My first touch with anything that could definitely be called Theosophy was in the year 504BC, when I had the wonderful honour and pleasure of visiting the great philosopher Pythagoras.'
5. C. W. Leadbeater, *How Theosophy Came to Me.*
6. Ibid.

7. In this context the word Indian implies native of the Indian subcontinent, including Ceylon.
8. Annie Besant's son, Digby, and daughter, Mabel, were reunited with her as adults. Their good relationship was one of the joys of her middle age. Both children ceased as adults to communicate with their father.
9. Annie Besant, *An Autobiography*.
10. Quoted from *Annie Besant* by Rosemary Dinnage.

Chapter Three: Make Straight the Way (pages 23–50)

1. Today this area falls into Andhra Pradesh.
2. The only other member of the Jiddu (or Giddu) family listed as serving in the civil service at this time is Giddu Kothanda Ramayya, MA. By his dates of service and seniority, together with the locality in which he operated, it would be reasonable to conjecture that this might have been Narayaniah's father, ie Krishnamurti's paternal grandfather. Kothanda Ramayya held the position of Deputy Collector between 1881 and 1901, after which official records of his employment cease.
3. Narayaniah's words, quoted from *The Boy Krishna* by Mary Lutyens.
4. According to Hindu reckoning, he was actually born on 11 May. A new day is not considered to have begun until 4 am the following morning. It is not entirely certain that Krishnamurti was born in the year 1895. His early history was adjusted by Theosophy's leaders for a variety of reasons. His passport always showed the year of his birth as 1897 – probably incorrectly, although it is now difficult to know why this amended date was used.
5. Narayaniah is not listed in the 1895 Madras Presidency Almanack as a named official. This does not preclude the possibility of his having taken the post at the close of 1894, as he himself claimed, the Almanack having gone to press only late in 1894. He is not listed as a named employee of the civil service prior to 1896. His occupation until becoming sub-magistrate at Rayachoti is therefore unknown.
6. The *Imperial Gazetteer of India* in 1908 lists only three schools in the entire Cuddapah district, one of which was in Madanapalle.
7. In later life Krishnamurti repeatedly and publicly emphasised how in childhood he had exhibited the normal characteristics of devout Brahminism, but how they had never in fact taken root. 'From childhood,' he said more than once, 'I never thought I was a Hindu.'
8. This was reported by Krishnamurti himself, in a 2000-word autobiographical sketch, written in 1913. He intended to continue the work

until 1945, by which time it would warrant its ambitious title, *Fifty Years of My Life*, but it was left incomplete. His references to auras reveals Leadbeater's influence – auras were one of Leadbeater's favourite areas of spiritual research.

9. Ibid.

10. Pupul Jayakar, *J. Krishnamurti: a Biography*.

11. Jiddu Sadanand lived in the care of his eldest surviving brother until his own death in 1948.

12. Quoted from a facsimile of Krishnamurti's manuscript (see note 8), photographed in Evelyne Blau, *Krishnamurti: 100 Years*.

13. Ernest Wood, in *Is This Theosophy?*, laments the exclusivity bred by organisations such as Co-Masonry, with its seductive secretism and pomp.

14. Ernest Wood, ibid.

15. Emily Lutyens, *Candles in the Sun*.

16. Arthur Nethercott, *The Last Four Lives of Annie Besant*.

17. This neatly corroborated Theosophy's conviction that all religions derived ultimately from the same source. They merely differed in cosmetic appearance and in the minds of men.

18. C. W. Leadbeater, *Man Visible and Invisible*.

19. Mary Lutyens, *Krishnamurti: the Years of Awakening*.

20. Annie Besant in the *Adyar Bulletin*, November 1922.

21. Ernest Wood in the *Theosophical Journal*, Vol. 6, 1965.

22. Ernest Wood, op. cit.

23. C. W. Leadbeater's letters to Annie Besant, reproduced in *The Theosophist*, June 1932.

24. Ibid.

25. See Pupul Jayakar, *J. Krishnamurti: a Biography*. A similar reference to this text was made by a Brahmin pandit to Krishnamurti in 1985. Krishnamurti was intrigued but sceptical.

26. See Krishnamurti's own account of the event, as reproduced in R. Balfour-Clarke, *The Boyhood of Jiddu Krishnamurti*.

27. Shamballa was supposed to be located in the Gobi Desert. The King of the World is equated in Hindu tradition with Sanat Kumara, the eternal-virgin youth.

Chapter Four: At the Feet of the Master (pages 51–72)

1. Lady Emily Lutyens, *Candles in the Sun*.

2. This theory and quotation from Rom Landau, *God is my Adventure*.

3. 'Our Relation to Children' by C. W. Leadbeater, *Lucifer*, Vol. XX, 1897.

4. Clara Codd, *So Rich a Life*.
5. Lady Emily Lutyens, op. cit.
6. Ernest Wood, *Is This Theosophy?*
7. Brockwood Park archives.
8. Letter from Annie Besant to J. Krishnamurti, copy at Brockwood Park archives.
9. Ernest Wood, op. cit.
10. It is worth noting that Narayaniah did not appear to be unduly concerned at the prospect of his sons travelling overseas for educational purposes, even though such travel also resulted in loss of caste, according to orthodox Brahmins.
11. Quoted from Lilly Heber, *Krishnamurti: the Man and his Message*.
12. C. W. Leadbeater, *The Masters and the Path*.
13. Alcyone, *At the Feet of the Master*.
14. Ernest Wood, op. cit.
15. C. W. Leadbeater, quoted in the *Adyar Bulletin*, November 1912.
16. Anecdote from Arthur Nethercott, *The Last Four Lives of Annie Besant*.
17. Ernest Wood, op. cit.
18. See the story of a boy known as Dibs, whose deficiencies uncannily parallel those of the child Krishnamurti, and who ultimately, after therapy, developed into a remarkably imaginative and articulate human being (*Dibs: In Search of Self* by Virginia M. Axline).
19. Quoted from Josephine Ransom, *A Short History of the Theosophical Society*. Madras missionaries also raked up stories of Leadbeater's immorality and claimed that the Krishnamurti 'cult' was religiously divisive rather than unitive.
20. *The Lives of Alcyone* had been published, in instalments, in *The Theosophist*.
21. Lady Emily Lutyens, op. cit.
22. Esther Bright, *Old Memories and Letters of Annie Besant*.
23. Major C. L. Peacocke, in the *Herald of the Star*, January 1912.
24. Clara Codd, op. cit.
25. C. W. Leadbeater, quoted from R. Balfour-Clarke, *The Boyhood of J. Krishnamurti*.
26. Ibid.
27. Quoted from Clara Codd, op. cit.

Chapter Five: Moulding a Messiah (pages 73–93)

1. Mary Lutyens, *To be Young.*
2. C. Jinarajadasa, *Occult Investigations: a Description of the Work of Annie Besant and C. W. Leadbeater.*
3. Ibid.
4. Quoted from Tillett, who quotes from C. W. Leadbeater, *The Hidden Side of Christian Festivals.*
5. Josephine Ransom, *A Short History of the Theosophical Society.*
6. Mary Lutyens, *Krishnamurti: the Years of Awakening.*
7. Ibid.
8. Quoted from letters between Krishnamurti and Annie Besant, 1915–16, Brockwood Park archives.
9. Quoted from Evelyne Blau, *Krishnamurti: 100 Years.*
10. Letter from C. W. Leadbeater to Krishnamurti, 5 March 1916, Brockwood Park archives.
11. Krishnamurti to Lady Emily Lutyens, 25 January 1920, quoted from Mary Lutyens, *Krishnamurti: the Years of Awakening.*
12. H. P. Blavatsky, *The Key to Theosophy.*
13. Lady Emily Lutyens, op. cit.
14. Sir Edwin Lutyens always retained an affection for the Jiddu brothers, who·became such a lively part of his family life.
15. Elisabeth Lutyens, Lady Emily's fourth child and a composer of distinction, particularly resented Krishna, and is the one member of the family who rarely had a good word to say about him.
16. Lady Emily Lutyens, op.cit.
17. Mary Lutyens, *Krishnamurti: the Years of Awakening.*
18. Krishnamurti to C. W. Leadbeater, 31 October 1913, quoted from Mary Lutyens, *Krishnamurti: the Years of Awakening.*
19. Krishnamurti to C. W. Leadbeater, 18 February 1915, ibid.
20. Described in Lady Emily Lutyens, op. cit.
21. Letter from Krishnamurti to Lady Emily Lutyens, quoted from Mary Lutyens, *Krishnamurti: the Years of Awakening.*
22. A. Besant, in the *Adyar Bulletin*, November 1922.
23. By expelling Steiner Besant appeared to be directly contradicting a claim she published in the *Adyar Journal* less than a year previously: 'All my life long I have worked for freedom of thought and speech for others ... and I am too old to surrender my own freedom at the dictation of a few members of the TS [including Steiner]. That they are disturbed by it merely shows that they are not willing to allow others the freedom

they claim for themselves, and which they use, quite freely, to attack me, knowing that in this they in no way imperil their membership, and that I am the first to defend their freedom of thought and expression.'

24. A. Besant, in the *Adyar Bulletin*, November 1922.
25. T. M. Nair, 'The Evolution of Mrs Besant'.
26. Letter from Annie Besant, quoted from Esther Bright, *Old Memories and Letters of Annie Besant.*
27. Sidney Field, *Krishnamurti: the Reluctant Messiah.*
28. Lady Emily Lutyens, op cit.
29. James Wedgwood, *Herald of the Star*, March 1914.
30. 'On the Liberal Catholic Church' by C. Jinarajadasa, quoted from Tillett, op. cit.
31. H. P. Blavatsky, 'Isis Unveiled', quoted from Tillet, op. cit.
32. Josephine Ransom, op.cit.

Chapter Six: Cracking the Mould (pages 94–115)

1. Krishnamurti to Lady Emily Lutyens, from Mary Lutyens, *Krishnamurti: the Years of Awakening.*
2. Ibid.
3. Lady Emily Lutyens, *Candles in the Sun.*
4. Mary Lutyens, *Krishnamurti: the Years of Awakening.*
5. Letter from Nityananda to Mme de Manziarly, March 1920, Brockwood Park archives.
6. Letter from Nityananda to Mme de Manziarly, 17 April 1920, Brockwood Park archives.
7. Quoted from Mary Lutyens, *Krishnamurti: the Years of Awakening.*
8. Ibid.
9. Mary Lutyens, *Krishnamurti: the Years of Awakening.*
10. Quoted in Arthur Nethercott, *The Last Four Lives of Annie Besant.*
11. An 1888 edition of the London newspaper, the *Star*, refers to the Bryanston Street house of Baroness de Pallandt as being a centre for Theosophical gatherings.
12. Krishna's main incentive in travelling to Eerde was to defuse the activities of B. P. Wadia, a renegade member of the Theosophical Society and one of Besant's fellow internees back in 1916, who was drawing members away from Besant's movement in an attempt to bring Theosophy back in line with the philosophy of its founder, Madame Blavatsky. The estate at Ommen was being used at that time for an open-air Theosophical gathering, and Wadia was thought to be spreading dissent.

Krishna distracted members from Wadia by organising lively sports activities.

13. Helen (Knothe) Nearing, *Loving and Leaving the Good Life*.
14. Ibid.
15. Mary Lutyens, *Krishnamurti: the Years of Awakening*.
16. Helen Nearing, op. cit.
17. Ibid.
18. J. Krishnamurti, 'Editorial Notes', *Herald of the Star*.
19. Ibid.
20. Quoted from Mary Lutyens, *Krishnamurti: the Years of Awakening*.
21. Letter from Nityananda to Annie Besant, 12 October 1921, Brockwood Park archives.
22. Brockwood Park Archives.
23. Mary Lutyens, *Krishnamurti: the Years of Awakening*.
24. Nityananda to F. Ruspoli, 2 July 1922, Brockwood Park archives.
25. Krishna's lectures and writings during this Australian visit sustain the decisive stance he had adopted in India, despite his restraining himself from any overt criticism of Leadbeater. He emphasises the spiritualisation of world politics and gives voice to a theme that was to be central to his later teachings, one that set him apart from the Theosophical Society elite: you are humanity – understand yourselves, see the Truth in your own lives and you will bring about positive change in humanity as a whole. External authority cannot achieve this for you; you must find out for yourselves.
26. Letter to Madame de Manziarly, 22 April 1922, Brockwood Park archives.
27. James Santucci, in the Foreword to *Krishnamurti and the World Teacher Project: Some Theosophical Perceptions* by Govert Schüller.
28. Clara Codd, *So Rich a Life*.
29. *The Theosophist*, May 1923.
30. Nityananda to F. Ruspoli, 2 July 1922, Brockwood Park archives.
31. J. Krishnamurti, Editorial Notes, *Herald of the Star*.
32. Ibid.
33. Nityananda to Lady Emily Lutyens, 13 July 1922, Brockwood Park archives.

Chapter Seven: In the Presence of the Mighty Ones (pages 116–140)

1. Soon after his initial experiences Krishna wrote to Leadbeater saying that he had found the light after seven years of being spiritually blind and locked in a mental dungeon. This would date his disillusionment

back to the period when Leadbeater emigrated to Australia and Arundale had refused to continue tutoring him, in 1915.

2. 'Ever since I left Australia . . .' J. Krishnamurti's account of his experience in Ojai in August 1922. Krishnamurti Archives, Ojai, California. Courtesy Krishnamurti Foundation of America.

3. 'In a long and narrow valley . . .' J. Nityananda's account of J. Krishnamurti's experience in Ojai in August 1922. Krishnamurti Archives, Ojai, California. Courtesy Krishnamurti Foundation of America.

4. Descriptions of such 'music of the spheres' are well-documented in reports of ecstatic trance. Some heard music of the Gandharvas at Krishna's 'pentecostal' incident, on 28 December 1911. Others heard it during the seances of Madame Blavatsky.

5. 'Ever since I left Australia . . .' J. Krishnamurti's account of his experience in Ojai in August 1922. Krishnamurti Archives, Ojai, California. Courtesy Krishnamurti Foundation of America.

6. Quoted from Mary Lutyens, *Krishnamurti: the Years of Awakening*.

7. The sources used in outlining the events between 3 September and 20 October 1922, together with the symptoms experienced by Krishnamurti, are composed by Nityananda and were seen by the author at the Brockwood Park archives.

8. J. Nityananda to C. W. Leadbeater, 25 January 1924, Brockwood Park archives.

9. J. Nityananda to Lady Emily Lutyens, 10 December 1922, Brockwood Park archives.

10. Nityananda wrote how disappointing it felt when the evening sessions came to an end, and that it was like the house lights coming up in a theatre, a return to the banality of ordinary life.

11. Several Kundalini scholars maintain that the emphasis laid on celibacy by so many religious cultures around the world is directly linked to the need for Kundalini energy (or whatever name is given to it) to be spiritually sublimated before divine realisation can occur. Krishnamurti himself said to a friend in 1928 that sex energy should be conserved in order to reach spiritual goals. 'Liberation is sex inverted,' he commented, echoing a tenet of tantric philosophy.

12. An excellent example is Mary Scott's *Kundalini in the Physical World*.

13. One celebrated and articulate account of a Kundalini awakening, by Gopi Krishna, bears an uncanny resemblance to Krishnamurti's experience. It describes the life-changing event as being accompanied by depression, terror, near madness, and a pain that was like 'a furnace raging in my interior', as if 'red-hot pins were coursing through my body'. Gopi Krishna goes on to say that the end result of his torture,

as with Krishnamurti, was that he had expanded mentally. 'It seemed as if my cognitive faculty had undergone a transformation.' His book concludes with the conviction that the kingdom of heaven and the fires of hell are both to be found within the psychosomatic matrix, and quotes the apocryphal saying of Jesus, 'Whoever is near unto me is near unto the fire.' The metaphor of rebirth, so often associated with Christian spiritual awakening, is frequently used by Gopi Krishna to describe the effect of Kundalini, and it could equally well be applied to Krishnamurti's experience.

14. Genesis ch 32, v 24.
15. Arthur Nethercott, *The Last Four Lives of Annie Besant*.
16. Mystical union and grief: the Ba'al Shem Tov and Krishnamurti', *Harvard Theological Review*, July 1993, v86 n3.
17. Interestingly, Leadbeater had clearly not been aware of the five apparently similar experiences witnessed by Warrington, nor the whole issue of the Kundalini injury.
18. C. W. Leadbeater to J. Nityananda, 1 January 1924, Brockwood Park archive.
19. Quoted from Mary Lutyens, *Krishnamurti: the Years of Awakening*.
20. Quoted in Pupul Jayakar, *J. Krishnamurti: a Biography*.
21. J. Nityananda to Annie Besant, 21 June 1923, Brockwood Park archives.
22. J. Krishnamurti to George Arunadale, 21 June 1923, Brockwood Park archives.
23. Mary Lutyens, *To be Young*.
24. Letter from Lady Emily Lutyens to Annie Besant, quoted from Mary Lutyens, *Krishnamurti: the Years of Awakening*.
25. A degree of playful flirtation on Krishna's part was probably approved by Besant, because she was keen to draw parallels between her protégé and his divine predecessor, Lord Krishna, whose amorous adventures with the mythical *gopis* were familiar to all students of Hinduism. Krishnamurti consciously aspired to the role-model of Krishna in other ways, much to the delight of his sponsors. He even attempted to learn the flute, in imitation of the god, whose 'flute is an extension of his beauty, for it makes heavenly music and imparts the essence of his blissful nature. The sounds that it produces are no earthly sounds; they fill the heavens and distract even the gods ... Its sound is like a summons calling the souls of men back to their Lord.' [Bassuk].
26. Elisabeth Lutyens, *A Goldfish Bowl*.
27. Annie Besant to Helen Knothe, quoted from Helen Nearing, *Loving and Leaving the Good Life*.
28. Elisabeth Lutyens, op. cit.

29. Some shaman traditions link head pain to the notion that supernatural spirits are inscribing a new language on the inside of the neophyte's skull.
30. J. Nityananda's diary, Brockwood Park archives.
31. Seventy years later, and long after the demolition of the Villa Sonnblick, one of Krishnamurti's devoted followers visited Ehrwald and, at a location which he later discovered to have been the site of the house, felt a distinct sense of sacred calm.
32. J. Nityananda to Annie Besant, 7 February 1924, Brockwood Park archives.
33. When Leadbeater read the text he dismissed it as not being in the Masters' style.

Chapter Eight: Journey to the Heart of Loneliness (pages 141–159)

1. J. Krishnamurti, 'The Kingdom of Happiness.'
2. Elisabeth Lutyens, *A Goldfish Bowl*.
3. Elisabeth Lutyens provides an amusing image of the pious 'busy non-activity' of disciples at Adyar: 'Under the odd tree one would come across plain European ladies, decked unbecomingly in saris, seated cross-legged, bunioned foot over bunioned foot, with closed eyes, presumably floating enjoyably on some astral plain.' Ibid.
4. Both quotes from the *Herald of the Star*, March 1925.
5. Arthur Nethercott, *The Last Four Lives of Annie Besant*.
6. Predictably the back-to-Blavatsky Thesosophists in Sydney and elsewhere poured scorn on the amphitheatre project. A Canadian Theosophist, D. McKinnon, included a mention of it in his widely circulated verse lampoon of Besant's Society: 'Our modern stuff is never rough – we make occultism simple/ To qualify you simply buy a share in our new temple/ In Sydney Bay; and watch and pray for Alcy's transformation/ From callow youth to Lord of Truth – our Christ by acclamation!'
7. The Manor was to remain Leadbeater's home until 1929 when he returned to live at Adyar.
8. Mary Lutyens, *To Be Young*.
9. J. Krishnamurti to J. Nityananda, 4 February 1925, Brockwood Park archives.
10. J. Krishnamurti to J. Nityananda, 10 February 1925, Brockwood Park archives.
11. J. Nityananda to C. W. Leadbeater, 1 March 1925, Brockwood Park archives.

12. Lady Emily Lutyens, *Candles in the Sun.*
13. Ernest Wood, *Is This Theosophy?*
14. Lady Emily Lutyens, op. cit.
15. Helen Knothe Nearing, quoted in Evelyne Blau, *Krishnamurti: 100 Years.*
16. Quoted from A. J. G. Methorst-Kuiper, *Krishnamurti.*
17. 'The Song of Life', J. Krishnamurti, *From Darkness to Light*, Harper-Collins, 1980, p.94.
18. Helen Nearing, *Loving and Leaving the Good Life.*
19. *There is No Religion Higher than Truth* by E. L. Gardner.
20. Krishnamurti later described what happened, when a friend asked him if it was true that he had actually conversed with the Master Kuthumi. 'He [Krishnamurti] told us that he had talked with Kuthumi on a number of occasions, usually in the early morning while he was meditating. One morning, just after sunrise, Kuthumi appeared in the doorway of Krishnamurti's room. They talked for a while, until Krishnaji, who had participated in similar discussions before, decided that he wanted more than verbal communication, not just words. He needed some tactile contact, to actually meet and touch Kuthumi. So he stood up, and walked to the sunlit door. Then came the telling words. "I walked right on through the figure. I turned around. There was no one there. I never saw the Master Kuthumi again."' (D. Ingram Smith, quoted in Evelyne Blau, op. cit.)
21. J. Krishnamurti, *The Collected Works of J. Krishnamurti*, vol. VI, Krishnamurti Publications of America, 1991, p. 15.
22. R. Balfour-Clarke, quoted in Evelyne Blau, op. cit.
23. *The Theosophist*, January 1926.
24. *Herald of the Star*, February 1926.
25. *Herald of the Star*, July 1926.
26. Radha Sloss, *Lives in the Shadow with J. Krishnamurti.*

Chapter Nine: Fires in the Forest (pages 160–186)

1. These talks, published as *The Kingdom of Happiness* sold 3000 copies in the US during its first month after publication, and 4000 in England.
2. Lady Emily Lutyens, *Candles in the Sun.*
3. Ibid.
4. Rom Landau, *God is my Adventure.*
5. Ibid.
6. J. Krishnamurti, *Early Writings*, Vol. 1.
7. Ibid.

8. Peter Washington, *Madame Blavatsky's Baboon*.
9. Quoted from Evelyne Blau, *Krishnamurti: 100 Years*.
10. The Auckland *Evening Post*, quoted in the Star Publishing Trust *Newsletter*, No. 3, 1934.
11. 'An Interview with Krishnaji, London, England, 20 June 1928', *International Star Bulletin*, August 1928. Krishnamurti was echoing the words of various mystics and teachers through the years, who have claimed dissolution of their own personalities in favour of the Christ spirit. St Paul wrote (in Galatians 2, 20): 'I am crucified with Christ: nevertheless I live; yet not I, but Christ liveth in me: and the life which I now live in the flesh I live by the faith of the Son of God, who loved me, and gave himself for me.'
12. Quoted from Arthur Nethercott, *The Last Four Lives of Annie Besant*.
13. Krishna's language in describing his meeting with the Beloved is sensuous, and brings to mind images of voluntary physical surrender, not unlike that involved in passionate human love. Mystics of many different religious persuasions have described this dissolution of the 'lower' self in the terminology of erotic love, and Krishnamurti is no exception. The Neoplatonist philosopher Plotinus, one of the forefathers of Theosophy, described man's union with the divine as 'that union of which the union of earthly lovers, who wish to blend their being with each other, is a copy'. (Quoted from Ellwood, *Mysticism and Religion*) In Hindu Vaishnavism the soul's passionate yearning for God finds literal expression in the gopis' erotic love for the Lord Krishna; and tantric gurus teach that divine realisation must be achieved through the union of Shiva and Shakti within an individual the metaphysical merging of male and female elements that represent, respectively, widsom and vital energy. The Old Testament's Song of Solomon, one of Krishnamurti's favourite texts, is a classic account of mystical experience interpreted in the language of earthly love; and Christian sages have also been known to use the same genre of terminology, such as John of the Cross, who describes the seeker's realisation of God through the explicit metaphor of a young girl making love to her beloved in a forest at night. (Quoted from Ellwood, op. cit.) Similarly, the Christian philosophy of the Church as Christ's bride, and nuns dedicating themselves in chaste wedlock to their Saviour, can be seen as reminiscent of Krishnamurti's mystical relationship with his Beloved.
14. J. Krishnamurti, *Early Writings*, Vol.1.
15. Ibid.
16. 'The Immortal Friend', K. Krishnamurti, *From Darkness to Light*, HarperCollins, 1980, p. 29.

17. *The Theosophist*, April 1927.

18. J. Krishnamurti, *Early Writings*, Vol.1.

19. Ibid.

20. Ibid.

21. J. Krishnamurti, the *Star Bulletin*, October 1928.

22. Reported in Arthur Nethercott, op. cit.

23. Annie Besant to J. Krishnamurti, 28 July 1927, Brockwood Park archives.

24. See Jinarajadasa to Annie Besant, 28 June [1928], Brockwood Park archive.

25. *Herald of the Star*, December 1927.

26. Gregory Tillett, *The Elder Brother: a Biography of Charles Webster Leadbeater*.

27. Adrian Vreede, 'An attack on Bishop Leadbeater', *The Liberal Catholic* 34/7 (February 1964), quoted from Govert Schüller, *Krishnamurti and the World Teacher Project: Some Theosophical Perceptions*.

28. Mary Lutyens, *The Years of Awakening*.

29. *Herald of the Star*, December 1927.

30. Lady Emily Lutyens, *International Star Bulletin*, September 1928.

31. J. Krishnamurti, *Early Writings*, Vol. 1.

32. Ibid.

33. J. Krishnamurti, *Early Writings*, Vol. 2.

34. C. W. Leadbeater to J. Krishnamurti, 18 July 1928, Brockwood Park archives.

35. C. W. Leadbeater in the *Australian Theosophist*, 15 October 1928. Krishna's name had been given the '-ji' as a mark of respect, starting from around the time of the December 28 1925 incident. Lady Emily astonished an informal young Sydney Field, who had become Krishna's friend in California, by insisting, at Eerde in 1926, that he now refer to his chum deferentially as Krishnaji.

36. J. Krishnamurti, *Early Writings*, Vol. 2.

37. Ibid.

38. J. Krishnamurti, *Early Writings*, Vol. 3.

39. Rom Landau, *God is my Adventure*.

40. J. Krishnamurti in an interview for the *Birmingham New Age Herald*, 1929, quoted from Peter Michel, *Krishnamurti, Love and Freedom*.

41. Quoted from Lilly Heber, *Krishnamurti: the Men and his Message*.

Chapter Ten: Farewell to Things Past (pages 187–212)

1. Krishnamurti to Lady Emily Lutyens, 26 December 1929, quoted from *Krishnamurti: the Years of Awakening*, by Mary Lutyens.
2. Ibid, 12 December 1929.
3. J. Krishnamurti, *Early Writings*, Vol. 7.
4. Quoted from *Krishnamurti*, by A. J. G. Methorst-Kuiper.
5. Gregory Tillett, *The Elder Brother*.
6. E. A. Wodehouse in the *Canadian Theosophist*, 15 February, 1931.
7. Jinarajadasa to Krishnamurti, 14 January 1932, Brockwood Park archives.
8. George Arundale in *The Theosophist*, March 1930.
9. Geoffrey Hodson, *Krishnamurti and the Search for Light*.
10. Annie Besant in the *Adyar Theosophist*, January 1930.
11. Ibid.
12. J. Krishnamurti, *Early Writings*, Vol. 7.
13. Alan Watts: 'Krishnamurti: the Messiah who became a Sage', *Tomorrow*, 18 November 1939.
14. J. Krishnamurti, *Early Writings*, Vol. 4.
15. Ernest Wood, *Is this Theosophy?*
16. Lady Emily Lutyens, *Candles in the Sun*.
17. Claude Bragdon in the *International Star Bulletin*, December 1930.
18. The Auckland *Evening Post*, quoted in the Star Publishing Trust *Newsletter*, No. 3, 1934.
19. Radha Rajagopal Sloss, *Lives in the Shadow with J. Krishnamurti*.
20. Radha Rajagopal Sloss confirmed to the author that, although Krishnamurti may not have advocated celibacy on paper, she had heard personal accounts of occasions when he did, both in interviews and discussions. There is, however, no printed evidence of this.
21. J. Krishnamurti, *The Collected Works of J. Krishnamurti*, Krishnamurti Publications of American, Vol. I, 1991, p. 166.
22. Christopher Isherwood *Diaries*, Vol.1, 1939–1960, ed. Katherine Bucknell.
23. Sydney Field, *Krishnamurti: the Reluctant Messiah*.
24. J. Krishnamurti, Seventh Public Talk, Ojai, 7 July, 1940, *The Collected Works of J. Krishnamurti*, Krishnamurti Publications of America, Vol III, 1991, p. 176.
25. Christopher Isherwood was present at Ojai on the occasion when Krishnamurti returned to the speaker's platform in 1944 and wrote; 'He really is very nice. Such a modest, slim, white-haired, boyish figure standing

in the sunny shadows. He obviously hates lecturing: he seemed terribly nervous and embarrassed, and winced visibly when people interrupted with questions. An extraordinary assortment of people go to hear him – boys from work camps, schoolteachers, apparently normal businessmen, small children, rich ladies, movie actors, farmers. And there are a few Theosophists of the old guard – bearded, smocked and sandalled – who sit regarding Krishnamurti with a kind of reproachful curiosity, because they firmly believe that, one day, he will announce his return to the movement and make a great historic speech in favor of Mrs Besant.' (Christopher Isherwood, op. cit.)

26. Christopher Isherwood, ibid.
27. Sidney Field, op. cit.

Chapter Eleven: Teaching the World (pages 213–244)

1. Evelyne Blau, *Krishnamurti: 100 Years.*
2. Quoted from Mary Lutyens, *Krishnamurti: the Years of Fulfilment.*
3. From the Order, approving settlement, etc. Case #79918, D. Rajagopal, et al. V. J. Krishnamurti et al., Superior Court of the State of California for the County of Ventura, quoted from Rhada Sloss, *Lives in the Shadow with J. Krishnamurti.*
4. Alan Rowlands quoted in Blau, op. cit.
5. Dr Deutsch's diary, quoted in Blau, op. cit.
6. Scott Forbes.

Chapter Twelve: The Empty Throne (pages 245–274)

1. Mary Lutyens, *Krishnamurti: The Open Door.*
2. Christopher Isherwood *Diaries*, Vol. 1.
3. Robert Ellwood, *Mysticism and Religion.*
4. The scholar Daniel Bassuk has pointed out that had Jesus been born in Bengal instead of Bethlehem, 'we could expect him to be hailed as an Avatar, for this would have been the appropriate expression within India for the same spiritual phenomenon that occurred in ancient Palestine.'
5. Evelyne Blau, *Krishnamurti: 100 Years.*
6. Mary Lutyens, *Krishnamurti: the Years of Awakening.*
7. Mary Lutyens, *Krishnamurti: the Open Door.*
8. Michael Krohnen, *The Kitchen Chronicles.*

9. E-mail to the author, 1999, from F. David Peat.
10. *Illustrated Weekly of India*, 25 May 1986.
11. U. G. Krishnamurti, *Mind is a Myth*.
12. Mahesh Bhatt, *U. G. Krishnamurti: a Life*.
13. Helen Nearing, *Loving and Leaving the Good Life*.
14. Mahesh Bhatt, op cit.
15. Quoted from Joscelyn Godwin, *The Theosophical Enlightenment*.
16. W. Q. Judge, *The Esoteric She*, quoted from Sylvia Cranston, *HPB: the Extraordinary Life and Influence of Helena Blavatsky, Founder of the Modern Theosophical Movement*.
17. In *The Key to Theosophy*, Blavatsky writes: 'The object of modern education is to pass examinations, a system not to develop right emulation, but to generate and breed jealousy, envy, hatred almost, in young people for one another, and thus train then for a life of ferocious selfishness and struggle for honours and emoluments instead of kindly feeling.

'And what are these examinations – the terror of modern boyhood and youth? They are simply a method of classification by which the results of your school teaching are tabulated. Now "science" teaches that intellect is a result of the mechanical interraction of the brain-stuff: therefore, it is only logical that modern education should be almost entirely mechanical – a sort of automatic machine for the fabrication of intellect by the ton . . . the education they produce is simply a training of the physical memory, and, sooner or later, all your schools will sink to this level. As to any real, sound cultivation of the thinking and reasoning power, it is simply impossible while everything has to be judged by the results as tested by competitive examinations . . . we should found schools where children should above all be taught self-reliance, love for all men, altruism, mutual charity, and more than anything else, to think and reason for themselves. We would reduce the purely mechanical work of memory to an absolute minimum and devote the time to the development and training of the inner faculties and latent faculties . . . We should aim at creating free men and women, free intellectually, free morally, unprejudiced in all respects, and, above all things, unselfish.' Quoted from Cranston, op. cit.
18. Pupul Jayakar, *J. Krishnamurti: a biography*.
19. Ibid.
20. Radha Burnier in *The American Theosophist*, Vol. 75/10, November 1987.
21. C. W. Leadbeater, *Man Visible and Invisible*.

Bibliography

Advance! Australia, Sydney (various issues).

Adyar Bulletin, Adyar (various issues).

Adyar Journal, Adyar (various issues).

Alcyone: *At the Feet of the Master*, Theosophical Publishing House, Madras, 1910.

American Theosophist, The (various issues).

Arundale, Francesca: *My Guest: H. P. Blavatsky*, Theosophical Publishing House, Adyar, 1932.

Arundale, George S.: *Alcyone and Mizar*, Argus Press, Chicago, 1912.

Arundale, George S.: *A Fragment of Autobiography*, Kalakshetra, Adyar, 1940.

Asylum Press Almanack, Madras, Vols 1888–1908.

Axline, Virginia M.: *Dibs: in Search of Self*, Penguin Books, London, 1984.

Balfour-Clarke, R.: *The Boyhood of Jiddu Krishnamurti*, Chetana, Bombay, 1977.

Bassuk, Daniel E., with a foreword by Ellwood, Robert S.: *Incarnation in Hinduism and Christianity: the Myth of the God-Man*, The Macmillan Press, London, 1987.

Bedford, Sybille: *Aldous Huxley: a Biography, Vol. 1* (1894–1939), Chatto & Windus, London, 1973.

Bedford, Sybille: *Aldous Huxley: a Biography, Vol. 2* (1939–1963), Chatto & Windus, London, 1974.

Besant, Annie: *An Autobiography*, T. Fisher Unwin, London, 1893.

Besant, Annie: *The Coming of the World Teacher*, Theosophical Publishing House, London, 1925.

Besant, Annie: *The Immediate Future and Other Lectures*, Theosophical Society, London, 1911.

Besant, Annie: *Theosophy*, T. C. & E. C. Jack, London (undated).

Besant, Annie: *The Path of Discipleship, Four Lectures delivered at the Twentieth Anniversary of the Theosophical Society*, at Adyar, Madras, December 27, 28, 29 and 30 1895, Theosophical Publishing Society, 1917 (seventh reprint).

Besant, Annie: *The Seven Principles of Man*, Theosophical Publishing House (undated).

Besant, Annie: *Popular Lectures on Theosophy*, The Theosophist Office, Adyar, 1910.

Bhatt, Mahesh: *U. G. Krishnamurti: a Life*, Penguin Books of India, New Delhi, 1992.

Blau, Evelyne: *Krishnamurti: 100 Years*, Stewart, Tabori & Chang, New York, 1995.

Blavatsky, H. P.: *The Key to Theosophy*, Theosophical Publishing House, Adyar, 1953.

Blavatsky, H. P.: *The Secret Doctrine*, Theosophical Publishing Company, London, 1888.

Brena, Stephen: *Pain and Religion: a Psychological Study*, Charles C. Thomas, Illinois, 1972.

Bright, Esther: *Old Memories and Letters of Annie Besant*, Theosophical Publishing House, London, 1936.

Brockwood Observer, The (various issues).

Brooks, F. T.: *Neotheosophy Exposed*, Vyasashrama Bookshop, Madras, 1914.

Brown, Mick: *The Spiritual Tourist: a Personal Odyssey through the Outer Reaches of Belief*, Bloomsbury, London, 1998.

Campbell, Bruce F.: *Ancient Wisdom Revived: a History of the Theosophical Movement*, University of California Press, Berkeley and Los Angeles, 1980.

Canadian Theosophist, The, Toronto (various issues).

Cleather, Alice Leighton: *H. P. Blavatsky: a Great Betrayal*, Thacker, Spink & Co., Calcutta, 1922.

Codd, Clara: *So Rich a Life*, Institute for Theosophical Publicity, Pretoria, 1951.

Collins, Mabel: *Light on the Path and Karma*, Theosophical Publishing House, London, 1917.

Cranston, Sylvia: *HPB: the Extraordinary Life and Influence of Helena Blavatsky, Founder of the Modern Theosophical Movement*, G. P. Putnam's Sons, New York, 1993.

Creme, Benjamin: *The Reappearance of the Christ and the Masters of Wisdom*, The Tara Press, London, 1980.

Davis, R. W. and Helmstadter, R. J. (ed.): *Religion and Irreligion in Victorian Society: Essays in Honour of R. K. Webb*, Routledge, London, 1992.

Bibliography

Dinnage, Rosemary: *Annie Besant*, Penguin Books Ltd, England, 1986.

Dunaway, David King: *Huxley in Hollywood*, Bloomsbury, London, 1989.

Ellwood, Robert S. Jnr: *Mysticism and Religion*, Prentice-Hall, New Jersey, 1980; revised 2nd ed. Seven Bridges Press, New York, London, 1999.

Field, Sidney, Peter Hay (ed.): *Krishnamurti: the Reluctant Messiah*, Paragon House, New York, 1989.

Foueré, René: *Krishnamurti: the Man and his Teaching*, (English ed.), Chetana, Bombay, 1952.

Friedrich's Newsletter, Rougemont, Switzerland, 1993–8.

Gardner, E. L.: *There is No Religion Higher than Truth*, Theosophical Publishing House, London, 1963.

Godwin, Joscelyn: *The Theosophical Enlightenment*, State University of New York Press, 1994.

Goodman, Felicitas D.: *Where Spirits Ride the Winds: Trance Journeys and other Ecstatic Experiences*, Indiana University Press, Bloomington, Indianapolis, 1990.

Happold, F. C.: *Mysticism: a Study and an Anthology*, Penguin Books, Baltimore, 1970.

Harvard Theological Review: 'Mystical Union and Grief: the Ba'al Shem Tov and Krishnamurti', July 1993, Vol. 86, no 3.

Heber, Lilly: *Krishnamurti: the Man and his Message*, George Allen and Unwin Ltd, London, 1931.

Herald of the Star (various issues).

Hodson, Geoffrey: *Krishnamurti and the Search for Light*, St Alban Press, Sydney, 1939.

Holm, Nils G. (ed.): *Religious Ecstasy*, Scripta Instituti Donneranni Aboensis XI, based on papers read at the Symposium on Religious Ecstasy held at Aåbo, Finland, on 26–28 August 1981, Almqvist 7 Wiskell International, Stockholm.

Holroyd, Stuart: *Krishnamurti: the Man, the Mystery & The Message*, Element Books Ltd, Shaftesbury, Dorset, 1991.

Howe, Michael J. A.: *The Origins of Exceptional Abilities*, Basil Blackwell, Cambridge, Massachusetts, 1990.

Huxley, Aldous, *Letters*, (ed. Smith, Grover), Chatto & Windus, London, 1969.

Imperial Gazetteer of India, Vols XVI, XI, Oxford, 1908.

International Star Bulletin (various issues).

Isherwood, Christopher: *Diaries*, (ed. Bucknell, Katherine), Vol. One 1939–1960, Methuen (Random House Group), London, 1996.

Jayakar, Pupul: *J. Krishnamurti: a Biography*, Arkana, London, 1986.

Jinarajadasa, C.: *Occult Investigations: a Description of the Work of Annie Besant* and *C. W. Leadbeater*, Theosophical Publishing House, Adyar, 1938.

Johmann, Kurt: *The Kundalini Injury, from the Computer Inside You*, http://www.webcom/jomann/index.html.

Johnson, K. Paul: *The Masters Revealed: Madame Blavatsky and the Myth of the Great White Lodge*, State University of New York Press, Albany, 1994.

Journal of the Krishnamurti Schools, Krishnamurti Foundation of India, Madras, July 1998.

Justice, editors of: *The Evolution of Mrs Besant*, Justice, Madras, 1918.

Keightley, Bertram: *Reminiscences of HPB*, Theosophical Publishing House, Adyar, 1931.

Keyserling, Count Herman: *The Travel Diary of a Philosopher*, Jonathan Cape, London, 1925.

Kneupper, Theodore L.: 'Three Major Paradoxes in Krishnamurti's Views on Education and their Resolution', paper presented at the Krishnamurti Centennial Conference, Miami University, Oxford, Ohio, May 18–21 1995.

Krishna, Gopi (with a psychological commentary by James Hillman): *Kundalini and the Evolutionary Energy in Man*, Robinson & Watkins, London, 1971.

Krishna, Gopi: *The Awakening of Kundalini*, E. P. Dutton, New York, 1975.

Krishnamurti Foundation Bulletin (various issues).

Krishnamurti Birth Centenary Souvenir, Krishnamurti Foundation of India, Madras, 1995.

Krishnamurti, Jiddu: *Early Writings, Volumes 1–7*, Chetana, Bombay, 1969–1971.

Krishnamurti, Jiddu: *The Collected Works of J. Krishnamurti*, Krishnamurti Publications of America, 1991.

Krishnamurti, Jiddu: *From Darkness to Light*, HarperCollins, 1980.

Krishnamurti, Jiddu: *The Complete Published Works, 1933–1986*, The Krishnamurti Text Collection and Index CD ROM, The Krishnamurti Foundation Trust, England, 1991.

Krishnamurti, Jiddu: *Editorial Notes*, Order of the Star in the East (no date).

Krishnamurti, Jiddu: *Poems and Parables*, Victor Gollancz Ltd, London, 1981.

Krishnamurti, Jiddu: *The Kingdom of Happiness*, Theosophical Publishing House, Adyar, 1926.

Kroft, Hans van der: *Waarheid zonder Weg, 100 jaar Krishnamurti*, Mirananda, Den Haag, 1995.

Krohnen, Michael: *The Kitchen Chronicles: 1001 Lunches with J. Krishnamurti*, Edwin House Publishing, Ojai, 1997.

Kundalini Research Foundation: *About the Kundalini Paradigm*, http://www.renature.com/krf/about-Kundalini-paradigm.html.

Landau, Rom: *God is my Adventure: a Book on Modern Mystics, Masters and Teachers*, Ivor Nicholson and Watson Ltd, London, 1935.

Leadbeater, C. W.: *How Theosophy Came to Me*, Theosophical Publishing House, Madras, 1930.

Leadbeater, C. W.: *Man Visible and Invisible*, Theosophical Publishing House, London, 1902.

Leadbeater, C. W.: *The Masters and the Path*, Theosophical Publishing House, Adyar, 1925.

Leadbeater, C. W.: *A Textbook of Theosophy*, Theosophical Publishing House, Adyar, 1912.

Leadbeater, C. W. and Besant, Annie: *The Lives of Alcyone: a Clairvoyant Investigation of the Lives throughout the Ages of a Band of Servers*, (2 Vols), Theosophical Publishing House, Adyar, 1924.

Leadbeater, C. W. and Besant, Annie: *Talks on the Path of Occultism, Volume I: At the Feet of the Master*, Theosophical Publishing House, Madras, 1930.

Lewis, I. M.: *Ecstatic Religion: an Anthropological Study of Spirit Possession and Shamanism*, Penguin Books, London, 1971.

Link, The, Rougemont, Switzerland (various issues).

Lucifer, Volume XX, London, 1897.

Lutyens, Elisabeth: *A Goldfish Bowl*, Cassell & Co, London, 1972.

Lutyens, Lady Emily: *Candles in the Sun*, Rupert Hart-Davis, London, 1957.

Lutyens, Mary: *The Boy Krishna: the First Fourteen Years in the Life of J. Krishnamurti*, Krishnamurti Foundation Trust Ltd, England, 1995.

Lutyens, Mary: *The Life and Death of Krishnamurti*, John Murray, London, 1990.

Lutyens, Mary: *Krishnamurti and the Rajagopals*, Krishnamurti Foundation of America, Ojai, 1996.

Lutyens, Mary: *Krishnamurti: the Open Door*, John Murray, London, 1988.

Lutyens, Mary: *Krishnamurti: the Years of Awakening*, John Murray, London, 1975.

Lutyens, Mary: *Krishnamurti: the Years of Fulfilment*, John Murray, London, 1983.

Lutyens, Mary: *To Be Young*, Rupert Hart-Davis, 1959.

Lutyens, Robert: *Sir Edwin Lutyens: an Appreciation in Perspective*, Country Life Ltd, London, 1942.

Marcault, J. Emile, and Hawliczek, Iwan A.: *The Next Step in Evolution*, Theosophical Society in England, London, 1932.

Meade, Marion: *Madame Blavatsky: the Woman Behind the Myth*, G. P. Putnam's Sons, New York, 1980.

Methorst-Kuiper, A. J. G.: *Krishnamurti*, Chetana, Bombay, 1971.

Michel, Peter: *Krishnamurti; Love and Freedom*, (English ed.), Bluestar Communications Corporation, Woodside, California, 1992.

Miller, William: 'Krishnamurti as Radical Response to our Postmodern Condition', paper presented at the Krishnamurti Centennial Conference, Miami University, Oxford, Ohio, May 18–21 1995.

Narayana Moorty, J. S. R. L.: Fragmentation, Meditation, and Transformation: the Teachings of J. Krishnamurti, *Journal of Indian Council of Philosophical Research*, Vol. V, No. 2, Jan–Apr 1988, ed. D. P. Cahttopadhyaya.

Nearing, Helen: *Loving and Leaving the Good Life*, Chelsea Green Publishing Company, Vermont, 1992.

Needleman, Jacob: *The New Religions*, Doubleday & Co, New York, 1970.

Nelson, Geoffrey K.: *Spiritualism and Society*, Routledge & Kegan Paul, London, 1969.

Nethercott, Arthur H.: *The First Five Lives of Annie Besant*, University of Chicago Press, Chicago, 1960.

Nethercott, Arthur H.: *The Last Four Lives of Annie Besant*, University of Chicago Press, Chicago, 1963.

Newland, Terry (ed.): *Mind is a Myth: Disquieting Conversations with a Man called U. G.*, Dinesh Publications, 1998.

Niel, André: *Krishnamurti, the Man in Revolt*, (English ed.) Chetana, Bombay, 1957

Nobel, Claus, and Krishna, Gopi: *Shaping a Brighter Tomorrow*, Kundalini Research Foundation Ltd, 1980.

Olcott, H. S.: *Old Diary Leaves*, Theosophical Publishing House, Adyar, 1941 (2nd ed.)

Owen, Alex: *The Darkened Room: Women, Power and Spiritualism in Late Victorian England*, Virago Press, London, 1992.

Pavri, P.: *The World-Teacher*, Indian Star Headquarters, Adyar, 1927.

Peat, F. David: *Infinite Potential: the Life and Times of David Bohm* (paperback ed. with new Afterword), Addison-Wesley, Reading, Massachusetts, 1997.

Perry, Michael: *Gods Within: a Critical Guide to the New Age*, SPCK, London, 1992.

Ransom, Josephine: *A Short History of the Theosophical Society*, Theosophical Publishing House, Madras, 1938.

Réhault, Ludovic (translated by Ina Harper): *Krishnamurti*, Christopher Publishing House, Boston, 1939.

Robinson, James Burnell: 'The Mystical and the Esoteric', paper presented at the Krishnamurti Centennial Conference, Miami University, Oxford, Ohio, May 18–21 1995.

Santucci, James: *Theosophy and the Theosophical Society*, Theosophical History Centre, London, 1985.

Schüller, Govert: 'Krishnamurti and the World Teacher Project: Some Theosophical Perceptions', *Theosophical History Occasional Papers*, Vol. V, ed. James A Santucci, Theosophical History, Fullerton, California, 1997.

Scott, Mary: *Kundalini in the Physical World*, Routledge & Keegan Paul, London, 1983.

Shringy, R. K.: *Philosophy of J. Krishnamurti: a Systematic Study*, Munshiram Manoharlal Publishers Pvt Ltd, New Delhi, 1976.

Sinnett, A. P.: *The Early Days of Theosophy in Europe*, Theosophical Publishing House, London, 1922.

Sinnett, A. P.: *Esoteric Buddhism*, Chapman & Hall, London, 1888.

Sinnett, A. P.: *The Occult World*, L. Trubner, London, 1881.

Sloss, Radha Rajagopal: *Lives in the Shadow with J. Krishnamurti*, Bloomsbury, 1991.

Smith, Stephen: 'The Priesthood of Mankind', paper presented at the Krishnamurti Centennial Conference, Miami University, Oxford, Ohio, May 18–21 1995.

Star Review (various issues).

Suares, Carlo: *Krishnamurti and the Unity of Man*, (English ed.), Chetana, Bombay, 1953.

Taylor, Anne: *Annie Besant: a Biography*, Oxford University Press, Oxford, 1992.

Theosophical Journal, London (various issues).

Theosophical Movement, The, (author anonymous), Cunningham Press, Los Angeles, 1951.

Theosophist, The, Adyar (various issues).

Tillett, Gregory: *The Elder Brother: a Biography of Charles Webster Leadbeater*, Routledge & Kegan Paul, London, 1982.

Washington, Peter: *Madame Blavatsky's Baboon: Theosophy and the Emergence of the Western Guru*, Martin Secker & Warburg Ltd, London, 1993.

Weeraperuma, Susunaga: *That Pathless Land: Essays on the Beauty and Uniqueness of J. Krishnamurti's Teachings*, Chetana, Bombay, 1983.

Weerapurama, Susunaga: *A Bibliography of the Life and Teachings of J. Krishnamurti*, E. J. Brill, Leiden, 1974.

Wessinger, Catherine Lowman: 'Annie Besant and Progressive Messianism (1847–1933), *Studies in Women and Religion*, Vol. 26, Edwin Mellen Press, New York/Ontario, 1988.

Wolffe, John: *God and Greater Britain: Religion and National Life in Britain and Ireland 1843–1945*, Routledge, London 1994.

Wood, Ernest: *Is This Theosophy?* Occult Book Society, London, 1936.

Index

Index